Competitive Fire

Michael Clarkson

Human Kinetics

Library of Congress Cataloging-in-Publication Data

Clarkson, Michael, 1948–
   Competitive fire / by Michael Clarkson
     p. cm.
   Includes bibliographical references (p.   ) and index.
   ISBN 0-88011-865-2
    1. Athletes--Psychology.   2. Sports--Psychological aspects.
    3. Sports--Competition.   I. Title.
   GV706.4.C53 1999
   796'.01--dc21
                                     99-17568
                                        CIP

ISBN: 0-88011-865-2

Developmental Editor: Kent Reel; **Assistant Editor:** Kim Thoren; **Copyeditor:** John Wentworth; **Proofreader:** Don Amerman; **Indexer:** Daniel Connolly; **Graphic Designer:** Nancy Rasmus; **Graphic Artist:** Tom Roberts; **Photo Editor:** Clark Brooks; **Cover Designer:** Jack Davis; **Photographer (cover):** Reuters/Peter Morgan/Archive Photos; **Printer:** United Graphics

Human Kinetics books are available at special discounts for bulk purchase. Special editions or book excerpts can also be created to specification. For details, contact the Special Sales Manager at Human Kinetics.

Printed in the United States of America   10 9 8 7 6 5 4 3 2 1

Human Kinetics
Web site: http://www.humankinetics.com/

United States: Human Kinetics, P.O. Box 5076, Champaign, IL 61825-5076
1-800-747-4457
e-mail: humank@hkusa.com

Canada: Human Kinetics, 475 Devonshire Road Unit 100, Windsor, ON N8Y 2L5
1-800-465-7301 (in Canada only)
e-mail: humank@hkcanada.com

Europe: Human Kinetics, P.O. Box IW14, Leeds LS16 6TR, United Kingdom
+44 (0) 113-278 1708
e-mail: humank@hkeurope.com

Australia: Human Kinetics, 57A Price Avenue, Lower Mitcham, South Australia 5062
(08) 82771555
e-mail: humank@hkaustralia.com

New Zealand: Human Kinetics, P.O. Box 105-231, Auckland Central
09-523-3462
e-mail: humank@hknewz.com

To Irene Clarkson and Jennifer (Vanderklei) Clarkson

Contents

Acknowledgments

Thanks to the many people who have made this book possible, either through their motivation to me or through information they provided.

My family has endured living with a writer and given me support and inspiration through years of ups and downs—my parents Fred and Irene Clarkson, my in-laws Tony and Kathleen Vanderklei, my wife Jennifer, and our sons Paul and Kevin.

In the newspaper business, there's been Clive Jacklin, John DeVisser, Murray Thomson, Mike Dempster, Dave Perkins, Steve Tustin, and John Nicol and, in writing, J.D. Salinger. I must thank all those athletes I coached and played with over the years who have become unwitting laboratory mice for this project, including my first coach Del Davidson, the teammates and players I coached at Niagara Christian College, and Harry Frith-Smith at the Calgary YMCA, who has the best three-point basketball shot of any psychotherapist I know. Arnold Fox, a Beverly Hills cardiologist and stress author, encouraged me to keep going on my research in the early years when publishers weren't interested.

Thanks to the *Toronto Star, Sports Illustrated,* the *Boston Globe Online, USA Today,* the Associated Press, the Canadian Press, *Psychology Today,* and the many users of the Internet for contributing much of the information contained in this book.

Finally, special thanks are due to all the elite athletes, coaches, neuroscientists, and psychologists who have contributed to my 10 years of research for this book by granting me interviews, to Human Kinetics editor Ted Miller for his encouragement and faith in my work, and to HK developmental editor Kent Reel for his insights.

Introduction

This book is largely about how human desires and needs can create powerful forces in the world of sports. Its main issue is that many superstar athletes reach peak performance more often than their opponents and stay at the top longer during their careers because they provoke and then control their stress emotions as an additive to performance both over the short term and the long haul. Their competitive fires are in a slow, steady burn over the course of their careers and occasionally erupt in supernova performances.

Many of their experiences in the so-called "arousal zone" of peak performance seem related to a need to defend their ego and self-esteem, resulting occasionally in a type of "fight or flight" on the playing field. Their insecurities often leave them with a strong need to prove themselves, driving them through years of rigorous training and career setbacks and sometimes triggering record performances. These insecurities and emotions often seem to come from a challenged, even dysfunctional, and yet resilient childhood and from a competitive sports system which fuels their competitive instincts.

Of course, talent has much to do with success, but, at the risk of oversimplifying a complex subject, they succeed because they turn their passions, and often their emotional and psychological needs and fears, into powerful fuels in two ways: Over the long-term, they are fueled by superior determination and drive or *emotional drive;* and during the short-term they trigger adrenalin, dopamine, endorphin, and other potent hormones for peak performances.

I am not a psychologist, although after more than 30 years of daily newspaper reporting as well as coaching and playing many amateur sports, I've been exposed to human behavior in heavy doses, especially to people dealing with stress. There are many brilliant thinkers who have devoted their lives to sports science and I am bringing together hundreds of top psychologists, sociologists, coaches, and players to help give insight to this complex subject.

This book does not contain a lot of new information, although in my research I have produced new findings linking successful athletes and their anger, as well as findings about elite athletes' unusual upbringings and rates of violence in their personal lives. What's especially new is the way old information and ideas are viewed. Much of the "evidence" that has been compiled is anecdotal and the conclusions drawn from it are speculative, but it's hard to dismiss some trends when they keep popping up over and over again. I've studied more than 50 of the all-time peak performances, from Jack Nicklaus in the 1986 Masters to Mike Powell smashing the long jump record, and found that anger was one of the quotients in most of them. I have also studied the lives of 500 high achievers, including many top athletes, and two things jumped out at me: They had a burning desire to succeed, the so-called *emotional drive*, which they often turned into intense emotions for short-term benefit. A second trend was that most of them came from a childhood with a serious issue—a dead or missing parent, a serious disability, or a smothering parent.

This book is somewhat controversial. It shows that insecurity and anger can sometimes get you places, that stars like Michael Jordan admit to sometimes putting themselves above their team, that NBA and NFL players have a higher rate of arrests for violent crimes than other sports players, that many top athletes may be psychologically or emotionally unhealthy.

This is also a book about how many top athletes are sometimes neurotically driven to defend their pride, ego, or self-esteem, as such legends have admitted—Michael Jordan, Billie Jean King, Jack

Nicklaus, Carl Lewis, Nancy Lopez, and Wayne Gretzky. It is also a study in animal response, human revenge, and the tactics that sports stars use to focus their strong feelings into production.

Being "in the zone" is one of the most overworked expressions in sports, yet the phenomenon remains a mystery, partly because we're fooled into over-simplifying it. When we talk of athletes being in the zone, there seems to be at least four different types of such states:

1. The Arousal Zone—A short spurt of arousal for one performance or part of one performance, often with "channeled" anger or another emotion as an additive. This results sometimes in *tachypsychia,* a phenomenon in which the action seems to transpire in slow motion. *Example:* Michael Jordan getting revenge on a foe who had embarrassed him in the media.

2. The Painless Zone—A short-term experience in which pain is temporarily numbed but which may result in a mind-body breakdown after the performance. *Example:* Kirk Gibson ignoring painful injuries to hit a ninth-inning homerun as his Los Angeles Dodgers won a 1988 World Series game.

3. Flow—The more romantic version of mind-body harmony, usually with less arousal than the Arousal Zone, but with numerous similarities, including superior concentration. *Example:* gymnast Nadia Comaneci recording the first perfect 10 in the 1976 Olympics. Over the long haul, flow is probably healthier than other states of mind.

4. Long-Term Zone—More of an *emotional drive* than the above three. *Example:* In 1997, Toronto Blue Jays pitcher Roger Clemens, with a "need to prove" something to the Boston Red Sox, the team that let him go, had his best season in years, winning the Cy Young when people said he was washed up.

Although there seems to be a connection among several of these zones, particularly in the "altered perceptions" reported by the athletes, we may make the mistake of trying to cram all four of them into one "zone." Perhaps that's one reason we have such a problem getting to the bottom of this subject and why many theories appear to clash.

This book, the result of 10 years' research, will concentrate mainly on the arousal zone. During the 1980s, it was said that the mind was sport science's last frontier, and all other systems to improve athletic performance had been exhausted. Yet out of that looms another frontier—the channeling of emotions. These emotions can be detrimental if they cause an athlete to "choke" during performance or lose control away from the playing field. Psychologists say some of the triggers elite athletes use to turn on their arousal systems are defense or coping mechanisms they have subconsciously developed to protect their egos over the years. While many athletes and teams employ sport psychologists to help them control their strong feelings for optimal performances, few admit they might have self-doubt, or even deeper psychological issues.

Professor Mihaly Csikszentmihalyi, who popularized the term "flow" and continues to write about how athletes and ordinary people can enrich their lives, not by trying to prove themselves but through optimal experiences, admits that my book is clearly more realistic while his work is more idealistic. But he adds: "I think both perspectives are needed."

I've been involved in numerous sports all my life as a player, coach, and college basketball scout. I've also covered sports as a journalist for 14 years. This book should be valuable to psychologists, coaches, and serious athletes who seek an extra edge in competition. Young and aspiring athletes should not follow the examples of some star players who are neurotic, immature, or angry. But all of us who watch and play sports would like to know why superior athletes act the way they do, where they come from, and what makes them not only tick but sometimes explode. The notion that sports are somehow romantic and pure has lost its glitter. Like the rest of society, it's both dazzling and dark; in other words, complicated. And perhaps it's getting more complex because of pressures increased by soaring salaries, corporate sponsors, and media scrutiny that's made our athletes kings, queens, and sometimes antiheroes.

It would be too lengthy to list all the attributions to the quotes and information in this book. They were gathered through hundreds of hours scouring libraries, the Internet, newspaper and magazine archives, and from interviews from more than 1,000 athletes, coaches, psychologists, and researchers over the past 10 years—from Ted Turner in 1993 to Michael Jordan during his comeback from baseball to Doug Flutie in 1998. Notes on this information can be found on the publisher's home page located at **www.humankinetics.com.**

PART I

Fight, Flight, or Fright

This section will focus on the arousal that athletes often experience in the heat of battle and how it can change them or their performances.

At peak moments of stress, athletes may go into a "fight or flight" mode. Chapter 1 discusses the physiological and psychological states of fight or flight and lesser mind-body alarms. It shows that many athletes attain record-breaking efforts when they are defending their pride or reputation, leading to a kind of controlling anger (and sometimes fear) in which their heightened hormones act as powerful additives. But, as shown in chapter 2, over- or underarousal can lead to subpar performances, so the optimal or desired levels of arousal for various types of sports and individuals are examined.

Arousal can lead to altered states of consciousness and some strange happenings, such as performances that appear to occur in slow motion and others in which an injured player feels no pain or has an out-of-body experience. These phenomena are discussed in chapters 3 and 4.

CHAPTER 1

The Athlete's Primal Defense System

> "Fear is a gift from God, for survival."
>
> Hall of Fame
> Running Back
> Jim Brown

Some of the most startling athletic performances are accomplished by athletes tapping into a reservoir of dormant hormones which they activate through "controlled" anger against their opponents or doubters. Arguably, the strongest animal instinct (in humans or otherwise) is self-preservation. When faced with a perceived threat, our autonomic system immediately kicks into a composite psychological and physiological reaction called "fight or flight." This instinct is built-in protection for the species, and for champion athletes, and it can also boost performance.

Fight or Flight

According to sport psychologist Patrick J. Cohn, PhD, athletes sometimes reach the zone of peak performance when they are defending their ego or pride. Their fight instinct operates at these times much as if they were in physical danger. This occurs not only in physical sports such as boxing and football but also in nonviolent games like golf. "When you feel fear about missing a short putt to win a match, the increase in adrenaline, heart rate, blood pressure, and respiration function to prepare your body and mind for action to deal with threat," says Cohn, who works with golfers on the PGA, LPGA, Nike, and Asian tours. He continues,

> Since you're never in physical danger when you play golf, the anxiety you experience is triggered by a perception of threat to your self-esteem or ego. The increased adrenaline you experience when trying to avoid a car accident is very helpful to your safety. When you get scared over making a five-foot putt for par, excess tension only ruins a fluid stroke. The worry, fear, and tentativeness you feel about missing a putt is not an abnormal reaction in that situation, but if you don't learn to control your emotions in that situation, anxiety gets the best of you. Everyone has similar feelings when under stress, but what separates a person who chokes from the person who copes is how he deals with those feelings.

Fight or flight involving a little white golf ball? A mind-body preparing itself for battle against another golfer or against himself while standing over a four-foot putt? If that sounds ridiculous, it shows us the absurdity of our evolution as human beings, says psychologist and stress expert Robert S. Eliot, former director of the Institute of Stress Medicine International in Denver. Eliot notes that while we've become terrifically sophisticated and civilized in many areas, we still react much the same to threats as our Neanderthal ancestors did. According to Eliot,

> We are still living in the bodies of our caveman ancestors in a world they never dreamed existed, and we will be for thousands of years to come. If they knew how we were using their adrenaline and endorphins, they'd be surprised. We have an arousal system designed to put us into physical activity under stress, but in our age we're invisibly trapped; all this energy gets turned inward, and the 30 or 40 little challenges we face every day are turned into physiological stress. In our society, we don't need to respond to physical threats as much, but we get psyched up in response to someone's criticism, or a driver who cuts us off on the way home from work, or the report card our son brings home from school. At

least in sports, there *is* a physical response to the threat of competition.

"Your emotions affect every cell in your body. Mind and body, mental and physical, are intertwined," says Thomas Tutko, PhD, a pioneer sport psychologist at San Jose State University, who has consulted for the Dallas Cowboys, the Oakland A's, and UCLA athletic teams.

> Whether the reasons for becoming emotional are real or imaginary, your reactions are similar. When you become anxious during a game—when you start to worry, "Will I make it? I've got to get this hit or we're gonna lose"—your body starts to react almost as if the danger were not a lost game but a lost life. We carry this behavior pattern with us from prehistoric times as a survival mechanism and it works without our having to think about it. This automatic response was valuable if you were about to be trampled by a mastodon, but it has its disadvantages if you are trying to settle down and concentrate on the next play in the game.

Tutko adds that fight or flight doesn't occur in most sports situations; athletes usually experience its symptoms in a milder form.

Physiological Response

Whether it's a high school girl aiding a friend in a car crash, an office worker trying to meet a deadline, or an athlete whose self-esteem is on the line, when faced with pressure or serious challenge most humans undergo a particular kind of physiological change. We have been programmed over millions of years to be able to summon extra strength, speed, or concentration when faced with a threat. Most of us have these "mind-body" alarm reactions every day in one form or another (see table 1.1).

As we become more technological and sophisticated with our robots scurrying around snapping photos on planets millions of miles away, we still don't know much about an everyday phenomenon back here on earth—our mind-body's alarm system. As far as we know it's as old as prehistoric man, yet we don't know enough about its potential. We do know that when faced with trouble, or what is

Table 1.1 Five-Alarm Fire

If we break it down to "fire hall" terms, depending on the expected degree of challenge or threat, we get:

Five-Alarm:	Full-fledged fight or flight. Defending one's health or, in extreme cases, one's ego or self-esteem.
Four-Alarm:	Threat to ego or pride during competition when others are watching.
Three-Alarm:	A blow up at work; a domestic quarrel.
Two-Alarm:	A phone call in the middle of the night. You prepare for the unexpected.
One-Alarm:	Nervous system on alert.

perceived as challenge, the mind-body can transform instantly through a complex series of changes. When a person feels strong emotion, such as fright, anger, or excitement, the body prepares itself for action. Its dormant weapons are gathered at warp speed in a military-style operation. Large amounts of adrenaline are poured from the glands into the blood. Heart rate and breathing speed up. Muscles increase activity and lungs work faster and longer. Blood pressure rises. Sugar releases into the blood giving extra energy. Pupils dilate for better vision. Thyroid hormones accelerate metabolism, and the body burns its fuel faster, providing speed. A sudden boost in blood cholesterol allows for long-distance fuel. Many systems, such as the digestive tract, shut down, allowing more blood to move to the muscles for action. In case of injury, endorphin, a potent painkiller, is released. Blood thickens, clotting bleeding from wounds. Concentration improves and judgments are more acute. At the optimal level, the five senses sharpen while the body's functions peak. The more threatening the situation, the more pronounced the reaction.

Documented Cases of Fight or Flight

• A 500-pound grizzly was mauling Deanne Lengkeek in Montana in 1991 when his five-foot, two-inch wife, Lorraine, became enraged and beat the bear off with a pair of binoculars.

• On March 2, 1993, four young female athletes and cheerleaders were returning home from a fashion show at Mandon High School in Bismarck, North Dakota. Their Ford Escort suddenly skidded off Interstate 94 and rolled down an 80-foot embankment. Missy Miller, the school's cheerleading captain, was crushed under the car and could barely breathe. The driver, Stacy Miller, scrambled out from the car with a broken collarbone. Afraid for her friend's life and worried that her father would be angry about the wrecked car, Stacy was able to push the 2,500-pound car enough for Missy to free herself.

• Pro golfer Mary Bea Porter was playing in a tournament in Phoenix in 1988 when she heard a child's cries coming from a swimming pool. She switched her mind powers away from her game to the rescue, climbed a fence, rescued the child from the pool, and brought the boy back to life.

• In 1987, five-year-old, 60-pound Rocky Lyons (son of former New York Jets' player Marty Lyons) saved his mother's life by pushing her out of a crushed truck and up a steep embankment.

• On January 11, 1992, North Dakota teenager John Thompson lost both arms in a farming accident. Home alone, his mind saved his life by preventing him from bleeding to death and giving him enough concentration to run to the farmhouse and, using his mouth and a pencil, telephone for help. "My mind took over," John recalled later. "It was like being hypnotized."

It isn't just thoughts or fears that set off arousal systems but also strenuous exercise and physical competition. During workouts, a variety of hormones are activated. A *hormone* (Greek for "to set in motion") is a chemical substance that carries out work. As well as their role in reacting to emergencies, they regulate a variety of functions, including body growth, food use, sex, and reproduction. There are some 10,000 hormones in the brain, many whose powers and duties remain unclear. *Adrenaline,* also known as epinephrine, is the most dramatic and widely known hormone unleashed during times of high arousal. Some experts believe that adrenaline can have negative effects as well and that it may react to our fears. It's generally accepted that adrenaline is a short-term chemical that causes energy peaks (and valleys), but when athletes report the highs and effects of adrenaline, they may be mistakenly attributing to adrenaline the effects of other hormones, such as dopamine or endorphin.

Other hormones, such as cortisol, valuable in centuries past in helping humans in their journey to find food, shelter, and clothing, can stay in your system for weeks or months. New hormones are being discovered all the time; oxytocin, for instance, contributes to good feelings toward others (as in a team concept) and to group achievements.

Mind Using Matter

Perhaps it isn't wise to generalize how people react to pressure situations. According to Karen Matthews, a professor of psychology at the

Hormones: Peak Performance Fuels

When athletes are faced with challenge, their emotional reactions send their minds and bodies hurtling through a series of chemical changes to help them deal with the situation. Among other things, it involves the brain, the central nervous system, and adrenal glands as the heart rate, muscles, and energy and concentration levels are brought to their most effective levels (although overarousal can impede performance.) Table 1.2 contains some of the powerful hormones involved in this complicated process. Scientists are learning new things about them every day and changing their opinions on how some hormones operate and mingle with other hormones. Some of these chemicals are pumped from the adrenal glands; others directly from the brain as neurotransmitters.

Table 1.2	Peak Performance Hormones	
Chemical	**Reaction**	**How It Is Triggered**
Dopamine	The body's rocket fuel, from which many other hormones follow. It stimulates aggression and awareness, coordinates muscle movement, and speeds up thinking.	From challenge. It responds to positive thinking more than adrenaline does and speeds up the momentum an athlete is headed in.
Adrenaline	Increases heart and respiration rates, widens air passages, increases blood pressure and muscle tension.	Mostly through fear and sometimes anger. It's more of a defensive "flight" fuel.

(continued)

Table 1.2	(continued)	
Chemical	**Reaction**	**How It Is Triggered**
Noradren-aline	Similar to adrenaline in increasing heart rate and muscle activity. Improves alertness and reaction time. Strengthens willpower.	Triggered when an athlete turns to aggression in a competitive situation. It's more of a "fight" fuel than adrenaline.
Testosterone	A fight, but not a flight, response, bringing strength, speed and power to maximum levels. Enhances the will to dominate an opponent.	Through a very competitive mindset and strong desire to overcome an opponent.
Cortisol	A long-term hormone that prolongs adrenaline and noradrenaline. Increases blood glucose levels, causes retention of salt, and makes the small blood vessels more sensitive to adrenaline. High levels can damage brain cells and accelerate aging.	Released when an athlete feels anxiety, anger, guilt, or frustration.
DHEA	Promotes well-being and joy and reduces anxiety. Gives added energy.	Released in the endocrine system by positive, loving thoughts. Athletes sometimes raise it with thoughts of loved ones at times of crisis.
Serotonin	Called the neurotransmitter of inner peace. Levels are raised somewhat by noncompetitive sports. A positive hormone linked with high self-esteem, confidence, and the ability to concentrate. Creates feelings of relaxation and happiness.	Appreciative feelings toward teammates. Stretching, walking, low-impact aerobics and meditative martial arts boost serotonin levels.
Endorphin	A powerful painkiller produced by the hypothalamus in the brain, it's the body's natural morphine. Suspected to produce runner's high.	Triggered by pain and other fight or flight feelings.

University of Pittsburgh, everyone's 9-1-1 reaction system is different depending on their metabolism and their view of the world. It is often attitude that determines the biochemical mix, Matthews claims: "Some people are more sensitive and are so-called 'hot reactors,' responding up to 30 times a day. Alarm reaction may be an early phase. Depending on your perception of the situation, you have behavior or response choices to make. If you think there is a threat, your response may be larger."

"In different situations, such as stresses in exercising, athletic competition, or public speaking, you have different hormones squirting through the body," says Jaylan Turkkan, associate professor of medicine in behavioral biology at Johns Hopkins University. "It depends on the defensive situation."

Of course, body-alarm reactions aren't always wonderful for those of us who live in the 1990s, when we get all worked up and even angry about a simple traffic jam. If we don't control them, or use them constructively, these overreactions can cause distress, reduce productivity, or even lead to disease or shorten our lives. According to Arnold Fox, a Los Angeles cardiologist who has written several books on stress, "overreactions can cause a person's skills or resources to seize up or 'choke' in pressure situations."

On the positive side, when it is used optimally, stress can help athletes achieve peak performances especially in explosion skills, claims Richard Earle, director of the Canadian Institute of Stress in Toronto. Earle says that Eastern Europeans were frontrunners in the stress-sports link. "The Soviets know the stories of little ladies picking up trucks. They know that most of lifting in weightlifting comes from focused energy and stress and not from muscle." Earle knows that, too. As a 163-pound power lifter, he once bench-pressed 390 pounds. "You need to focus energy and stress, to harness them."

Stress and Sport

• If the punch that Muhammad Ali (then Cassius Clay) floored Sonny Liston with in the 1964 world heavyweight championship seemed "phantom" to some people, perhaps its force had something to do with the fact that Ali's pulse rate had reportedly rocketed to 200 just before the fight.

• In the 1984 Olympics, Great Britain's Daley Thompson got so worked up before his final discus throw of the decathlon competition that the hairs on his arms and legs stood on end—a condition designed to make cavemen seem bigger than they were when confronted by a foe. Thompson's throw won him the gold medal and an Olympic record.

• On Sept. 3, 1997, Toronto golfer Gordon Grieve was so pumped up after sinking his first hole in one on the Thunderbird Golf Course that he aced the very next par three on the course—a feat with odds stacked against it at 64 million to one.

The examples listed here may be extreme examples, but they give an idea of what we as humans are capable of. Often it doesn't take an extreme reaction to make a difference for athletes in competitions where an inch or a fraction of a second separate winners from losers. Steve Backley of Britain, a former world-record holder in the javelin throw and now a sports researcher and author of *The Winning Mind*, once said that psyching himself into optimal arousal during competition could improve his performance by 10 percent over his performance in training. When he maintained control, his arousal made him stronger and more alert. "I never think of stress as a negative thing," he said. "I think as soon as you do admit that stress can be a negative factor, then it will be."

Psychological Response

"When you mess with my pride, somebody's going to be in trouble."

Pete Rose

In our civilized, sedentary society, the reactions of our mind-body alarm system are often misused, and the reasons they kick in have altered drastically. They are often subconscious reactions through which athletes protect their pride, ego, or self-esteem, or cope with stressful or threatening situations.

The Ego Defense

According to Carole Seheult, a British sport psychologist and chartered clinical psychologist, many athletes react to competitive situations with knee-jerk psychological and emotional reactions that have been programmed in their past. Seheult and other sport psychologists refer to these reactions as "defense mechanisms," and they can provide extra energy, intensity, and determination at crucial times. According to Seheult,

> The area of competitive sport, particularly at the elite level, is likely to provide ample opportunity for the exercise of an individual's defense mechanisms. . . . Head-to-head competition or involvement in major championships, where an athlete or player has to be prepared to put him- or herself on the line, to ask of themselves testing questions regarding levels of skill and commitment, and to extend limits of performance, will undoubtedly trigger instinctual feelings of anxiety against which the ego will need to protect itself. Further pressures may also come from external sources such as relationships with coaches, sponsors, officials, and family, as well as internal feelings regarding rivals and opponents."

Without getting too scientific, these defense mechanisms include denial, repression, and isolation. They can be positive or negative, "adaptive" or "maladaptive"—resulting either in a powerful and successful performance or a self-destructive one. For example, when facing a tough match against a seemingly unbeatable opponent, an athlete may react with denial. Successfully used, this denial may help the athlete maintain a high performance level, as he or she is unafraid of the favored opponent and does not accept the danger of the possibility of losing, even when behind late in the match. That's the *adaptive* reaction. The *maladaptive* reaction would be for the athlete not to understand the challenge he or she faces in the powerful opponent and fail to make the required effort to win. These defense mechanisms are often subconscious, automatic reactions of the mind-body system, Seheult notes, but becoming aware of them can enhance an athlete's performance. "A better understanding of the way an individual athlete is likely to respond in situations such as trials, qualifying competitions for major championships, or even Olympic finals can only be regarded as useful."

Psychologists say these defense mechanisms—the ways an athlete learns to react to stressful situations—can be shaped in childhood, adolescence, or in the highly competitive world of sports.

For instance, it may have been that Mo Vaughn of the Boston Red Sox was defending his pride with his performance in a game against the Toronto Blue Jays on Sept. 17, 1997, when he launched two unexpected home runs. Prior to the game, media and hometown fans had turned against Vaughn because he had openly criticized Red Sox management over the handling of his contract negotiations. Believing their beloved slugger had become another overpaid crybaby, the crowd of 23,648 at Fenway Park roundly booed Vaughn as he came to the plate. Clearly upset, Vaughn smacked a two-run homer to give Boston a 4-3 victory. "Mo's a very emotional person," teammate John Valentin said after the game. "He lives and dies for this city. I think he's a little hurt with the way things are going."

Fight or flight in baseball is not uncommon. Many players and coaches believe that slugger Albert Belle is more productive when he is angry and defending his pride. "Belle motivates himself by being mad at the world," wrote *Baseball Weekly* writer Tim Wendel. In the 1995 World Series between Belle's Cleveland Indians and the Atlanta Braves, Belle had just one hit as the Indians lost the first two games. Teammates hoped his anger would erupt ("Albert has not been as frustrated as I want him to be," Cleveland outfielder Kenny Lofton said), and it did prior to Game 3. Belle walked into the clubhouse prior to the game and faced journalists, whom he disliked for intruding into his personal life. He started shouting at them: "All you media a——, get the f—— out of here now!" Most of the reporters left, but NBA announcer Hannah Storm did not. "I'm talking to you, you a——!" Belle yelled at Storm. "Get the f—— out!" A short time later out on the field, Belle's bat exploded: He drove in his first run in Game 3, then homered in the next two games. "He uses his emotions to propel him," said Frank Mancini, a Cleveland clubhouse attendant and a close friend of Belle. "Albert thrives on his anger."

During spring training the following year, Major League Baseball fined Belle $50,000 for his five-minute tirade against Storm and directed him to seek anger-control counseling. Belle was furious, and he showed it by homering in his first at-bat the next day.

Belle seems able to keep his anger at a controlled, productive pace for long stretches as well. In 1994, he was suspended for using a corked bat. He angrily denied the charge. When he returned to the lineup, he hit .426 over the next 20 games. "He looks at a game as a battle," Mancini said. "It's war. Anybody who's not on his team is against him. That's the enemy." Of course, this type of avenging angel can turn against you. During a bench-clearing brawl in 1996, Belle nearly broke the forearm of Fernando Vina of the Milwaukee Brewers. At the next game, Vina got pumped up defensively to rob Belle, snaring his hard ground balls three times at second base. "We robbed him three times. . . . That was nice, to get him back a little bit," Vina said.

© RON VESELY

After the strike year of 1994 had left baseball fans disenchanted with the game, Mark McGwire (70 homers) and Sammy Sosa (66 homers, next page) brought a unique brand of excitement to 1998, an invigorating year that sparked new life in the game and renewed fan interest.

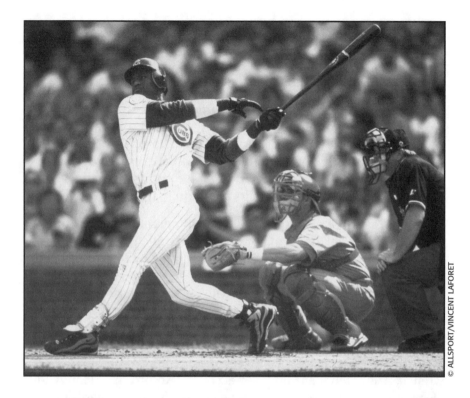

An example of joy under pressure would seem to be St. Louis Cardinals' baseball slugger Mark McGwire with his record-shattering 70 homeruns in 1998. While McGwire has battled emotional demons throughout his career and has regularly seen a psychotherapist, he said there were numerous factors as to why he shattered Roger Maris' hallowed record of 61 homers: his strong mind and positive thinking, a willingness to embrace the media pressure, and the fun and excitement of his season-long race against Sammy Sosa of the Chicago Cubs, who had 66 homers.

In basketball, Michael Jordan admitted that he reached the zone more often when he took criticism or challenges personally. When opponents like Shaquille O'Neal, LaBradford Smith, Gary Payton, and Larry Bird questioned his ability, especially his ability to beat them one-on-one, Jordan raised the level of his quickness, his defense, and most of all his shooting and scoring to prove to them he was the king of the court.

Such reactions often trigger anger and fear—and those are the biggest boosters of powerful hormones, according to Yuri Hanin, a pioneer Russian sports researcher, now professor and senior researcher at the Research Institute for Olympic Sports in Finland. In fact, many professional and international athletes are not as successful as others because they don't tap into the so-called "negative" emotions, such as aggression, fear, and anxiety. Hanin adds,

> High-level mobilizing energy comes from negative emotions; they are often untouched reserves. Positive emotions (joy, contentment) are not as quick to act or as intensive as negative emotions. Not all athletes are ready for competitions because they don't have enough negatives, or they don't channel or allocate them in the right way.

Hanin notes that studies show about 40 percent of elite athletes need a high level of precompetition anxiety to perform well. "They are more efficient when they're tense or nervous. That's helpful to them."

These uncomfortable, nervous feelings are often products of the mind-body defense system. "It's a type of defense, a response to a threat," says Hanin. "The whole person reacts, not just the mind or the body. It's a holistic response. The successful [athletes] are those able to establish a clear link between the uncomfortable feelings and what has triggered them, and then act on it." According to Hanin, this "fear energy" defense system can be genetic from a human's primal programming, but it can also be learned from childhood or through the world of competitive sports.

"The secret of great athletes is converting the pressure and their own insecurities into a powerful force and harnessing the electricity, the stress of the moment," says Brooks Johnson, former college and U.S. Olympic track coach. It seems as though athletes' self-defense systems can also be productive for long-term success, motivating them to strengthen their games through practice, conditioning, and strategy, like Roger Clemens on his 1997 mission to prove the Red Sox wrong for letting him go. "He went on a mission," Joe Carter said. "It's almost like you pin somebody up against the wall, and what Boston did to him was sort of like that. He came out firing on all 12 cylinders to prove those people wrong."

When Michael Jordan returned from his hiatus in baseball in 1995, critics said his basketball game was not up to par. Jordan was miffed and worked hard all summer on his skills and conditioning. "My challenge has always been to never give [the public] room for any conversation about my abilities," he said. "Everyone's looking for just one little slip-up so they can create a big hole in my game. And whenever I see that, I work to close that as quickly as possible. When I came back (from baseball), I created a big hole, and I worked all summer to close that hole. I have to make sure no holes evolve in my game. [People will] say, 'Oh, Pippen's the best player on this team,' or 'Penny Hardaway's the best player in the East,' or 'Hakeem Olajuwon or Shaq are the best players in the game.' Well, I stopped all that conversation. The bottom line is, while I'm still on the court, don't try to move anyone into my spot. I'm the only one who will decide that. Only me."

For a player with such abundant offensive skills, Jordan, like other competitors, spends much of his time defending what he has earned. But it's not always *self*-defense. Athletes have produced remarkable efforts when defending their national pride in international competition, defending their race—such as Jesse Owens in the Berlin Olympics—or defending their age group, such as Carl Lewis winning his ninth Olympic gold medal at age 35 after critics said he was too old.

CHAPTER 2

Impact of Optimal Arousal

"It all seemed to happen in slow motion."

Reggie Miller, Monica Seles, Wayne Gretzky, and many others in describing an optimal state of arousal experienced during athletic performance

Golf legend Jack Nicklaus welcomes arousal, but he believes that the majority of his opponents do not. That's just fine with him. During his prime, the terrific pressure of playing in the top competitions was a key factor in Nicklaus' high percentage of victories in the four "majors"—the Masters, British Open, U.S. Open, and PGA Championship. From 1960 through 1980, he played in 289 nonmajor events and won 50, for a 17.3 winning percentage. In the majors, despite playing against more talented fields, Nicklaus won 17 of 76 events, for a 22.4 percentage. "In the majors, you knew when it got closer to the final day, the pack ahead of you would fall back because of the pressure," Nicklaus said. In other words, their tension affected their strokes, and their scores ballooned, while Nicklaus kept his cool.

Until recently, many sports researchers and psychologists have agreed that a high level of pressure and arousal are usually detrimental to performance, especially in sports involving fine motor skills. Sport psychologist Thomas Tutko has said that more athletes succumb to feelings of arousal than benefit from them. "It is far more common in athletics for anxieties and tensions to be disruptive—both physically, affecting your playing ability, and mentally, affecting your concentration and judgment."

Lately, more reports are coming forth that even in golf, tennis, and other fine-skill sports, athletes sometimes have improved concentration and results under a high state of tension or pressure. One thing remains agreed upon: under pressure, most athletes usually perform better or worse than without pressure—there is almost always *some* effect. Most records are broken by athletes under the stress of competitive arousal; they are seldom broken during practice. And yet many athletes perform better under relaxed conditions than they do under the gun.

Much depends on the task, or skill, being performed, says psychologist Charles Spielberger:

> A football lineman is very focused on a task in terms of blocking or rushing a passer. Anger might facilitate that type of performance and energize more vigorous activity. But you don't want to have a quarterback angry most of the time. He has to read defenses, have peripheral vision, and to make quick decisions. Anger might interfere.

Skills Best Influenced by Arousal

Different skills require different arousal levels, sports researcher Dan Landers says. Conceding exceptions such as Nicklaus, Landers claims that generally speaking there is, "for each task . . . a different level of stress that might be needed. In archery and shooting, where you need steady nerves and precision, you don't want high levels of arousal. It could cause too much tremor. But in other events, you want more excitement." In a sport such as football, arousal levels should vary for players of different positions depending on the skills they use during a game. "Linemen wonder why coaches are always yelling in their faces while the quarterbacks get treated with kid gloves," Landers says. It's because it's often effective to get a lineman worked up, whereas a quarterback needs to remain calm.

In football, the tasks of the various positions are rather obvious, but even in a sport like gymnastics, some skills or tasks flourish under a high level of arousal, whereas others fail. The vault, for instance, requires psyching up to a high level of arousal, while the beam requires the arousal level to come way down. Falls on the beam are often attributed to a too-high arousal level that distracts focus.

Most experts do agree that high arousal tends to help performance in explosive sports that involve power and short-term speed. Sports such as ski racing, where competitors live on the edge, require high arousal. Former Canadian skiing standout Steve Podborski says, "Downhill skiing is the classic fight or flight syndrome. The only thing I want to do when I am going fast is to go faster. You don't think. There is no thought process in skiing. You react like an animal."

"All athletes have to learn how to get the arousal that most matches the challenges of their sport," says Jay T. Kearney, a psychologist who works with the U.S. Olympic team. "You can't take the explosive anger component for a shot-putter and have a golfer or marksman in that level of arousal. And you probably can't be a marathon runner and have the same kind of aggressiveness as (sprinter) Ben Johnson. There's an incredible balance in all of that."

Robert Weinberg, PhD, professor and chair of the physical education and sport studies at Miami University in Ohio, agrees that sport skills that require short, quick bursts of energy and power (e.g., track and field, hockey, some skills in football) apparently benefit most from high levels of arousal, whereas precision skills (e.g., archery, shooting free-throws in basketball, and putting in golf) benefit from a much lower optimal levels of arousal. Weinberg has prepared a chart matching sports skills to their ideal arousal level (see table 2.1).

Exceptions

Of course no rule is without exceptions. While most skills consistently match up with Weinberg's chart, there have been exceptional athletes and exceptional performances that go against the tide. Bowlers, tennis players, golfers, and other athletes in fine-skill sports have reported how a high level of arousal boosts their skills and concentration. Here are some examples:

• Corunna, Michigan. On Dec. 18, 1993, Troy Ockerman got himself pumped up with heavy metal music and then bowled three straight perfect games—36 consecutive strikes. He then turned sheet white as all the blood drained from his face, which is usually a fight or flight symptom.

• Wimbledon, 1997. American Michael Joyce trailed British crowd favorite Chris Wilkinson 0–3 in the second set, when a British fan shouted "miss it" as Joyce tried an overhead smash. Joyce became

TABLE 2.1 Arousal Level According to Skill Performed

Level of arousal	Sport skills
5 (Extremely excited)	Football blocking and tackling 220- and 440-yard runs Weight lifting Push-ups, sit-ups, bent-arm hang test
4 (Somewhat excited)	Running long jump Running very short and long races Shot putt Swimming races Wrestling and judo
3 (Aroused but not excited)	Most basketball skills Boxing High jumping Most gymnastic skills Most soccer skills
2 (Somewhat aroused)	Baseball pitching and hitting Fancy diving Fencing Football quarter backing Tennis
1 (Slightly aroused)	Archery and bowling Basketball free throws Football field-goal kicking Golf putting and short irons Skating figure eights
0 (Normal state)	

Modified from Robert Weinberg after interview with author.

angry and forged back to win the match. "I am a fighter. I play my best tennis when my back is against the wall."

• Jimmy Connors, tennis champion. "I thrive on emotions," says Connors. "They're reflected in my game with aggressive play, with going forward all the time . . . and with a heightened awareness of what's going on that I'd compare to an animal's instinct in hunting down its prey. The emotional energy allows me to raise my level of play." Connors generally saved his biggest emotional bursts for late in a match when he needed the points.

• Hale Irwin, golf champion. "I try to make pressure and tension work for me," Irwin says. "I want the adrenaline to be flowing. I think sometimes we try so hard to be cool, calm, and collected that we forget what we are doing. There's nothing wrong with being charged up if it's controlled."

Michael J. Mahoney, psychology counselor at the University of California, reminds us that athletes should be wary of arousal levels that are too low. For instance, the ice hockey goalie whose arousal level is too low "may be distracted by the crowd or bench activity. Under extremely low arousal, he may fail to attend to opposing skaters moving into the play from the periphery."

Choosing Optimal Levels of Arousal

Exercise physiologists say that modern athletes spend an increasing amount of time dealing with the teeter-totter of their emotions, and how to use the stress hormones to maximize performance. How they provoke, or deal with, pressure depends on their personal makeup, the skills they require for their sport, and, perhaps, the importance of the event. Some athletes need to psyche themselves up for competition whereas others need to gear down.

Some observers at the 1995 USA Track and Field Championships were startled by how Meredith Rainey prepared for the start of the 800-meter run. While her opponents took deep breaths and shook their arms to compose themselves, Rainey went a little frantic: She jumped up and down, tossed her arms about, and swung her body much like a high-impact aerobics instructor. She then went on to win the race. Rainey says,

> I always do jumps at the start; I need to compete aggressively, to run with courage, and confront any fears I have about the race. To do that, I try to psyche myself up more than calm myself down. . . . It's a mental and physical feeling. When I'm getting ready to go to the line, all my nerves are standing at attention. Whatever part of my body I need to call upon is ready to respond.

In the past, much time was spent trying to control arousal and the fight-or-flight response, but athletes and researchers are now discovering ways to *unleash* it. Indeed, for Rainey, a Harvard graduate and 1992 Olympian, being relaxed can backfire. At one indoor meet, she recalled, "I felt so relaxed. I thought, This is great. I ran completely passively and never got my rhythm. Afterward I realized that, for me, being relaxed is the worst way to feel."

In the early 1980s, Yuri Hanin developed the concept "zone of optimal function" (ZOF), which holds that all athletes have different emotional states that help them perform at their peak. Hanin found variation in anxiety levels among ice hockey players, runners, and other athletes. Some needed to be excited, others relaxed. Jack Raglin, PhD, a kinesiologist at Indiana University, researched ZOF along with Hanin and found that it's wrong to believe that reducing anxiety always gives athletes a chance to store psychological energy. "It's quite an individual thing and very complex," Raglin said. "There are athletes with increased anxiety who exhibit no change in stress indicators such as blood pressure."

Individual Differences

Researchers are learning that arousal is a complex phenomenon and that how a person deals with it, or the degree of success they achieve, differs from athlete to athlete. For instance, studies suggest that one in three runners needs high anxiety before a race in order to run well.

We have also learned that an athlete's attitude and emotional state might influence the effect of arousal on performance as much as the type of sport he or she is in. Bob Weinberg says, "Individual differences have to be factored in, because in addition to the type of sport skill, an athlete's individual makeup is an important factor in determining optimal arousal levels. Some athletes perform better under high pressure conditions, whereas others perform poorly."

Jimmy Connors, who often got angry at himself during tennis matches, after scoring a vital point would clench his fists, pump his arms up and down, and arch his back, said this type of animal behavior is not for everyone. "It worked for me . . . but you shouldn't try to pattern your emotional responses after someone else's," he says. "What works for the person you're imitating may not work for you. . . . And it's impossible to play at a feverish emotional peak for long . . . your body would use up far too much energy to keep you at that high level."

The more average the athlete, the more his performance will suffer under pressure, says John D. Curtis, health professor at the University of Wisconsin. "In pressure situations, most athletes tend to get too aroused; that's why they remain average athletes. They need to relax and let their body and training do their jobs." Elite athletes, though, can stand increased levels of anger and the adrenaline and other hormones it generates when they are performing a skill they've been highly trained to do, according to psychologist Charles Spielberger. For example, baseball slugger Darryl Strawberry has said he has his worst slumps when he's not emotional enough. He claims to see the ball better when he is frustrated or angry. "Strawberry can do that because he's channeling his emotions into focus. He's concentrating on one thing—the ball coming at him at 100 miles

"I thrive on emotions," says former tennis great Jimmy Connors. "The emotional energy allows me to raise my level of play."

an hour—and he's got well-coordinated reaction developed over many years. He's an expert," Spielberger said.

Benefits of Arousal

Michael Johnson credits prerace pressure and physiological excitement to helping him record a stunning 19.32 seconds in the gold medal race of the 200 meters in the Atlanta Olympics, a sizeable .34 better than his old record. "Where the hell did that come from?" he said with a puzzled expression when looking up at the scoreboard timer after the race. But after he had cleared his head and reflected, Johnson credited the pressure of *needing* to win the race with charging him with extra energy, including a tremor throbbing through his body at the "on your marks" that sent him blasting out of the starting blocks .16 seconds after the starter's pistol sounded. He then roared down the curved track at 25 miles per hour. Johnson related after the race,

> There was pressure from the 80,000 people there who expect you to win, not to mention having the Olympic schedule changed for you, and all the years of magazine covers, photo shoots, people calling to try to take off the pressure but just making more pressure, and the fact that Frankie [Fredericks] and Ato Bolden were running really, really well. . . . I thought that if I didn't win this, a lot of things were going to be said that I would not want to hear. . . . It dumped a whole ton of pressure into the mix. It was like one of my competitors coming up and hitting me. It was perfect because I always race better under pressure."

Along with extra speed and strength, psychologists believe that high stress can increase athletes' motivation and endurance and allow them extra energy. One January day in 1996, Roy Jones, Jr., awoke all excited because what was ahead of him that day—he would become one of the first athletes to compete in two professional sports on the same day. "I woke up early, all restless, like it was Christmas morning," he said. Jones went on to play that afternoon for the Jacksonville Barracudas of the United States Basketball League.

Benefits of Arousal

1. Added power (physiological and psychological), speed, and energy
2. Added drive, determination, and endurance
3. Sharpened concentration and heightened awareness
4. A feeling of being in the zone
5. Short-term pain-killing for even serious injuries

That night he successfully defended his IBF world super middle-weight championship against Eric Lucas.

World cross-country champion Lynn Jennings, of Newmarket, New Hampshire, said that many times she receives increased power, confidence, and momentum knowing that her arousal hormones will kick in during a race. Describing her victory in a race in Connecticut, she says, "I pulled the trigger with about 150 meters left. I felt like Wonder Woman going up the hills."

Many athletes report that high stress vaults them into a brief "twilight zone" where everything seems to happen in slow motion and they seem to have more time to react (a condition called *tachypsychia*, discussed in the next chapter). For instance, Indiana Pacers star Reggie Miller described it this way: "I rose above the floor, and it was like I had a camera, filming the game . . . no, actually I felt like a movie director, telling everybody what to do from above. Everybody was in slow motion." This is the state of mind that amateur athletes dream about but many never attain: that magic period of time where complete control is attained—or at least you *feel* as if it is attained, which can mean the same thing when it comes to performance.

When it is well understood, practiced, and used wisely (and sometimes luckily!), a high level of arousal can be the difference between success and failure or normal performance and optimal performance. However, accompanying the significant potential benefits of arousal are several possible drawbacks that athletes at all levels try to avoid.

Drawbacks of Arousal

Perhaps the most common drawback of overarousal is "choking," a term derived from the Greek, meaning a narrowing of the esophagus. When an athlete reacts with too much stress, the esophagus can constrict, the body can get flooded with adrenaline, and any number of bad things can happen. Choking can occur in any type of sport at any time. In the Atlanta Olympics, Canadian shot putter Brad Snyder threw far below his personal best, explaining, "It was like someone had their hands around my neck. I couldn't breathe." But there may be more chances of it happening in finesse events, says psychology professor Roy Baumeister. "There are two main ingredients to most athletic performances: skill and effort," he said. "Pressure seems to impair skill but improve effort." He believes that in highly skilled events, such as diving, gymnastics, and golf, competitors are most affected by sudden bouts of self-consciousness, but in sports involving sheer effort and determination, such as running and weightlifting, self-consciousness is less likely to result in choking.

Drawbacks of Arousal

1. Too much power and speed, resulting in overkill
2. Muscles can seize up or motor skills break down
3. Concentration distracted
4. Concentration too narrow, leading to tunnel vision and other distortions
5. Errors in judgment

Scott Norwood, who missed perhaps the most famous field-goal try in NFL history, a 47-yarder as his Buffalo Bills lost to the New York Giants in the 1991 Super Bowl, said he got too pumped prior to the kick. "I was so pumped up for the kick that my plant leg went about three or four inches ahead of where it should have been, and I ended up pushing the kick," he said. There was plenty of distance, but it drifted four feet wide to the right.

Nowhere is the seizure of life and limb more obvious than on the golf course, where amateurs and pros alike can blow easy shots. Seasoned pros like Greg Norman, who keeps coming up short in major events, and Tiger Woods, Loren Roberts, and Curtis Strange, who have struggled in the Ryder Cup, attest to the fact that even the most experienced athletes are not exempt from tightening up.

In baseball, a study of World Series games between 1924 and 1982 revealed that when seventh games were necessary, the home teams won only 40.8 percent of the time, compared to 59.2 percent for the visitors, thanks at least in part to more errors by the home teams. One of the study's researchers, Roy Baumeister, believes the home teams felt more pressure to win in front of their fans and were more self-conscious. (Of course, entire teams choking may be more complicated than individual athletes.)

There are other potential drawbacks to high emotions, to be examined later in this book, such as athletes getting so psyched that they cheat or become violent, and so accustomed to a heavy hormonal flow that they eventually become addicted to the highs that it brings.

Mastering the Beast

If the impact of arousal on performance is due largely to an athlete's attitude and ability to channel emotions, then he has great powers to affect the outcome of a match. Can we harness our mind-body systems and their extra powers? John Krystal, director of the laboratory of clinical psychopharmacology at the U.S. Department of Veterans Affairs in West Haven, Connecticut, believes we can. "It's very clear that this (arousal) system is very sensitive to learning. There's a difference between stress and distress. It's stressful for an athlete to compete, but he learns ways to relax and keep control. It's an adaptive process. That's why athletes are so healthy."

All great athletes have choked under pressure, including Michael Jordan in the 1995 playoff losses to the Orlando Magic, Brazil's Ronaldo in the 1998 World Cup of soccer, Roger Maris hitting .105 in the 1961 World Series after hitting a record 61 homers during the regular season, and record-smashing Ukranian pole vaulter Sergei Bubka, who failed to clear any height in the 1992 Summer Olympics. And yet successful athletes seem able to get over the wall of pressure and pain more often than not.

When Jordan feels the butterflies in his stomach, he knows extra powers are at his disposal, that the pressure can liberate him or smother him, and he has brilliantly learned how to get them flying in formation most of the time. "Of course I've failed in the clutch many times, but some people will say that's why in the end I'm so successful," he said.

There are many talented athletes, but is it possible that what separates the consistent winners from the rest of the pack is their ability to evoke and manipulate intense emotions which produce amazing hormones and, hence, these unusual experiences where more things seem possible? Some athletes have made a career out of using their emotions, and perhaps their survival instincts, to raise the level of their play even beyond what was thought to be their abilities; hockey player Maurice Richard, baseball Hall of Famer Ty Cobb, and football linebacker Dick Butkus come to mind. Such athletes with uncommon desire and drive, who consider sports more than a game, seem to trigger and control a higher emotional response than others.

The Golden Age of Psychology

With sport psychologists and techniques such as visualization and positive thinking to help them, there are more opportunities these days for athletes to master their mind-body emotional system. As elite sports get more scientific, researchers will study the body alarm systems like fight or flight. This is an avenue for athletes to increase their production through their own natural drugs rather than artificial steroids.

In part III of this book, we'll examine the ways that elite athletes are learning to get into the arousal zone with techniques involving imagery, breathing techniques, and channeling, such as changing fear to anger to dispassionate response, which seems to change the mind-body's chemical state from negative to proactive. Many how-to methods are springing up. At the Institute of HeartMath in Boulder Creek, Colorado, researchers are examining ways to bring human defensive responses from the primitive to intelligent stages. "For many high achievers, including athletes, anger may be a wake-up call, and they've learned to transform that energy, that emotion, into fuel, but there are more efficient ways to get into the 'zone,'" says Bruce Cryer, executive director of corporate programs for the institute which is teaching zone-inducing techniques to turn anger and fear into the "positive" hormone DHEA by getting athletes to focus on the heart and its electrical system—and their loved ones—in crucial times during a match.

Arousal Debate

Psychologists and biochemists agree that arousal alters performance, but there is debate about the differences between nervousness, fear, and anxiety. "Despite the abundance of data, no theory has gained universal acceptance," said John F. Murray, a psychologist at the University of Florida and a former tennis professional.

Murray believes that arousal should be distinguished from anxiety and stress. "Although anxiety usually involves increases in arousal, it is also accompanied by worry, concern, and negative thoughts and feelings. Stress refers to any external or internal stimulation that tends to grossly disturb stability."

Athletes can learn to raise their arousal levels as they increase their skill and learn to perform under pressure, many psychologists say. "But you have to be careful you don't get beyond your arousal curve," said John Anderson, PhD, a sport psychologist who works with Olympic athletes and lectures around the world.

> As you continue to experience pressure, you begin to understand more and more where your point is. You may discover you can learn to handle 6 out of 10 on an arousal scale, but if you go beyond that and you haven't been there before you begin to worry. Then you forget to trust your internal system and focus on external things. Then the arousal state is not functional.

Anderson added that superstars and world-class athletes have learned to perform on an arousal scale of 10 out of 10. They, too, can sometimes "choke," but they do it less frequently than their opponents. "They learn to trust their performance system under high arousal, and it gives them an added boost. And they learn that their feelings of nervousness are often a good sign," Anderson said.

Even very young athletes are prone to arousal during competition, says John Anderson.

> You only need to watch them come off the field or the court after a match and you see kids crying. There's a very strong

emotional component. Even in T-ball at age six or seven, the kids have a rally, somebody gets a key hit, and they get excited and start cheering and yelling. They get pumped and there's adrenaline flowing. But the kids on the other team have their heads hanging and they're hitting their gloves against their legs.

The father of a talented five-year-old athlete once came to Anderson to ask his advice about quickly shaping the child into an elite, aggressive athlete. But Anderson told him to let the child have fun, that he was too young to be aroused. And yet, if a child wants to climb the competitive sports ladder as he gets older, he must get used to the feelings of arousal under pressure because it will have a significant effect on his performance. That's something all serious athletes get to know rather quickly.

CHAPTER 3

Altered States

The experience does not happen to an elite athlete every day, but every once in a while, usually during times of intense feelings and often in the "moment of truth" in a match, a safe hole opens up in the tornado. The calm in the eye of the arousal storm can be a magical place of altered mental states, where "centered" athletes move around in slow motion, where they seem to have more room in time to react, and where they sometimes even have what they describe as out-of-body experiences.

The sensations and enhanced concentration and skills which elite athletes report during high arousal seems to parallel the unusual experiences of others caught in pressure situations, such as police officers in gun battles, workers facing extreme deadline situations, rescuers at accident scenes, and even patients having out-of-body experiences during surgery. In these varied instances, they reported:

- Sharpened concentration and skills, making their target seem larger;
- A feeling of slow motion, offering more reaction time (a phenomenon known as tachypsychia);

- A feeling of power and control;
- Little or no pain; and
- Detachment from what was happening around them.

The Big Slowdown

The seemingly magical state of calm control is a precious, precarious state of mind, body, and emotions that remains terribly understudied because it's difficult to take apart in a lab setting and because sports science is still relatively superficial and not tied enough to human reactions in the real world. To assess the point, then, let's step outside athletics for a moment to consider a related example of a professional suddenly gaining enhanced mental abilities. In 1984 in Woodstock, Ontario, Corporal Ron Thompson of the Ontario Provincial Police was confronted with an armed suspect holding his police partner hostage. He recalls his superhuman mental powers, which came to him in the extreme heat of the moment: "A grey mantle, like a blanket, was rolled down. Suddenly everything was gone—the street, the traffic, the moon, my partner. All that was left was the gunman and me. His head was transformed into a white oval egg. Very sharp. I shot him between the eyes and killed him. Then the mantle disappeared and everything was normal." Thompson did not tell his colleagues about his twilight zone experience because "they would have thought I was crazy."

Sometimes—often when they are seriously challenged—athletes report experiencing a similar sensation. While their situations are not as grave, to them they are harrowing enough to their self-esteem to trigger their mind-body alarm systems and perhaps even fight or flight. Some examples:

1. Former NBA great Isiah Thomas: "My anger drove me to a high level of performance, but then I went beyond that into a zone of calm and peace. Everything seemed effortless. The plays were in slow motion and the rim seemed this big [he stretched his hands wide] ... You are aware of every detail around you. You can even hear your own breath. It's a real high, like drugs. But then the next night, I couldn't get past the anger stage. It was frustrating."

2. Roger Bannister, upon becoming the first man to run the mile in less than four minutes: "The world seemed to stand still, or did not

Roger Bannister, the man who broke the 4-minute mile: "The world seemed to stand still, or did not exist. . . . There was no strain. My mind took over."

exist. I was relaxing so much that my mind seemed almost detached from my body. There was no strain. My mind took over. It raced well ahead of my body and drew compellingly forward. I felt that the moment of a lifetime had come. There was no pain, only a great unity of movement and aim."

"What these experiences had in common was a focus so intense that the athlete felt detached from the rest of the world, and also a high degree of arousal, which probably raised the level of hormone release and mixed the various hormonal combinations as they squirted through their bodies," suggests Jaylan Turkkan of Johns Hopkins University. "It's possible," she says, "that the experiences of athletes are related to others of police officers, accident victims, and other rescuers in times of high stress—they are by-products of the mind-body defensive reflex. Sometimes in extreme cases, even fight or flight."

A common feeling is the slow-motion effect. Former National Football League quarterback John Brodie reported: "Often in the heat of the game, a player's perception and coordination improve dramatically. It seems I have all the time in the world to watch the receiver run his patterns, and yet I know the defensive line is coming at me just as hard as ever. It's a beautiful dance in slow motion." And yet opposing players may be in a zone of their own. Former linebacker Dan Wicklum sometimes intercepted such passes: "There were times when I saw the ball leave the quarterback's hands in slow motion. I had the time to consider the spin on the ball, and I could see the gap in the white stripe. It didn't happen all the time and seemed to be related to my level of concentration."

Basketball champion Patsy Neal is in awe of such occurrences. "There are moments that go beyond the human expectation, beyond the physical and emotional ability of the individual. Something unexplainable takes over and breathes life into the known life. One stands on the threshold of miracles." And yet it may be explainable, if not with scientific proof, at least with recurring anecdotal evidence. The euphoria of such experience comes from "internally generated physiological reactions," according to Gary Wells, a psychologist at Iowa State University in Ames, Iowa, who tests people's reactions to pressure situations.

> Runners experience these things during races and sometimes it happens after the race. It's a natural thing. Endorphins and other hormones are released into the system. You find it among other people, too. Police don't like to admit it, but after they're shot at, a short time later, they get this rush from the endorphins, the opiates. They don't know what to think, or why they feel this way. But these are biochemical reactions, not unlike a dreamlike state.

Such states are hard to prove biologically, Wells said. "We have to rely on anecdotal reports. In experiments, we can re-create the event, but they're hard for us to manipulate. There are ethical boundaries, too. We may have to pull guns to create high arousal in some people."

Tachypsychia

It's widely known that athletes and other people who challenge themselves in pressure situations have a chance at improving their mental skills and even sometimes reaching states like *tachypsychia*, some researchers say. Exercise improves brainpower, concentration, creativity, and problem solving, said Thaddeus Kostrubala, author of *The Joy of Running*. "During running, when the heart is pumping hard, that blood flow is increased and that changes the biochemistry of the brain," he said. "There's an increase in oxygen."

Tachypsychia, Greek for "speed of the mind," slows an athlete's perception to action, an effect created by the mind-body as it speeds up its metabolism to deal with an emergency (or a perceived emergency), releasing dopamine, adrenaline, noradrenaline, cortisol, DHEA, and endorphin at breakneck speeds, according to Massad Ayoob, a police captain in New Hampshire who has interviewed athletes. "It's an illusion, like a video camera on fast forward," Ayoob says. "The more the danger, the more pronounced the slowdown. Factors large and minute are recorded as the brain throws all its vast capability into fight or flight, and because we are not used to that much detail being recorded by the mind in a short time frame, we remember it as if it had taken much longer." (It also illustrates how poorly most of us concentrate at times of low arousal, but more on that later.) There is more slowdown when the person sees the threat coming and often not as much when someone is taken by surprise, Ayoob said. And that goes for football players as well as cops or a Wall Street tycoon faced with a crucial deadline.

Science (never mind athletics) has virtually ignored tachypsychia, and no rigorous studies have been done, says Jaylan Turkkan. "Scientists say, 'Yeah, I've heard of it,' but it's hard to pin down and study." The biology behind such phenomena is difficult to trace, says Calgary endocrinologist Alun Edwards. "There are hormones present in the brain we haven't even identified yet. During these very human experiences, there are changes in the brain function, but we can't take the brain apart to investigate."

Sports researcher Dan Landers of Arizona State University confirms the existence of tachypsychia, not only in sports but in his personal life. In the 1960s, during his college days in California, Landers was a passenger in a car. He was not wearing a seat belt and went flying when the car slammed at 50 mph into the back of another car in fog. "It seemed to take an eternity for the crash. It seemed like I was given a lot of time to reach out and brace myself from crashing through the windshield, yet it all happened within a split second. I was able to escape with only a scratch."

The Out-of-Body Experience

The out-of-body phenomenon is known in psychologist's jargon as "excorporation," in which the athlete has the perception of seeing himself or herself perform from outside his body, or "psychological splitting," in which the athlete thinks there are two of him: the passive self who stands watching as the active self responds physically to the situation. According to Barbara Harris, a researcher at the University of Connecticut Medical School, the phenomenon is partly the result of endorphins and adrenaline being released by the brain stem. Harris, who had an out-of-body experience herself in 1975 during surgery, believes that "science needs to expand and create new tools to find the answers."

Bannister's feeling of being outside his body is the transcendental state that many runners seek to reach. The activity can produce a positive addiction to one's own natural drugs, says psychologist William Glasser. "It's a trance-like, transcendental mental state that athletes seek as much as trophies."

"There is a link between muscular and emotional states," writes John Jerome in *The Sweet Spot in Time.* "Getting blissed out might explain the depth of commitment that some endurance athletes have for their sports." The man who is considered the father of modern sport psychology, Bruce Ogilvie, calls this calm in the storm "an elevated sense, almost an out-of-body experience, a disassociation, a displacement."

> It becomes an ideal harmony of mind and body. The athlete is one with the performance world, with the setting he's in. He has total faith in his performance, a trust in his motor skills. He becomes egoless. There's no yardstick down his backbone anymore.

In his days as a world-class runner, Roger Bannister was a disciple of rigid training. But now, as a researcher and neurologist, he says there is more to heaven and earth:

There seems to be a connection with peak performance in sport and people who are drowning or who have these out-of-body experiences or other fight-or-flight situations. Many people near death say their life passes before their eyes. That's happened in heightened sporting events, as well. As the psychology of sports becomes much more researched, there'll be more studies in parapsychology.

NBA star Reggie Miller says that when he's psyched up (usually angry at opponents or fans), he sees himself directing the game from above the floor. "It takes me to another level and I shoot a lot better." In a 1994 game at Madison Square Garden, Miller's Indiana Pacers were facing defeat at the hands of hated rival New York Knicks. Miller's friend and rabid Knicks' fan, movie director Spike Lee, started rubbing it in with insults from his seat in the front row. Miller started taking the barbs personally and, while exchanging trash talk with Lee along the way, became vaulted into the zone. He went wild, firing in three-point shots from all over the court while in his head he seemed to be floating above it. He scored a whopping 25 points in the fourth quarter to single-handedly lead the Pacers to a comeback victory.

Miller claims such confrontations vault him into an out-of-body experience. He sounds like Rod Serling when he describes it: "When I get shooting like that, I'm suspended over the court, watching myself directing the game down below. Everything's going in slow motion. I seem to have more time to move around, to dictate plays and to make shots. When I shoot, I see the ball go in a split second before it actually does. . . . It's a wild feeling, and yet very natural when it happens. These things happen more on the road than in the Pacers' home gym, Market Square Arena, Miller admits. "I love being the enemy in the other team's building—it takes me to another level and I shoot a lot better," Miller said.

While in such cases athletes may be defending their pride or ego to trigger emergency resources, ironically it is the sudden release of all ego and anger that propels them to the final state of the zone performance, Ogilvie said. "In the moment of truth, the great athletes lose total self-awareness and even lack of consciousness of what's going on," he said. "They turn themselves over to their talent and their genes and let their ego get out of the way. It becomes an ideal harmony of mind and body, an out-of-body experience, and the athletes have total faith in their performance and a trust in their motor skills. They may go into an alpha brain state." Reaching such states often takes mental discipline and visual imagery, Ogilvie added. "They mentally rehearse their task and even the pressure attached to it, then they feel comfortable with it when it comes." Researcher Brad Hatfield, of the University of Maryland, said that entering such intense states of concentration is associated with profound changes in the brain.

Precognition and Other Altered Perceptions

Football great O.J. Simpson had a feeling of precognition while scoring the winning touchdown on a 64-yard run for the UCLA Bruins in 1967: "It was like watching myself in a daydream. I just took off and ran. When it was over, I felt good. But somehow I knew it was going to happen, even though it was a spontaneous thing." Baseball Hall of Famer Hank Aaron had two precognition feelings—which he relayed to teammates—moments before hitting two homeruns in 1974. Former Canadian men's skating champion Toller Cranston says this is often self-willed, an extension of a person's confidence, triggering adrenaline and other mind-body resources and skills to the ultimate. "I've seen the *expression* take over the face of the athlete who *knew* he or she was going to win. It happened in the Calgary Olympics with Brian Boitano, and then Elizabeth Manley. It was almost a supernatural power that took over, and they allowed it to take over. They called on invisible gas pumps in their bodies. The slow motion thing comes into effect, too. It's got something to do with not thinking at all about the results. You allow your body to go into automatic pilot and amazing things happen; you become reckless, you become fearless; even if you're outnumbered like Cortez, you feel protected. You really become the instrument of another force."

Flow

Even more rare than an individual "zone" is several athletes or even members of opposing teams feeling it at the same time. Hall of Fame

NBA player Bill Russell recalls:

> It would usually start with three or four of the top players serving as catalysts. Then the "feeling" would spread to the other guys, and we'd all levitate.... At that special level all sorts of odds things happened.... It was almost as if we were playing in slow motion.... I could almost sense how the next play would develop and where the next shot would be taken.... These were the moments when I had chills pulsing up and down my spine.

Psychology professor Mihaly Csikszentmihalyi of the University of Chicago calls some of these experiences being in the "flow" state and says they are probably related to the release of endorphins, adrenaline, and other hormones, although he's never investigated the biological basis. Csikszentmihalyi is the man who coined the term "flow," the rare mind-body state in which athletes lose themselves in total concentration.

"Being able to enter flow is emotional intelligence at its best; flow represents perhaps the ultimate in harnessing the emotions in the service of performance and learning," said Daniel Goleman, PhD, an author who covers behavioral and brain science for the *New York Times*. "In flow, the emotions are not just contained and channeled, but positive, energized, and aligned with the task at hand.... Yet flow, or a milder microflow, is an experience almost everyone enters from time to time, particularly when performing at their peak or stretching beyond their former limits." In flow, he added, the brain is in a cool state, its arousal and inhibition of neural circuitry attuned to the demand of the moment. When people are engaged in activities that effortlessly capture and hold their attention, their brain quiets down."

Unlike the arousal zone, the true "flow" does not involve anger or defense of ego, Csikszentmihalyi has said. It is not necessarily optimal arousal, but optimal experience and the mix of hormonal chemicals shooting through the mind-body that might be different than it is during high arousal, he added, although he has never studied the hormonal background of such feelings. Flow, he says, is an experience in which "attention can be freely invested to achieve a person's goals because there is no disorder to straighten out, no threat for the self to defend against. We have called this state the flow experience because this is the term many of the people we interviewed had used in their descriptions of how it felt to be in top form: 'It was like floating. I was carried on by the flow....' The battle is not really against the self, but against the entropy that brings disorder to consciousness. It is really a battle *for* the self; it is a struggle for establishing control over attention. The struggle does not necessarily have to be physical, as in the case of the climber. But anyone who has experienced flow knows that the deep enjoyment it provides requires an equal degree of disciplined concentration."

Csikszentmihalyi added there is a lot of play and give in the nervous system and "we can achieve somewhat impossible things; we can achieve miracles." Some flow states in athletes seem the same as the flow felt by soldiers on the battlefield, he says. "But war experiences can be more exhilarating than anything encountered in civilian life." Let's not overlook, though, how important the outcome of a game can be to the pride of athletic warriors John McEnroe and Martina Navratilova!

CHAPTER 4

The Painless Zone and Other States

". . . the adrenaline kicks in, and the body miraculously blocks the pain."

Dr. Carol Frey

Let's slow down and take stock of this complex subject.

All this talk about athletes in an aroused state and others being in states which seem to go from hyper to a more relaxed "flow," or even to slow motion, can be confusing. It's sometimes difficult to separate these states and hard to document them scientifically because of the unwieldy aspects of trying to hook up an athlete during the heat of battle.

Many experts believe there is more than one so-called "zone" of strange phenomena for athletes. We touched on this in the introduction, but it's worth repeating. The four zones we mentioned are

1. *Arousal zone,* where the athlete has a short spurt of arousal for one performance or part of one performance, often with "channeled" anger or another emotion;

2. *Painless zone,* where athletes can ignore or disconnect from pain for a short time;

3. *Flow,* where there is mind-body harmony, usually with less arousal than the arousal zone; and

4. Long-term zone, which is a sustained *emotional drive* that can last a few games, a few months, or even an entire season.

It's not clear about the interaction or connection among some of these experiences, says stress researcher Archibald Hart. "The experiences are hard to catalogue because they happen infrequently and because of the difficulty in studying them scientifically." Professor Csikszentmihalyi believes a connection exists between some of the zones at times, but he's also cautious because of the lack of formal research.

Discussion about types of zones gets puzzling "if we try to pin down too exactly the meaning of a colloquial term, such as the zone," wrote Andrew Cooper, PhD, in his book *Playing in the Zone*. "The term is used widely in sports culture, but agreement about its meaning is only general. When it comes to specific details, there is plenty of room for interpretation. . . . an athlete who speaks of being in the zone is describing the experience of any number of qualities clustered around them," said Cooper, who practices martial arts and meditation.

According to John Douillard, a former professional triathlete who teaches both arousal and calming techniques to amateur, pro, and Olympic athletes, there may be a number of mental/emotional states that remain out of reach because athletes rarely live up to their potential. "Neuroscientists say humans use only a small percentage of our brain power," Douillard said. "There are many potential states that we never reach. There are at least 100 trillion neuron junctions in the brain. What if we could just get access to many of them? Our athletic performances and performances in other areas of life would really soar."

Performing With Pain

In this chapter, we'll look at the "painless zone," a magical state athletes sometimes reach when they're battling pain or injury. It can help them produce seemingly impossible feats, yet, according to Douillard, this zone is merely a temporary protective shell that collapses on or before the end of a performance.

Some of sports' greatest performances have been accomplished by athletes in considerable pain. Is it possible that their mind-body defense systems, perhaps even fight or flight, not only made these efforts possible, but even enhanced the results with a combination of powerful hormones?

One of the defining moments of the 1996 Summer Olympics was the sight of U.S. gymnastics coach Bela Karolyi carrying sprightly 18-year-old Kerri Strug after her final, near-perfect vault on a badly-sprained ankle gave the Americans their first gold medal in women's team competition. President Bill Clinton called Strug's performance "miraculous." Experts believe that Strug's intense will to win and her little body's stress system triggered the internal wonder drugs—endorphin, dopamine, and serotonin among others—to allow her the golden moment. Keith Franklin, professor of neurobiology at McGill University in Montreal, believes that in such cases athletes use their fight-or-flight systems to trigger those "neurotransmitter" hormones, plus noradrenaline, from their brains into their bloodstream. "Endorphin increases your tolerance to pain and shuts off pain sensitivity, and it improves your coordination," he said. "Noradrenaline liberates more energy to the muscles and improves concentration, while dopamine makes things appear that they've slowed down."

As she charged down the runway of the arena in searing pain, Strug chanted to herself: "I will, I will, I will!" It is such positive thinking and determination that sparks the release of dopamine, Franklin said. "It's released all the time in anticipation of a successful outcome for the task. You could call it a positive hormone."

Natural Chemicals

During periods of high stress or pain, the brain's opioid system secretes endorphins to blunt the pain, says Daniel Goleman, PhD. "The system also becomes hyperactive . . . the opioids are brain chemicals that are powerful numbing agents, like opium and other narcotics that are chemical cousins," Goleman wrote in his book *Emotional Intelligence*. "When experiencing high levels of opioids, the brain's own morphine, people have a heightened tolerance for pain—an effect that has been noted by battlefield surgeons who found severely wounded soldiers needed lower doses of narcotics to handle their pain than did civilians with far less serious injuries."

Serotonin

Another neurotransmitter valuable to athletes under high stress and pain is serotonin, which can also be responsible for feelings of well-being, personal security, and relaxation, according to Joel Robertson, clinician and director of The Robertson Institute, which provides neurochemical evaluations and treatment techniques for athletes, corporations, and mental health facilities.

Endorphin

Endorphin is another fascinating drug of which we have all felt the effects. It is released, along with other hormones, from a place in the brain called the "E-spot" (a term coined by Los Angeles cardiologist and author Arnold Fox). In the modern brain, where the cerebral cortex (new brain) meets the limbic system (primitive brain), lies the magical E-spot. It is here where thoughts are converted into bio-chemical and electrical messengers, then dispersed throughout the body to carry out a person's wishes. This E-spot converts positive thoughts and enthusiasm into endorphins and dopamine. Fox coined the term to single out endorphins, which are hundreds of times more potent than morphine. They block chronic pain, enhance the immune system faster than any drug known to man, and can lift depression and fight disease. A study at the University of Tennessee Center for Health Sciences proved that thoughts can raise endorphin levels in the body.

Adrenaline

Adrenaline and its by-products probably were also released into Strug's system in the seconds prior to the final vault, according to Carol Frey of the American Academy of Orthopaedic Surgeons in Rosemont, Illinois. "What happens is that the adrenaline kicks in, and the body has a miraculous way of blocking pain. The mental edge is what makes you a winner."

Former world champion figure skater Elvis Stojko uses such edges to overcome pain. In the 1998 Winter Olympics, he was suffering from the flu and a torn adductor, a pinched nerve in his groin. For a skater who relied heavily on athleticism and powerful jumps, this should have been curtains, but Stojko dealt with the situation in the arena corridors as he prepared for his performance. "After I had done the warmup, I felt really small," he said. "I could feel everything closing in on me. And then I got pissed off with myself. I said to myself, 'You've spent 20 years working for this. Give it 100 percent or don't do it at all.'" There was also a brief question and answer period with his mental self: "'Okay, am I pissed off? Yes. Why am I so pissed off? Because I was dealt with this card. Okay, deal with it.' You've got to deal with it as a positive or else you'll never make it through. It'll eat you up."

Stojko then went out and delivered a performance that earned him the silver medal, although the groin injury prevented him from attempting a quadruple jump that could have given him the gold. He believes his mental outlook activated hormones to help him through the pain: "The adrenaline [and perhaps endorphin?] almost acts as a pain reliever. I thought to myself, 'Okay, I've got all the crappy stuff out of my system. Now, don't try to bypass the pain. Go straight towards it.'"

Secrets to sports science and psychology are being unearthed from the deep past. The skills and instincts of our brain, particularly the primitive parts, often go untapped, yet they can be effective tools to reaping high achievement, neurobiologists say.

Mind Control

Some athletes, such as former baseball player Kirk Gibson, seem to show us the missing links between primitive and present. During his storied, 16-year career in major league baseball, Gibson was often a Neanderthal in pinstripes—stubble-faced, physically intimidating, and reckless in his style, even rude and crude, albeit very street smart. And yet, adding modern methods of so-called "visualization," he may have tapped into pathways of a primitive part of the brain that has somehow taken on sophisticated skills—and the result was powers that made Gibson remarkable in the sports world.

> People say I'm a physical person, but I've been able to accomplish some incredible things through mind control," he says. "You have to control your mind, or it will control you. If you set a thermostat at 70, and the temperature drops below that, the heat will come on. Your mind's the same way. If you see yourself shooting 50 for nine holes of golf, your mind will move you toward 50 at the end. If you're shooting 40 with two holes to play, you'll get 10 for the last two holes.

Gibson's pinch-hit, two-out homer in the bottom of the ninth inning off pitcher Dennis Eckersley on October 15, 1988, was viewed by hundreds of millions of TV viewers across the world. Gibson's Los Angeles Dodgers faced the favored Oakland Athletics in the opening game of the series. By all reason, Gibson, plagued by several injuries, shouldn't have even dressed for the game, but he summoned amazing resources to belt the homer, and the memory of his crippled trot around the four bases is etched in the psyche of ball fans everywhere. It was a crisis Gibson had been bred to face up to. "All my life I've waited for these moments where I have to prove myself," he said.

For his great feat, Gibson summoned a form of visualization. He created a vision in his mind of the possibilities: "If it came down to the bottom of the ninth, I saw the fans goin' nuts as I came out of the dugout for the first time with my bat. I'd walk to the plate and suddenly all the pain would be gone. It would be just me and Dennis Eckersley, a hitter against a pitcher and nuthin' else in the way. All lateral distractions would be gone. It would be just me and him. I'd competed against him my whole career, and I had a good scouting report and game plan."

Visualization can work if it's deeply practiced, said Keith Franklin. "You can utilize the memories in the brain circuitry," he said.

> If you acquire a deep knowledge of a skill, you can visualize that it will happen when you need it. A classic case was Beethoven, who produced one of history's greatest works of music years after he'd gone deaf and couldn't hear the sounds! His wasn't visualization, but nearly the same thing, a sort of 'audioization.' His memories of the notes were stored in the same brain circuits he used to get his original perception.

The 6-foot-3, 220-pound Gibson bore down like a bull in the batter's box. He concentrated so intently on Eckersley, all distractions disappeared. Suddenly everything irrelevant vanished—the crowd noise, any consciousness of his broken-down swing, Athletics' catcher Ron Hassey and the other players in the ball park and, most of all, the pain in Gibson's worn-out body. "I refused to think about the pain. I put all other thoughts out of my mind except for one good swing . . . I was totally locked into Eckersley. In those situations your desire and your focus are better. It was the fiercest war you could imagine. I was locked into him big time. It was a physical, mental, and emotional battle. It was outstanding."

These unusual moments during high arousal are reported in all competitive sports. When tennis fans think of the top-ranked players, they think first of their big serve or baseline footwork or their ability to dazzle opponents with topspins, but it is often the will to win and "hormone control" that separates someone like Pete Sampras from the pack and sends him into the zone. In the quarterfinals of the 1996 U.S. Open, Sampras was sick as a dog, but he overcame Spaniard Alex Corretja in an incredible match 7-6, (7-5), 5-7, 5-7, 6-4, 7-6 (9-7). Exhausted in the heat and humidity, fighting a queasy stomach and dehydration, Sampras leaned on his racket like a crutch between long rallies. In the middle of the fifth-set tiebreaker, he vomited on the court and looked like he would pass out. Corretja, who broke down and cried after the long ordeal, said that Sampras was more dangerous, like a wounded animal, when he got sicker. "I saw him get really tired and sick, but then he was more dangerous; he'd serve at 124 miles an hour."

According to Brian Hainline, a tournament physician, Sampras has an amazing ability to block out distractions, such as illness, and focus on his task—as well as using outside influences as motivators. Sampras said he endured the pain of the Corretja match by thinking about his coach and best friend, Tim Gullikson, who had recently died of brain cancer. "This one's for Tim; Tim was out there with me," Sampras said after the match.

Overcoming Pain and Illness

• 1997 NBA finals—Michael Jordan, saddled with a stomach virus that left him nauseous, weak, dizzy, dehydrated, and with a headache, probably shouldn't have played in game five of the Chicago Bulls' series with the Utah Jazz. But he did, scoring 38 points including the winning three-pointer.

• 1996 Stanley Cup playoffs—While his Pittsburgh Penguin mates were on the ice playing the Florida Panthers, Mario Lemieux was sick with the flu in the dressing room, getting an IV injection of saline. He came out to set up one goal and score another as the Penguins won.

• 1992 NBA game—Boston Celtics' Larry Bird shouldn't have played with an Achilles injury, but he scored 49 points to lead Boston over Portland.

• 1991 Indianapolis 500—A.J. Foyt, in severe pain from a 1990 crash, qualified at 222 mph.

• 1991 college football—Lehigh receiver Rich Clark caught 26 passes in four games with two broken hands.

• 1991 American League baseball game—With serious back problems as well as heel and finger injuries, the Texas Rangers' Nolan Ryan threw a no-hitter at the Toronto Blue Jays.

• 1988 Olympics, women's figure skating—Sick with the flu and an ear infection, Canada's Elizabeth Manley scored a near-flawless performance to defeat favored rivals in the free skate.

• 1988 Olympic men's 10-meter platform diving—American Greg Louganis won the gold medal after smashing his head on the diving board, cutting himself and requiring four stitches.

• 1988 NBA finals—Detroit Pistons' Isiah Thomas badly twisted his ankle, then scored 25 points in one quarter while hobbling around.

• 1984 Olympics 1,500 meters—Britain's Sebastian Coe was ill all week, had infected lymph glands, and was worn down from heat and smog, then he recorded a remarkable 13.4 seconds down the 100-meter homestretch to defeat the fastest field ever and win the gold medal.

• 1984 Olympic men's figure skating—American Scott Hamilton won the gold medal with an ear infection.

• 1978 World Heavyweight Championship fight—Leon Spinks pulled off one of the biggest upsets in boxing history over Muhammad Ali, despite a rib cage muscle tear so painful he couldn't throw a punch before the fight.

• 1977 NFL game—Tired and queasy with flu, the Chicago Bears' Walter Payton rushed for a record 275 yards against the rival Minnesota Vikings.

• 1972 Heavyweight Fight—Muhammad Ali fought for 11 rounds with a broken jaw against Ken Norton.

• 1970 NBA finals, seventh game—New York Knicks' Willis Reed shouldn't have played with knee and hip injuries, but he led the Knicks to a dramatic win over the Los Angeles Lakers.

• 1968 Olympic s1,500 meters—After collapsing in an earlier race from a gall bladder infection and being sick on the day of the race, Kip Keino won the gold medal.

• 1964 LPGA Tournament (Midland, Texas)—Nagged by injuries, Mickey Wright came from 10 strokes behind to win the tournament.

• 1932 U.S. national track and field championships—After having severe stomach pains the night before, Babe Didrikson broke world records in four competitions.

The Illegitimate Zone

John Douillard cites many experiences as occurring in the "illegitimate zone," a fight-or-flight response intended to mask serious pain, injury, or fatigue. He believes they often result from a breakdown between mind and body, as opposed to the harmony of mind and body in a "flow" zone.

> What happens is, during intense exercise or during intense pain, the body starts to produce stress-fighting hormones to help the athlete endure the ordeal—endorphins, enkephalons, and other substances which have morphine qualities. Yes, the pain is killed and you start to feel numb swimming in a flood of endorphins. And you can even feel euphoric. But the mind can become out of touch with physical reality.

Runners sometimes feel a type of this experience in "runner's high," Douillard added, although in a healthy "runner's high," the fight-or-flight response reaches only 50 percent capacity. His exercise program teaches athletes to have a 50-50 split between mind and body responses, allowing brain waves to go into an alpha state, a "legitimate zone where mind and body become inseparable."

As more research is conducted and sport psychology continues to examine the role of emotions and stress hormones during performance, perhaps the link among these various "zones" will become more clear.

PART II

Warring Athletes

This section will look at how many elite athletes get super production from looking on themselves as warriors caught up in a contemporary battle.

Chapter 5 uses Michael Jordan, the ultimate competitor, as a springboard for discussion, showing how modern-age warriors have attached themselves to the athletic world. They are not protecting their bodies or their families from harm, but rather protecting their territory, their pride, their ego. For them, it is not an insignificant war.

In chapter 6, I look at the incredible drive that elite athletes possess and the various places there motivation may come from. In chapter 7, I discuss the elite athlete's upbringing, showing that a high percentage come from dysfunctional or challenged backgrounds and how they turn that adversity into an advantage. This follows with a chapter on the heavy influence that parents have had on professional sports. To complete this part of the book, in chapter 9, I look at how the competitive sports world is a breeding ground for insecurities and defense mechanisms that athletes use as powerful weapons.

CHAPTER 5

The Athlete as Warrior

> "I won't forget what happened, or who did it to me."
>
> Michael Jordan

When an athlete looks at him- or herself as a modern-day warrior, the powerful and ancient defense arousal systems can kick in.

No one has perfected the primitive techniques like Michael Jordan. For years, his secret weapon was known only to NBA insiders, fans sitting at courtside, and, of course, the victims he brought to their knees. Many people outside that realm were led to believe that the often-smiling Jordan succeeded solely because his talent was so much richer than anybody else's. But people close to him whispered secrets such as this: In the 1985 NBA rookie all-star game, Jordan, then a cocky rookie out of North Carolina, believed that Isiah Thomas of the Detroit Pistons and George Gervin of the San Antonio Spurs tried to embarrass him and put him in his place. The next day, while pumping quickly on a stationary bicycle, a sweaty Jordan grumbled to a journalist: "I won't forget what happened, or who did it to me." Two nights later, Jordan torched Thomas and the Pistons for 49 points and later in the season, he destroyed Gervin's Spurs for 48.

Behind the Smile

CNN interviewer Larry King once wondered what fueled the intense drive behind "the most beautiful smile in sports." Jordan wasn't smiling during the 1993 playoffs, when a national TV audience got a glimpse into what everybody in the NBA already knew: that Michael Jordan, the most famous, successful, and respected athlete in the world, becomes an angry warrior when it's good for production. For most of Game 5 that year, the New York Knicks' Doc Rivers had answers for Jordan's sophisticated moves and shots. He was thwarting the game's best player with physical yet clean defense, limiting him to nine points after three quarters. To start the fourth quarter, Rivers blocked Jordan's drive to the basket but was called for a foul as Michael hit the deck. With dramatic timing, Jordan leaped to his feet and cursed at Rivers. As a hidden TV camera zoomed in, Jordan thrust his face a few inches from the calm Rivers to yell, "You're a nuthin'. You're a zero! You can't cover me!" Rivers looked embarrassed that a person of Jordan's stature had lowered himself to such drivel. But it worked. Over the next few minutes Jordan became a revitalized player. He broke free from Rivers' shackles, scoring important baskets as the Bulls overcame a deficit to defeat New York.

Said Rivers: "You don't get to Michael very often, but I did with my physical play. He didn't appreciate that I wasn't in awe of him. He started insulting me to try to get the edge back, and he did. I understand why he had to do it. It's a war out there, and you need every edge, every psychological and emotional edge. It's a virtual war." Yet as soon as the game was over, the assassin's expression receded from Jordan's face, along with his tongue. He walked over to Rivers, shook his hand, and called him a champion.

Later, with the passing of the 1996-97 season, Jordan's "secret" was out for good. His angry outbursts had become well-documented in the press. Even his cerebral coach, Phil Jackson, admitted that "there were four or five games this year when Michael used his anger against people." Here are a couple of examples from 1996-97, another championship season for the 34-year-old Jordan and his Chicago Bulls:

• Victim: New York Knicks. Knicks' coach Jeff Van Gundy says in the *Chicago Tribune* that Jordan is a con man who softens up his opponents by befriending them, then destroys them on the court. Whoops. That night, Jordan scores 51 of his team's 88 points in a Bulls' victory and yells something at Van Gundy that would embarrass any con man.

• Victim: New Jersey Nets. Nets' coach John Calipari warns his rookie guard Kerry Kittles about covering Jordan: "Do not make him mad, do not talk junk . . . just let him play his game and leave the building." But Calipari should have given the same lecture to his assistant Don Casey who needled Jordan after Kittles scored 17 points on him in the first quarter. An infuriated Jordan blasted Kittles 14-0 in the second quarter and nearly melted the fiberglass backboard with the look he gave Casey.

The Trump Card

How *dare* other players try to cover me, Jordan told himself. This is a man who once said his father's murder was God's way of testing him. Jordan rose to repel every challenge that came along because for the second and glorious stage of his rocket career, Michael Jordan honed his final and perhaps most devastating skill: his fighting emotions. He sharpened his vindictiveness to the point that it was the most feared weapon in the NBA, his trump card. Jordan became the ultimate warrior, combining the fighting and survival instincts of primal man with his unrivalled fundamental skills and the sophisticated techniques of today's basketball. Behind Jordan's sweet smile was a hunter with a sharp spear. And his "controlled" anger seemed good for business. When some players get mad, their fundamentals break down, but with Jordan, his dribble got faster, his defensive step quickened, and his shot started rotating like Mars. With all he accomplished, you wouldn't think Jordan would care much about what other people think about him. Through 1998 he had ten NBA scoring titles, five MVP trophies, and six championship rings. His salary was the size of some state budgets. But he did worry what others thought of him and his abilities. "I tend to take things personally," Jordan said after a playoff game in 1996 in Seattle in which he traded insults with the SuperSonics' Gary Payton, then scorched him as the Bulls won. In many of these high-level performances, Jordan has reported that the action seemed to transpire in slow motion, that he seemed to have more time to cut and dribble and shoot than normal, while opponents were traveling at normal speeds.

It could be that Jordan has brought warrior instincts into the modern age of sports and added to it a sophistication that will be copied by elite athletes who follow him. According to Marie Francine Raymond, assistant to the director of the athletic department at the University of Toronto, many other elite athletes are able to use their animal instinct to varying degrees of success, but that often they cross over the line during high arousal and their anger becomes self-destructive. "Either you deal with arousal intelligently and use it to influence your performance and your environment productively or you lose it," said Raymond, a former international rower for Canada. "It all depends on the messages your coaches have sent you through the years and your values and your education and whether you have access to a sport psychologist. You can let the arousal spill over in a game and then it becomes just an animal response which was made to help you fight for your life. Then you can get into a situation of fouling your opponent, fighting, or verbally abusing him. The reaction of defending yourself in sport is very different than that of defending yourself from harm. In a sport, you've got to keep perspective."

Raymond says you need look no further than Jordan's former teammate on the Bulls, Dennis Rodman, to find an athlete who steps over the line too frequently. Rodman has been the best rebounder in the NBA in the 1990s, but he is also one of the most frequently suspended players for his fighting, fouling, and verbal abuse of opponents and officials. "I would hope that young athletes learn from the way Jordan deals with pressure; they'll be better off than becoming a Dennis Rodman and getting into confrontations," Raymond said.

The Anger Zone

It's too bad that science doesn't have the technology (yet) to test superstars like Jordan and golf whiz Tiger Woods and baseballer Ken Griffey, Jr., in the heat of their battles. (In 1993, researchers at Syracuse University attached brain-wave monitors to basketball players' heads in practice, but the test proved too unwieldy.)They might discover that what separates super athletes from the pack night after night is not as much talent as it is *drive*—long-term determination and short-term explosions, perhaps hatched out of a desire to prove something to somebody—a warrior's attitude. Nancy Lopez used anger to dramatically win the LPGA championship in 1985 after she felt she'd been unfairly penalized for slow play: "I made anger work to my advantage. I went into tunnel vision," she said. "I didn't see the galleries, the TV cameras. I was going to show the LPGA and its officials that I could win in spite of them all. I promise you, nobody could have beaten me that day. I got into a zone where I could see every shot before I hit it, and every shot was perfect in my mind. It was a matter of pride."

Many athletes report this "anger" zone. And many others report playing better than normal when aroused by other emotions. These strong and yet controlled feelings can provide a hormonal additive for underdog athletes and teams, such as the 1997 Ryder Cup team from Europe. The powerful U.S. squad, led by Tiger Woods, was heavily favored, but sparked by fiery captain Seve Ballesteros, motoring from hole to hole on a golf cart to rally his troops and urged on by a home Spanish crowd singing and chanting "Ole!" the emotional Europeans upset the Americans by one point.

Concentrated Emotions

When we study elite athletes and their celebrated performances, we find many strange and fascinating characteristics: strong desires and perhaps even *needs* to succeed, a lifetime of training and coaching help, and a consistent ability to seize the moment. It is within this moment of truth that concentrated emotions, particularly anger and fear, are often found. Some athletes can trigger arousal states, albeit infrequently, through precompetition thoughts, and these states can also be reached physically on occasion through the rigors of intense exercise, says neurologist Roger Bannister. "More athletes should enter the 'zone,' but there's a lot we have to learn."

Warriors love the pressure situations and try to use their nervousness as an added power. "It feels real good to be nervous, to have sweaty palms again," Woods said before winning the 1997 Western Open. "I like being in contention: the pressure gives you a better chance of winning—you feel your nerves, the butterflies going through your stomach." Woods knew what all the greats have learned through trial and error—that pressure of the big match and the inner resources it can spark can send their game over the top, or it can bring it crashing to earth if they choke.

"Emotions run the show in sports," says James E. Loehr, EdD, sport psychologist to such superstars as tennis player Monica Seles

© CRAIG JONES/ALLSPORT

Nancy Lopez: "I got into a zone where I could see every shot before I hit it, and every shot was perfect in my mind."

and speed skater Dan Jansen. "But it's a delicate process, very intricate. Some emotions, like fear and rage, are disempowering and move you away from your optimal performance level, your ideal performance state. Others are empowering, like challenge and determination, and they move you towards it."

There seem to be many components that go into an unforgettable performance, including an athlete's fitness, training, and perhaps even biorhythms—not to mention, of course, what the opponents are doing against him that night. But the athlete's attitude, particularly if it is unusually aggressive or even angry, appears to loom large. Here are a few more examples of athlete warriors throughout sports history:

• On Oct. 1, 1932, Babe Ruth was said to predict his World Series home run against the Chicago Cubs. But some witnesses claim that Ruth was not pointing to the bleachers but threatening Cubs' pitcher Charlie Root. Ruth was so furious at Root and Cub fans for insulting him and his wife and for pelting him with fruit, he belted the ball out of Wrigley Field.

• In perhaps the best golfing exhibition ever, a previously slumping, 46-year-old Jack Nicklaus shot six-under on the back nine to seize the 1986 Masters over a young bunch of hungry Europeans. Nicklaus admitted he was ticked off after reading in the papers prior to the round that he was too old to win. "Hmmm, I sizzled . . . then I went out and did it."

• Billie Jean King came from far behind to defeat Chris Evert in the 1975 Wimbledon because she was angry from a previous loss to Evert in which she felt cheated by officials. "I willed the victory," she said.

• Prior to an NBA game between the Philadelphia Warriors and the New York Knicks on March 2, 1962, a coach walked up to the Warriors' Wilt Chamberlain and showed him the New York newspapers in which Knicks' players were quoted as saying Wilt was "too slow, lacked stamina, and we're going to run him ragged." A fuming Chamberlain went out and scored 100 points in a performance that may never be duplicated.

• Another record that still holds up is Rennie Stennett's seven hits in a major league baseball game as his Pittsburgh Pirates beat the Chicago Cubs on Sept. 16, 1975. In his previous visit to Chicago, Stennett had been hit in the head by a pitch and hospitalized. "I was mad," he said. "The only way to get back at them was to hit them. I just knew I was going to get the hits. . . . I saw them before they happened."

While the above cases happen once or twice in a lifetime, other performances in which anger, or at least *controlled* anger, seems to be an important fuel cross the sports' pages every morning. While the sporting community reluctantly acknowledges these outbursts happen from time to time, it remains a dark topic even among some sport psychologists.

The Emotional Link

While sports has finally embraced the link between mind and body in the past couple of decades (check locker rooms and book shelves for the number of sport psychologists), it's still slow to admit, or even fully recognize, the link between emotions, especially so-called negative emotions like fear and anger, and performance, says Jack Raglin, a kinesiologist who says many athletes are motivated by worry or fear. It gives them the high arousal they need to go over the top and it focuses them to persist on their task. Although many stars seem consciously strong and very confident, this insecurity may be subconscious (or in the case of the enlightened Jordan, at least semiconscious), and they may not be aware that it's helping to drive them, Raglin added.

> It may be a subconscious lack of confidence. But my position on anxiety and stress in sport differs from the majority of sport psychologists. They make a lot of money by teaching athletes mostly about confidence and that they need to relax before a performance . . . and yet many athletes are motivated by lack of confidence and need a high level of anxiety for performance. There's a lot of work and research to be done in this area.

Anger Prevails in Toyko

The biggest hormonal bang for athletes is provided by feelings of fear and anger, often when they feel they must prove something to somebody or are defending their pride. Perhaps the world's most sought-after sports record was finally smashed after 23 years—not by the most talented athlete, but the most angry and desperate. In the 1968 Olympics, Bob Beamon long-jumped an incredible 29 feet, 2.5 inches, beating the existing record by two feet. The jump had the advantage of being performed in the rare air of Mexico City and many track and field experts felt it would never be broken. If anyone could do it, it would be American Carl Lewis, arguably the best athlete of all time, and during King Carl's reign throughout the 1980s and into the 90s, the media kept repeating this.

But it was unheralded Mike Powell, never winner of an Olympic gold medal and loser of 15 straight long jumps to Lewis, who defeated Beamon's record in a stunning upset at the world track and field championships in Tokyo in 1991. And he said he did it largely through a strong desire or need to defend his pride and ego against

Lewis and the world's press. "I was really mad and angry that everybody was counting me out," Powell later said.

Powell awoke the morning of the world championships thinking through every step of his jump, scheduled for seven o'clock that night. He kept on the schedule of a careful plan he'd been thinking through for years, set up with scientific thought, rigorous training, top coaching, and adjustment of jumping techniques. Powell described his visualization technique in training: "I went through everything in my head: My approach along the runway, the start, the kick off the board, the time in the air — each body movement. All day I focused on it, deliberately keeping my eyes down to the ground if I saw people in the athletes' village. I felt this was my moment for something big. In my mind, I'd already broken the world record a thousand times." Most of the day, Powell sat quietly in his room and jotted down on paper the things he would get out of a world record performance.

1. The satisfaction of beating Carl Lewis for the first time.
2. A sense of accomplishment of being the best in the world and breaking a record people said was untouchable.
3. Putting himself on a new level professionally.

And then Powell made a stunning prediction: he'd eclipse Beamon's unreachable world record with a jump. "I'd show them," he said. "They didn't think I could do it. It was a personal insult. I'd show everybody."

The moment finally came: a muggy Friday evening in Tokyo, hot and humid. The world championships, men and women representing their countries, running and jumping in an air of thick pea soup, waving their national flags before 60,000 spectators. In his first of five jumps, the intense Powell became so emotional, he hyperventilated and felt faint. His performance suffered as he jumped less than 26 feet, a typical "choke" response of overarousal. "I wanted to go out and break the world record on the first jump. I tried too hard, got too crazy, and my mechanics broke down," Powell said. "My technique was terrible. I had to get focused, get relaxed and channel my emotions to the exact moment I'd need them, instead of letting them escape. I had to put it all into one jump."

Meanwhile, Lewis soared with his usual grace for an early jump of 28 feet, five and three-quarter inches — a meet record, but a long way off Beamon's world mark. Lewis, who had been chasing Beamon for a decade, was hoping to retire with it under his belt — "then I could walk off into the sunset." At 30, Lewis was getting old to stay on top with such elite competition, some experts felt, yet he remained dangerous. Noted an observer: "His manner was contained and businesslike, but his appetite was voracious."

Powell was inspired by Lewis' leap. "He (Lewis) threw his fist in the air. I looked into the stands at my coach and I got that feeling," Powell recalled. "Overcoming the odds always gets me going. It seems natural for me to step up and perform during The Moment of Truth. I need this motivation. I may not have as much training, and some may say not as much talent as some other track stars. But I got charged from head to toe. Something was flowing through me. My body and mind were ready."

Powell recovered with improved jumps in his subsequent tries, but Lewis was still leading when it came down to the final jump for each competitor. The anger was building in Powell and the 15 straight defeats to Lewis was tasting like bile in his mouth. Powell had something to prove to Bob Beamon, too. Years before, Beamon had presented medals at a track meet in which Powell was entered. But Beamon walked away as Powell was about to jump. "I said to myself, 'Don't you walk away when I'm jumping!'" Powell said. (Powell then recorded the winning jump of the competition.)

Faced with his final try, Powell *visualized* how he would succeed. "Before the last jump, I knew what was going to happen—the whole process. It was eerie. I saw it all again in my mind, but this time it was like precognition: the good speed on the runway, the good timing and good takeoff on the board, that super extra burst of strength. It really was eerie. It felt like it was supposed to happen."

Sports Illustrated described Powell's last attempt: "He had meditated on the images of what he had to do, took four walking steps with his arms swinging loosely, gathered into a run, hit full speed as his singlet slipped over his left shoulder, struck the board hard two inches from the end, drove high off his left foot, performed a hitch kick with his head thrown far back, broke the sand in the vicinity of the nine-meter marker, swung right and burst from the pit thrusting his arms with what seemed righteous anger."

What the magazine didn't mention was the yelp Powell let out while he was airborne — releasing the frustrations of a career into the sticky Japanese skies—and the intense concentration, which turned Powell's quantum leap into something out of the Twilight Zone, the gold earring in his left ear twinkling as he soared. "It all happened in

© VICTAH SAILER

"When anyone tells me I can't do something, you can be sure I'm gonna do it soon."

slow motion. I can remember every movement of my body, especially when I was in the air. In the air I remember thinking, 'Soon I'll be hitting the sand and the crowd will go Ooooh!' Then it will be announced that I've broken the record."

For 30 seconds after his superman effort, Powell nervously wandered around the infield until the measurement was announced: 29 feet, four and one-half inches. He had demolished Bob Beamon's indestructible record. Powell skipped and danced like a child. "In your face!" he snarled at Lewis, who looked almost bewildered.

But Powell had to put his celebration on hold because Lewis had one jump left. Powell could still be the dreaded number two again. Lewis was an old warrior at responding to pressures of battle, armed with his cliche: "You feel like your whole life is at stake and it is because you have put out your whole life for this one chance."

Powell, heart pounding, folded his hands, as if silently pleading to a god who would take sides in this clash of egos. The fate was finally out of Powell's hands. "I thought he'd still beat me," Powell said. But Carl Lewis came up short in his last jump, setting off a celebration in the Powell camp. Powell scrambled up the aisles crammed with 60,000 screaming Japanese and hugged his coach, Randy Huntington. "We got him!" Huntington shouted, referring to Lewis (or was it Beamon?). Later, Powell would remind reporters that he'd predicted his record jump right down to the inch.

At the same championships, Lewis had his moment of triumph, proving he was the World's Fastest Human. He broke the world record for the 100 meters—9.86 seconds, powering past five rivals who also broke the coveted 10-second barrier. Lewis did it, he said, for his dead father. The following year, in the 1992 Olympics at Barcelona, Lewis won four more gold medals, including a "revenge" win over Powell in the long jump.

Meanwhile, Powell couldn't rest on the laurels of his fantastic record in Japan. "I have to prove things to myself every day, every morning when I wake up. I challenge myself—in soul-searching, in finding just the right mate to become the father I never had, in helping young people on the street, and in the weight training room with my friend. Really, when you look at it, all I did in Toyko was jump in dirt."

War Minus the Shooting

Writer George Orwell once called sports a war minus the shooting. (In fact, it's said that a soccer match once started a war between Honduras and El Salvador). If so, is it any surprise that athletes sometimes go into fight or flight, especially in games of aggressiveness and violence?

"My favorite period of history is the ancient Romans," said tennis legend Martina Navratilova. "I'm fascinated by the gladiators in the arena. I think of them sometimes when I'm waiting to go into the great bowl of the U.S. Open or the old green stadium at Wimbledon. It's the same idea: two warriors, the fight to the death, the crowd rooting for its favorite. I always accepted the notion of winning and losing, of surviving on your wits and your courage and skill."

"The emotional roots of athletics are deep. A great deal of the jargon and many of the attitudes about sports have been carried over from the days when games were rites of passage in primitive societies," said sport psychologist Thomas Tutko.

> The British, for example, were said to have won their wars on the playing fields of Eton, where the officer class learned as children the importance of sacrificing to win. Games are a sublimation of combat between individuals or between cities, regions or countries. . . . In modern games, warfare metaphors still abound: competing sides alternately play offense or defense, the team destroyed that one, so-and-so has killer instinct, a long pass is a bomb, overtime play is sudden death (note the equating of death-as-losing, and the emphasis on sudden losing as opposed to sudden winning). As great warriors have always been great heroes, the warriors of our time, the professional athletes, now often receive the social benefits of generals.

Track-and-field athletes need a warrior mentality to succeed, said veteran track coach Brooks Johnson.

> The field events couldn't be invented today. They wouldn't be politically correct. You have to realize that all the tools in these events are implements of war. That was how the events began, as competition between soldiers. The javelin. The shot. The 35-pound weight. All weapons. The pole-vault. The idea of the pole vault was that I vault over the wall and go up behind you and slit your throat. You have to act like these are implements of war. When you have that discus in your hand, you have to have that kind of mind. You have to say 's— -!' when you let go. You're trying to kill someone. That is how you have to feel.

This is the way many top generals, er, coaches motivate their troops; by appealing to their killer instincts. The battle is not about food and shelter or the meadow across the river anymore, but about the territory of pride and winning one for the team.

Some athletes try to bring this attitude to life. Goalie Patrick Roy of the Colorado Rockies of the NHL had the words *Be a Warrior* inscribed under his blocker. In his 1997 boxing match with Oscar De La Hoya, Hector Camacho entered the ring in a cape and a Darth Vader–like mask. In a 1997 football game, all-American Juan Roque of Arizona State University smeared war paint on his face and called his opponents "the enemy." Such tactics—or antics, depending on whom you're talking to—are common today in physical sports, such as football and hockey.

Many sport psychologists and researchers say such intense emotions are triggered by the athletes as a sort of reflex mechanism to defend their egos or self-esteem. Their need to "defend" often, they say, comes from a challenged upbringing (research shows that a high percentage of stars had a missing, dead, or abusive parent) or from insecurities developed while playing competitive sports from a young age.

Many coaches and sport psychologists seek ways to harness an athlete's reactions to pressure. Stress expert Massad Ayoob of New Hampshire advises athletes to recognize their nervousness for what it is (a type of fear), then quickly turn it briefly to anger, then finally to dispassionate attention to the task. Biochemists suggest that this mindset could even trigger a physiological switch in hormones squirted throughout the body, causing adrenaline (mainly a fear and defensive hormone) to ignite noradrenaline, testosterone, and dopamine, which are attacking hormones. "But there must be a flow to the whole process or it will break down," Ayoob said. "It must be practiced under stressful situations in order to develop your reaction system."

The best way for an athlete to successfully use arousal, according to Thomas R. George, a sports psychologist at the University of Michigan, is to use emotional and psychological insecurities as subconscious motivators, but during the performance, the athlete must focus consciously on technical aspects of his or her event. Such methods will be examined at length in part III of this book.

CHAPTER 6

The Incredible Drive of Elite Athletes

> " What I have learned about myself is that I am an animal when it comes to achievement and wanting success. There is never enough success for me."
>
> Golfer Gary Player

Many coaches believe that an athlete's success depends on four factors: physical ability, physical training, mental training, and desire or *drive*. The percentages of these four factors may vary from athlete to athlete and even with the same athlete from game to game.

Many psychologists say that it is the desire, the passion, and the ambition, that separates high achievers from the rest of the field, even from others with equal or more talent, whether they're a banker, an author, or a baseball player. "Superstars have almost too much drive to succeed and that sets them apart from the pack," said Steven Berglas, a clinical psychologist at Harvard Medical School who works with professional athletes.

Inner Drive to Excel

Legendary players like baseball's Pete Rose (who was not drafted by a major league team) and basketball's Larry Bird didn't necessarily have legendary physical prowess, but they made up for it with their motivation to succeed. They *wanted* it more than others did, so they did what it took to get it. They practiced harder, they studied their skills and their opponents, and they worked harder in games. They sacrificed their personal lives and gave up vacations. They took more risks. Their motivation seemed to come from desire, sometimes bordering on manic desire.

In his childhood, through his adolescence, and into his all-star days with the Boston Celtics, Bird seem to have an athletic inferiority complex. He recalled of his early years in the NBA: "A lot of the time I thought about establishing myself as a professional, to prove I wasn't too slow and all the other things that my critics said I was, or wasn't."

Martina Navratilova also admitted to manic desire. "God, I want to win so bad, I'll die if I don't," Martina Navratilova told herself just prior to winning the U.S. Open women's tennis title for the first time in 1983. But sometimes even that is not powerful enough when an athlete comes up against an opponent with even more desire, as Navratilova found out when she tried to win her ninth Wimbledon title in 1989 against Germany's Steffi Graf. After winning the match, Graf sobbed in her sideline chair and later confessed: "I wanted it so badly that I put a little more pressure on myself than usual. It's an overwhelming feeling." Graf had won.

Martial arts pioneer Bruce Lee called such intense drive by star athletes who have won time and time again "an unquenchable thirst for competition." Lee had it in spades, too, and forged a name for himself in competition and blazed a trail to meld Eastern and Western philosophies into sports.

Sprinter Donovan Bailey confessed it was not enough to become the world's fastest man, as he proved in record time in the 100 meters in the Atlanta Olympics, but to keep proving he was over and over again. "I guess the more success I get at whatever I do, there's a craving for more," he said. The drive not only to win but just to compete has compelled many athletes back into sports after serious injuries, like San Francisco 49ers quarterback Steve Young, who suffered three concussions in 10 months and yet made a comeback despite the urgings of his parents and family that he retire and despite the potential for permanent brain damage.

Thomas Tutko, one of the leading sport psychologists and researchers in North America, has done numerous studies of athletes. The first thing he talks about is an elite athlete's "push . . .this want they have to excel." This drive can be the engine behind them improving their game, training hard, planning, and making goals for themselves. It can encourage them to become risk-takers. It can even improve their maturity and allow them to accept responsibility when something goes wrong. And it can give them a humility which allows them to learn from their mistakes, Tutko said.

Emotional Drive

Motivation can lead to success and subsequently confidence and positive thinking. And it can encourage the athlete to practice hard to develop his game. Strong motivation is what helps them develop their skills, say psychologists Miriam and Otto Ehrenberg in their book *Optimum Brain Power*: "The skills of an artist or athlete are developed through a strong emotional drive for mastery. Without that motivation, the persistent application required to develop those skills is not possible."

"Emotional drive is a good name for it," says John Anderson, a sport psychologist.

> These days, we're hearing a lot about emotional quotients and emotional intelligence, that emotions are the source of our energy. When we talk about logic, the left brain stuff, people just don't get cranked up about it. But when they let their emotions come in, that's when you see the excitement come in with an athlete; that's when they get energized, over the long haul and the short term.

Sometimes the competitive spark seems dormant in "placid" athletes until the game starts or until the moment of truth comes, when they are threatened by defeat or by opponents. Look at the fire that can suddenly energize hockey's Wayne Gretzky, boxing's Evander Holyfield, baseball's Mark McGwire and Sammy Sosa, golf's Nancy Lopez and Tiger Woods, football's Joe Montana and Steve Young, and tennis great Martina Hingas.

If emotional drive is an athlete's long-term motivation, then arousal during a performance is the short-term drive. From now on, let's refer to these two motivations as (1) emotional drive and (2) arousal. Both systems, psychologists say, are fueled partly by hormones.

The Power of the Holy Grail

The *emotional drive* to win can manifest itself in dramatic fashion. On an afternoon in mid-July of 1997, long after the ice had melted on another National Hockey League season, friends, family and teammates of Detroit Red Wings' star Vladimir Konstantinov huddled in a Michigan hospital to try to save his life. Konstantinov had been in a coma for more than a month, either in a conscious or semi-conscious state. He was injured when their limousine crashed on its way back from a charity golf tournament, suffered serious brain trauma, and for weeks did not respond even to family and friends. He seemed in a dream-like state, unaware of the world around him. It was feared he would die. Few things seemed to work, not even comfort from his wife and eight-year-old daughter, nor prayer vigils from hundreds of fans lighting red and white candles. But then his loved ones came up with a startling and desperate strategy: they brought the Stanley Cup, the Holy Grail of hockey, into his room at the William Beaumont Hospital. It was the same championship trophy Konstantinov had hoisted over his head a few weeks earlier when his Red Wings had won the playoffs for the first time in 42 years. When some of his teammates brought the Cup into the room, they kept it covered up and Konstantinov paid it little attention. But then someone unveiled it, revealing its shiny silver luster and all the names of the great men who had won it. Suddenly, the semiconscious Konstantinov seemed to pay attention. "He never took his eyes off it," hospital spokesperson Colette Stimmel said. "He touched it and stared at it. He was staring very intently at it. He did seem to recognize what it was." Within months, Konstantinov had recovered sufficiently to watch a Red Wings' practice.

Did the Stanley Cup really have the power to help bring Konstantinov back to life? If so, how? That's likely an intricate issue for doctors and psychologists to tackle. It might have even been the shiny silver qualities of the cup, although hospital officials stressed that he seemed to recognize the cup. If that was the case, it probably had nothing to do with a piece of silver but a hockey player's view of the world and what was important to him. Obviously, winning was extremely important to him, as it is to most serious athletes.

The Need to Win

Bruce Ogilvie says with many athletes winning becomes "an absolute obsession." In four decades of following sports, much of it as a psychologist, he's seen some explosive performances. One of the biggest motivators, he says, is when an athlete is on the verge of a dream, like winning the Stanley Cup or the Wimbledon tennis tourney. "One tremendous force is precipitating expectation that the dream or the goal can be realized. It becomes like standing at the edge of the cliff and you leap out and realize your fullest potential. It's as though you see the potential realization of your dreams."

An Olympic gold medal is apparently as important as life itself for some athletes. Gabe Mirkin, who wrote *The Sports-Medicine Book*, polled more than 100 top runners and asked them if they could take a pill that would make them Olympic champions but would also kill them within a year, would they take the pill? Incredibly, more than half the athletes said they would indeed take such a pill.

Tutko worries that an increasing number of athletes have unhealthy drive because of the way sports has changed. "We've put too many perks into sports. There is a lot of money and notoriety and a lot of nationalist pride. Winning has become too important because of these perks. If an athlete has a feeling of inadequacy, the sports world is a place to prove themselves. Many athletes don't seem to have an understanding of their games. They're too preoccupied with winning."

Types of Motivation

Besides wanting to win, what motivates some athletes to try so hard? Psychologists usually break motivation down into two areas: intrinsic (internal) and extrinsic (external). Examples of intrinsic motivators are athletes doing something for the challenge or excitement of their sport or the achievement of goals, while extrinsic motivators are things like social approval from peers or playing for big contracts and trophies. According to William J. Beausay, retired president of the Academy of Sports Psychology, there are seven motivations for athletes, each influenced by a combination of several at one time:

• Money. "It's a heck of a motivator early in a career (especially to provide for family), but becomes less so as an athlete makes more and more."

• Ego. "It's the need we all have to feel important. In psychology we say 'You never get enough of that wonderful stuff.' That usually means sex, but that's actually No. 2. Our greatest need is to satisfy our egos."

• Camaraderie. "It feels good to be one of the guys."

• Expectations. "They feel like they must live up to the expectations of others."

• Achievement. "Some athletes simply have an innate need to get things done."

• Excellence. "It's a need to be the best at what you do."

• Love of the game. "Some athletes just love what they do so much, they can't give it up."

Over the long haul, it's impossible to motivate people unless they motivate themselves, according to psychologists Edward L. Deci and Richard Ryan, who founded a human motivation program at the University of Rochester. "People think about how to motivate as something you do to someone else," Ryan said. "Our theory is that the readiness to be motivated exists and it's a matter of facilitating that natural process." People are most motivated and do their best work when they are engaged in activities, such as sports, "simply for the feelings of excitement, accomplishment and personal satisfaction they yield," Deci said.

Of course, the best athletes seem to have the strongest self-motivation. But where does it come from?

Genetic Influence

Part of the drive may stem from a restlessness in childhood with a young athlete having an unusual amount of natural energy and needing to find an outlet for it. Even as a toddler, hockey star Eric Lindros was a growing concern, walking on his own at seven-and-a-half months old, according to his father/agent Carl. "He was a very busy kid—sometimes he was a terror—and we had to find activities for Eric to put his energy into. He ran and played flat out from day one. He played baseball and ran cross-country, but eventually he focused on hockey. I'm not sure why. I guess he was attracted to it because of the combination of speed, finesse, physical play, and teamwork it offered."

Some athletes probably get at least some of their drive genetically, such as Pete Rose, who had the same intense makeup as his father, Pete Sr., who played pro football into his 40s. Biology does play a key role, said New York psychologist Gloria Witkin who believes elite athletes and high achievers in other fields "may have a better sensitivity to their adrenaline system than others. They use and control their adrenaline better than others, as a fuel to get ahead." This is particularly helpful, she added, if the athlete has had a difficult childhood because the adrenaline can help them control depression brought on by their surroundings. "It helps them psychologically and gives them mastery and an increased sense of control."

Intense motivation is often a personality characteristic, said John Anderson. "Studies show that about 40 percent of athletes' motivation is genetically based, then the developmental jump comes from what happens to them as a young kid."

Los Angeles cardiologist Arnold Fox, author of several books on stress, said that some people are born with more spark, which may be a type of drive or resiliency to overcome obstacles. "Some babies come to your attention right away in the incubator, before their mothers and fathers ever touch them. They have a different spark than the other babies," Fox said.

Jim McGee, director of psychology at Sheppard Pratt Hospital in Baltimore and a former consulting psychologist with the Baltimore Orioles, believes that elite athletes have different hormonal and neurological makeup than other people. "I think they're wired differently and you could say that they're neurological freaks. It's hard for the rest of us to understand them, that their bodies do almost always what they want them to do. You can pick them out when they are still children. They are the ones doing things quicker than the other kids, more effectively."

Retired psychoanalyst Maurice Vanderpol, MD, a long-time member of the Levinson Institute, believes that although many motivations are nurtured in childhood, some of them may be genetic. "We're all born with certain assets and talents and drive mechanisms that protect us. Super achievers, including athletes, seem to survive and even flourish with a minimum of nurturing. We don't talk about this enough. The givens at birth are not always taken into consideration."

Environmental Influence

Some people call the influence of environment on a person's personality makeup *social* or *cultural programming*. In our Western culture, with its achievement orientation, there's a strong sense of the need to become number one. In other cultures, being at the top is not nearly as important. India has one of the world's largest populations, but one of the lowest number of Olympic winners because competition is not stressed as much as participation and cooperation.

Some Darwinists and others who view evolutionary patterns as illustrating "a survival of the fittest" believe that if humans didn't have a basic desire, a basic emotional drive, we wouldn't have "conquered" (some say *exploited*) the world as we have. If such a drive is in fact innate in humans, it makes sense, perhaps, that some may have a higher degree of the drive than others. Perhaps these individuals are predisposed toward striving for excellence in all facets of life, including athletic fields and arenas.

The Hunter Mentality

Many anthropologists say that an arousal defense system, including the fight-or-flight response, is programmed into all humans and has remained virtually unchanged for millions of years, When we feel threatened—physically, verbally, or professionally—our mind-body goes through the same hormonal changes as it did when we lived in caves and warred against other barefoot tribes. Of course, we no longer have to fight for a daily existence in the wilds; instead, our battles are fought in the offices, on the assembly lines, and on the sports fields. In fact, athletics is one of the few areas remaining where it's acceptable to be aroused, to battle, to have a killer instinct and tear away at your opposing tribe.

"We were hunters for a million and a half years. It was a learned behavior, but it's conditioned us all," says C. Loring Brace, a Neanderthal expert and a professor at the University of Michigan.

> All our basic emotions and capabilities and reactions have been shaped by that. It has had an effect on our emotional and adrenaline aggression systems, but it isn't focused. If we want it to, it can make us a professional scholar, or an athlete. That's part of our heritage. We enjoy doing those things, so that's where we focus. That's what made Pete Rose so successful in baseball.

Will our emotional drive and arousal system change in our lifetime? Not according to Professor Brace. "It's going to take 150,000 to 200,000 years for that to change. I expect we'll lose some of that edge slightly, but our fight-or-flight responses are still sharp. Our hormonal reactions are probably the same as they were long ago."

The Intense Psychological Needs of Top Athletes

"It isn't the money. It's the hunger, the desire, and it's hard to turn it off. It's about pride, and it's about ego."

Chris Evert, who used her pride and ego to become the world's number 1 female tennis player 5 times and win 18 Grand Slam titles.

Bob Beamon says that when people are watching, athletes are capable of some grand accomplishments. "Competing is somewhat natural to humans, particularly if other people are listening or watching." In the 1968 Olympics in Mexico City, the whole world was watching as Beamon produced one of the most brilliant performances in track and field history—leaping 29 feet, two and a-half inches to break the world record in the long jump by nearly two feet.

Many world-class athletes have a need to impress others (of course this is true of amateur and recreational athletes, too—one study showed that joggers speed up when they realize people are watching them!). Prior to the Atlanta Olympics, as he prepared for the 200- and 400-meter races, American sprinter Michael Johnson said: "I want all eyes on me. Not on the Dream Team [men's basketball] or anyone else" (18).

Driven By Insecurity

Many psychologists say high achievers are driven by their insecurities, but that isn't necessarily a bad or unhealthy thing to a goal-oriented athlete, according to Dan Landers, a sports researcher at Arizona State University. "You need to create a bogeyman in your mind, a self-doubt that makes you work harder to overcome it," he said. Landers and some ASU coaches plant the seeds of insecurity by whispering to their athletes prior to a contest, "The fans are saying you're too old. Some are betting against you."

Brooks Johnson, former world-class sprinter, college coach, and U.S. women's Olympic track coach, believes many athletes have strong mental health, but those at the very top are not necessarily healthy and they use their needs as powerful machines to produce a sort of ego energy. "Well-adjusted, happy people do not make great athletic competitors," he said. "The secret is converting insecurities into a powerful force. A great match is theater and drama with performers shamelessly demonstrating their psychological needs." He says these needs separate winners from those of equal talent who are not as driven. Some athletes may even suffer from neurosis or psychosis and need therapy, Johnson added, "so we shouldn't be surprised when some get into trouble away from the playing fields." Boxers are among the most psychotic, he added. "They have to be psychotic because of the risks and the pounding they're going to take."

Selwyn Liderman, PhD, a clinical psychologist who works with professional athletes in New York City, agrees with Johnson. "Reggie Jackson became known as Mr. October because he loved that time under pressure," he said. "Many athletes have an over-arching need." Liderman has felt this need himself while getting his PhD to prove wrong a teacher who had denied him an earlier shot at it. "I just said to myself there is no sonovabitch in this world that is going to stop me from getting my PhD. It was an adaptive approach to defending the ego."

American track legend Jackie Joyner-Kersee had such insecurity and need for recognition that Brooks Johnson said "for her [an event] was like a theatrical performance with 90,000 people watching in the stadium. She really wanted to be a dancer. She gets on this magnificent stage in front of all those people, and she simply performs. She wants to be recognized and loved. Jackie watched the 1976 Olympics on TV and said, 'Wow, I want people watching me'." And when they did, she didn't let them down, winning two Olympic gold medals in the heptathlon and another in the long jump. Christian Laettner, who led the Duke University Blue Devils to two NCAA men's basketball championships and went on to a successful NBA career, says that top athletes have unusual psychological needs and often seem arrogant in order to protect themselves. "As much as we want to be normal, we're not all that normal," he said. "I have an arrogance; it's there to protect me." Laettner also seems to have a strong need to win in everything he does, from hoops to tennis to ping-pong to swimming.

American track legend Jackie Joyner-Kersee: "I want people watching me."

Even one of the NBA's "nicest guys," Grant Hill of the Detroit Pistons, confesses to having a hidden mean streak when his ego is on the line. "I don't show it, but I'm very cocky and very confident underneath," he said. "I feel I'm the best player out there and no one can stop me. I want to beat you and embarrass you bad. But I don't want people to know that. It's like a little secret I keep to myself."

Need for Attention, Love, and Support

Many Olympic and professional athletes are searching for indiscriminate love and acceptance, Brooks Johnson adds. Of American runner Mary Decker-Slaney, Johnson said, "Mary Slaney has a desperate need for love and support. These people are performing for the fans and from acceptance from them. All the great ones are like that. All of them." When Johnson first started coaching Slaney when she was 15, she finished a race in Germany and immediately leaped into her coach's arms. "She wasn't concerned about beating the Russians; she wanted to know if I approved of her," he said. "Nowadays to excel on a national or international level, you require an overcompensation mechanism that clinically makes you abnormal,"

Johnson said. "It usually comes from a sense of feeling inadequate and produces an overcompensation drive."

Another former coach of Decker-Slaney, Tracy Sundlum, added that, "Mary judges her worth as a person solely by what she accomplishes on the track. It's scary to contemplate, but the competitive nature we so admire in the woman is actually a huge personality flaw."

Many superathletes are driven to great heights by issues of ego, says Toni Farrenkopf, PhD, a clinical and sport psychologist, who works with athletes in Portland, Oregon. Often they suffer from an obsessive-compulsive disorder in which they overcompensate for their insecurities and emotional needs through incredible achievement. The people who make it to the top in this competitive society, including the sports world, succeed with this attitude, Farrenkopf added. If the athlete can channel this into peak performance, "there is a good side to the outcome. Achievement is a good outcome, whether you're in athletics or a business. There's a built-in reward, but the price to get there is psychologically high."

Tom Tutko believes there are healthy and unhealthy inner drives. "When a young person sees it being modeled in his or her family, when the father or mother is striving to be the best they can be and constantly taking on challenges, that's healthy," he said. "If parents promote that, it can provide a positive start for an athlete. But there is a neurotic drive coming from a feeling of inadequacy where a person feels he has to prove he's worthwhile. His competition comes from clobbering others and not from enjoyment of the game. It becomes an unhealthy neurosis."

Figure-skating champion Elvis Stojko, considered a "healthy" competitor by many coaches and psychologists, says trophies and gold medals are not his ultimate goal, but rather he strives to see how much he can improve his performance, how far he can push his limits and physical capabilities. "Everyone gets caught up in (the pursuit of Olympic gold) because of the glamour and everything, but internally no one can see or get a feeling for what it feels like inside to produce what you want to produce beyond the medal, beyond winning, and how gratifying it is," Stojko said. "Only the athlete knows. That's what keeps you alive. That's what keep you hungry."

But clinical psychologist and sports author Robert W. Grant believes motivations such as seeing how much an athlete can improve his performance or playing for the "love of the game" are way down on the list of many elite athletes. "No one in real life dedicates himself to a game just for the fun of it," Grant said. "Motivators such as fun are not strong enough to push and sustain athletes through the painful gauntlet that must be run to reach the top. Such a path is fraught with tension, anxiety, and continual pressure to stay in shape on top. For these individuals, almost all areas of life must be structured around training. If people are in it for fun, they are either extraordinarily gifted, independently wealthy, or just plain crazy."

Instead, Grant adds, athletes are driven by psychological needs deeper than what is obvious to themselves and others:

> All elite athletes are driven by issues of identity. . . . They have literally trapped themselves in their sport. The more of their lives and self-esteem they put into it, the harder it is to let go. . . . Athletic supremacy is a gateway to life's riches on and off the court. Success usually brings a great deal of material from which one can create and repair a damaged ego or enhance an already stable and strong identity.

Ego Satisfaction

Remember William J. Beausay's quote: "Our greatest need is to satisfy our egos." Many top athletes are constantly defending their egos and reputations, said Dan O'Brien, the 1996 Olympic gold medalist in the decathlon who admits that in races he often ran out of fear of losing—not necessarily the race, but his pride and self-esteem. "At times, I ran scared because I was defending my pride and all that I stood for," he said.

Unlike O'Brien, who has had the benefit of many sport psychologists, many athletes seem unaware of what makes them tick or are in denial about it. Baltimore Orioles Mike Mussina pitches better when he has something to prove to others, according to his pitching coach Ray Miller. When the 1997 American League playoffs opened, Miller was glad that Mussina was matched up against the ace of the Seattle Mariners staff, Randy Johnson. "Everything was about Randy Johnson," Miller said. "I like it when Mike gets real quiet. Tonight, when he was warming up, the first five pitches hit the glove right where it was. I said, 'Oh boy, here we go.'" But Mussina denied that he got motivated to face Johnson. "I like to watch him pitch, but it doesn't make me do anything different," he said. Mussina went on to win the game and was MVP of the playoff series.

Tutko says that Wayne Gretzky, Larry Bird, and Magic Johnson have been the most mature and healthy-minded athletes he's ever seen. "Gretzky has a healthy drive, and in that regard he's the greatest of the greats." However, many hockey writers say that it's a bogeyman that often revs Gretzky's motor, providing strong ego energy. When people said he was too skinny to play in the NHL, and later that he was washed up, he bore down to prove himself over and over again. And he has gone out of his way to show writers that they have been wrong in criticizing him in the papers. "Gretzky is very thin-skinned and defensive when people have the audacity to criticize him, and he'd go out of his way to prove you wrong, then needle you with it later," said one veteran Toronto hockey writer. "Hockey is more than a game to him." Gretzky's former coach in Edmonton, Glen Sather, agrees, but added that "The Great One" was often motivated by more than one force. "Wayne channeled his anger very well, but he didn't outwardly expose himself to the public about it," said Sather, who won four Stanley Cups with Gretzky. "He could be very motivated by things in newspaper articles, what people said about him. If somebody said something about him being a whiner, he really got ticked. It was purely a pride thing." When Gretzky gets motivated, his face tends to get red with little splotches and his skills become sharper and deadlier as he stickhandles and passes through opponents. "People think that Wayne is all skill, but he's a killer. It's a personal thing. He's driven by pride. How else could a guy five feet, 10 inches and 175 pounds survive in this sport, at this speed?" Sather said.

Many modern athletes are sensitive to criticism because their every move and every mistake is under a media spotlight, Landers said. Baseball all-star Ken Griffey Jr. says he's constantly under pressure to prove himself to media, fans, and a society that he feels doesn't respect him. Even after winning the American League's MVP award in 1997, Griffey complained he wasn't getting the respect he deserved from the media. Posing at the plate after hitting a home run, like Griffey always does, or dancing for the crowd in the end zone after a football touchdown, as Deion Sanders of the Dallas Cowboys does, is an ever-increasing ritual by players of today, says Landers. "There's so much more media attention on athletics, compared to years ago, and there has been a constriction on the sports focused on in the media, like baseball, basketball, and football. Now their salaries and trade

© ALLSPORT/TIM DEFRISCO

Larry Bird's calmness in pressure situations hid a strong need to prove he was good enough.

negotiations and their business sides are discussed in public. They've got no private life, almost like a Hollywood star."

Sport psychologist Bruce Ogilvie knows that this narcissistic, look-at-me attitude can help some players to perform their best, but he admits he hates it. "Wherever I go to meet coaches these days, the first question they ask is, 'I've got another narcissistic athlete; what do I do?' There's no perfect strategy. Some become so self-centered, there's no therapy in the world that can help them. It's almost psychopathic. Their problems go way beyond sports."

CHAPTER 7

Turning Adversity Into Advantage

"We never had enough to eat, and I became angry, and my anger stayed with me through my career. It drove me."

Former Detroit Piston
Isiah Thomas

If top athletes feel a strong need to prove themselves, to defend their pride, ego or their self-esteem, this attitude may come from one of several factors, including genetics, their childhood, the sports world, or a combination of all three, psychologists say.

"A lot of athletes get their intense drive from their upbringing," said Dan Landers, sports researcher. "It may be sibling rivalry, poverty, or pushy parents with undue expectations. If a family splits up, the child may think it's his fault and the way to get the parents back together, or get dad to respect him, is to excel at a high level of sports. It may be subconscious."

"Sports is a breeding ground for youths looking to prove themselves," Tom Tutko said. "It can give them attention and accolades and make them feel special, especially if they're from a large family. . . It can help children with psychological or emotional problems, enhance their self-image."

Research of the backgrounds of 100 of the top athletes of all time revealed that 62 had a missing, abusive, or dead parent while another 30 had an authoritarian or unusually pushy parent. Many grew up in poverty or had a serious illness. Baseball great Hank Aaron was raised in a house with no windows; boxer Muhammad Ali's father had a history of alcohol and crime; Roger Bannister learned to run out of fear as a child from Nazi air raid sirens in his English neighborhood; young Bobby Charlton survived a plane crash that killed most of his teammates, then went on to become England's most celebrated soccer player; tennis great Martina Navratilova and her parents suffered Communist repression and her father's suicide, and Olympic diver Greg Louganis was ill, had a reading disability, and kept his homosexuality secret.

If the best seem to thrive on pressure, maybe it's because they're used to it—used to fighting serious battles since they were young, most of which they've won. Maybe what doesn't kill you makes you stronger. Elite athletes and high achievers in all fields have an advantage over competitors because they are battle experienced from a tough childhood, said Michael Boyes, associate professor of developmental psychology at the University of Calgary. "A classic motivating force is children wanting approval, particularly from their parents. When they don't get it, one response is to fold up, but the other is to try harder." This theory seems to stand up across the board. In research of the backgrounds of 500 high achievers, including athletes, politicians, scientists, and explorers, 72.4 percent came from a home with serious parental problems, including 41 percent who had at least one parent die before they were 20. Some 31.6 percent had an absent, abusive, or alcoholic parent, and nearly 9 percent were raised in poverty or watched their parents' finances collapse.

As they seek out and overcome more and more challenges, says University of Nebraska psychologist Richard Dienstbier, "the tough should get tougher." Mental resiliency can vary from person to person, athlete to athlete, claims sport psychologist James Loehr. Research shows that some athletes may have a more resilient genetic underpinning which Loehr calls mental toughness.

Bouncing Back

"Superior athletes use adversity as a showcase for life-defining moments."

Sport psychologist
Phil Towle

"We all have our own demons driving us," said four-time World Champion figure skater Scott Hamilton, who claimed his childhood illness and people taunting his shortness motivated him to prove them wrong. Cathy Rigby sucked her thumb until she was 12, but she developed a feeling of indestructibility after surviving death several times as a child and went on to become a pioneer American gymnast.

Escaping poverty has been a motivator for many youths who rose to stardom, including boxers Rocky Marciano and Mike Tyson, basketball greats Bill Russell and Julius Erving, and track star Florence Griffith-Joyner. The motor behind former NBA star Isiah Thomas' strong drive came from his hunger growing up in the streets of Chicago. "We never had enough to eat.... I became angry, and my anger stayed with me through my career. It drove me," he said. It drove Thomas to become an NBA all-star for 12 consecutive years and to some remarkable individual "arousal zone" performances.

In recent times, more and more athletes have risen from the inner cities of America to the high-rises of national and international sports, including the majority of the players in the NBA. The rise from rags to riches is a global phenomenon. Brazilian soccer hero Ronaldo emerged from the poverty-stricken suburbs of Rio de Janeiro to become the world's best soccer player. At one time he couldn't afford bus fare to join a new club, but then he became one of the richest athletes in the world—similar to the path taken by the great Pelé who couldn't afford soccer shoes as a boy.

Peter Westbrook, the most successful U.S. fencer in recent times, learned to survive with his fists, growing up in the projects in Newark, NJ "If you live in the projects, you can't communicate verbally. Talking goes out the window. You start to use their language. . . . I had a lot of anger, even when I started fencing," Westbrook said. "It was a young man's anger, like I was after something too much." That anger drove him to 13 U.S. national saber championships and he became the first American fencer to win a medal in the Olympics. That violent world took Westbrook's mother,

© ALLSPORT

Twelve-time all star Isiah Thomas of the Detroit Pistons—one of the best examples of an athlete who had to fight for everything he achieved in his career.

Mariko, who was beaten to death in 1994 on the Newark bus she took every day for most of her life. She was identified by a trading card found on her—of her son in his white fencer's uniform.

U.S. sprinter Gwen Torrence was from a broken, violent home and grew up lonely in the East Lake Meadows projects in Atlanta where everybody protected their territory and she learned to fight the boys.

"Torrence possessed the mortar that builds great athletes: neurosis and a need for individual expression. What's more, her mother had instilled an up-from-the-projects work ethic," wrote Joe Drape in the *Atlanta Constitution*. "I am an angry little girl. I always have thought that anything anyone did to me was intentional," said Torrence, who accused her rivals of using drugs in the Barcelona Olympics. "I've got a wall around me that I'm trying to bring down. I'm trying." Eventually, she became the world's fastest woman.

Obsessiveness

Many athletes turn what they perceive as the unfairness of life into anger, and they put that anger into their training and their careers and become obsessive, according to psychologist Selwyn Liderman. "There is a lot of anger which comes from childhood and is aimed at what is seen as the unfairness of life," he said. "It's often an act of revenge against those people who were our early masters. It becomes part of our conscience." The most famous case, he said, was that of Ty Cobb, who at age 19 became enraged at the accidental shotgun death of his father by his mother. "He took that anger, mostly aimed at his mother, and turned it outwards and he became one of the best baseball players of all time."

Greg Louganis took up diving at age nine. Little wonder. "It was the perfect vehicle to shield a painful upbringing," wrote Larry Reibstein in *Newsweek*. Louganis said that as a young boy his confidence was low for many reasons—for starters, his parents were unmarried teens who gave him up for adoption soon after birth. After nine months in a foster home, he was adopted by an alcoholic father who was at the same time neglectful and overbearing, beating him when he wouldn't dive off a nonregulation springboard. At school, children called him names because he was dark skinned and had dyslexia. Depressed, he became a drug user and attempted suicide at age 12. As a young man, he had a stormy relationship with a man who once raped him at knife-point. But in diving, Louganis could escape; he raised his confidence and skill levels to the point that he won both the platform and springboard gold medals in two Olympics.

Dan O'Brien was another adopted child, a poor student who turned to drinking to try to drown some of his problems. "I was always a troublemaker as a kid," he said. "I was always searching to find my niche in life, my group of people I felt I could fit in with. A lot of decathletes come from that type of background." Besides drinking, he found an outlet in track and field and went on to become one of the best decathletes of all time.

Sibling Rivalry

Strong drives can be formed in childhood less dramatically, according to Ken Dryden, who was the goalie for six Stanley Cup hockey championships with the Montreal Canadiens, author of two sports books, and is now president and general manager of the Toronto Maple Leafs. Dryden said his emotional drive was enhanced by trying to match up to his brother Dave, an all-star goalie in youth hockey, who was six years older than Ken. Dave recalled Ken becoming very intense in road hockey battles near their home—"he became a perfectionist." Almost a daily contest in the summer would see Dave toss a ball up onto the sloping roof of their house and the two brothers would battle to see who could jump higher to catch it as it fell down. "It wasn't until he was 16 that he was finally able to out-hockey me for the ball," Dave laughed. Dave, too, made the NHL, but was considered just an average goalie while younger brother Ken made the Hall of Fame.

Sibling rivalry seems common in the background of elite athletes:

• The race for her three gold medals in the Seoul Olympics for American Janet Evans actually may have begun when she was a tot and jumped into a YMCA pool to join her older brothers who were taking lessons.

• The six Sutter brothers of Viking, Alberta, were not talented, but they drove one another to make the National Hockey League, which they all did.

• Salevaa Atisanoe (Konishiki) learned to fight among his eight siblings in Hawaii; then he grew up to be the world's best sumo wrestler.

Tony Dorsett was a shy and introverted boy, but touch football foes motivated him by constantly comparing him to his talented siblings. "You can't even play the game," taunted an opponent in junior high school. "You're going to be the sorriest Dorsett of them all." Tony shot back: "No, I won't. I'll prove you wrong."

Years later, after he'd won the Heisman Trophy as college football's best player and become one of NFL's all-time rushing leaders with nearly 13,000 yards, Dorsett reflected on those words in the schoolyard:

"His comments triggered something in me. It wasn't so much anger as motivation to do well. I think after that I became more focused, more driven to succeed at playing football."

Carl Lewis believes he may have received some of his long-lasting drive to become the best track star ever from trying to live up to his parents and his siblings. "Being the loser in my family was so frustrating," recalled Lewis of his boyhood days in Willingboro, N.C. Lewis was the son of two talented athletes who became teachers and track and field coaches. Carl, the third of four children, used to sneak his mother's track medals out of the house to use for neighborhood races. When their parents went to school to coach other children, they would leave Carl and his younger sister Carol in the long jump pit to play by themselves. "That pit became our babysitter," Carl recalled. Carl was shy and tried to express himself through running and jumping, but he quickly found himself losing to the other brothers and sisters who became all-state or even all-American.

Even Carol crushed him in races. "I was the runt of the family, the nonathlete," Carl said. "I thought I was the one [without talent] for our family." When he entered official track meets against boys his own age, Carl lost. "I became tired of losing." He persevered and at age 12 finally won a race, but his parents weren't satisfied. "They always treated us like adults. . . .They were toughest on me," Carl said. "At times I resented the way my parents worked me. . . . they knew how much it hurt me to be the worst in the family, knew how much I wanted to succeed, and they spotted some talent in me before anyone else did. They thought if they pushed me, they could help me develop that talent."

Childhood Defense Mechanisms

Is it possible that the way Carl Lewis reacted to his Olympic opponents may have been related to the way he was treated by his siblings in their intense rivalry as children in North Carolina? Is it possible that Michael Jordan's reaction to NBA opponents and threats late in playoff games may be related to the way he felt he was treated when he was cut from his high school team, or the way he was treated in a rough series against the Detroit Pistons early in his NBA career?

"No matter how good some athletes get, they carry their early-life insecurities with them," said Stanley Titelbaum, PhD, who counsels

Track and field star Carl Lewis, who went from worst in his family to best in the world.

© VICTAH SAILER

baseball, football, and basketball players in New York City. "They still feel insecure or they only feel as good as their last game," he said. "They need validation from the media or the fans. But like after having a good meal, they get hungry again tomorrow. There's not always a strong correlation about how they do on the floor and how they feel about themselves. It's a need they have to keep bolstering their sense of OKness."

"We all have mental and emotional as well as physical traits, from childhood that are maladaptive, immature, and downright silly," said former gymnast and college professor Dan Millman. "In most people, these traits remain hidden from their own awareness, only to surface momentarily in times of upset, pressure or crisis. Not being aware of motives, which typically have a long developmental history, is the primary reason athletes choke — not only in actual competition, but also in the choice of team and coach and, most specifically, in the design of training routines," said Robert W. Grant.

Maurice Vanderpol, MD, a retired psychoanalyst and child psychiatrist, calls these childhood defense mechanisms. Becoming a superachiever in sports, or any other field, is often a way that a child deals with a problem situation, he said. "It serves a purpose of not only achieving, but also gives the child a safe haven or defense mechanism. They have a resource (such as athletic skill) to defend themselves with. It makes them feel safe and respected." In problem homes, there is often guilt that an athlete takes on subconsciously, Vanderpol said, "and the super achieving helps to channel that. It allows them to keep their guilt in manageable quantity." These childhood defense mechanisms are often subconscious, he added. "When we find ourselves in unusually stressful situations, we often react in ways we never would have believed. We carry these things from childhood with us without realizing it. . . . The whole idea of protective mechanisms and resiliency of survivors is fairly new. We're just starting to understand them."

And yet athletes may become conscious of what drives them. Amy Van Dyken had asthma and a self-esteem problem in high school. Fellow students teased her and called her a nerd. "I was six-feet tall. I towered over the crowd, and I think that's why people picked on me," she said. She was such a poor swimmer that her teammates made fun of her, but she worked hard, developed her skill, and in 1996 in Atlanta became the first American female to win four gold medals at a single Olympics. "To the girls that gave me a hard time in high school, I'd like to say thank you," Van Dyken said. "I don't think I would have the drive I have if it wasn't for them. . . .This is a victory for all the nerds out there. For all the kids out there struggling, if they can keep plugging away at it, something good will come of it."

Of course, the resiliency and survivor capabilities of top athletes are what endears them to fans, said Dick Ebersol, president of NBC Sports. "Our surveys show that people — about 80 percent — want to see the athletes struggle. . .their survival against amazing odds, and then their subsequent moment of victory or sadly, often times, their agonizing moment of defeat."

"You Can't Keep Me Down!"

50 Athletes Who Overcame Adversity or Serious Challenge to Succeed

Ali, Muhammad	Family violence; father history of alcohol and crime; dyslexic
Ashe, Arthur	Grew up without his mother
Beamon, Bob	Mother died when he was a young child
Bird, Larry	Father's suicide; teenage marriage failed
Brown, Jim	Father abandoned family; raised by alcoholic grandparent
Clemens, Roger	Parents divorced; stepfather died
Cobb, Ty	Authoritarian principal/father killed by mother
Comaneci, Nadia	Parents allowed her to be recruited in kindergarten
DiMaggio, Joe	Father always working; 9 kids; poverty
Erving, Julius	Fatherless; poverty; never happy as child
Fixx, Jim	Father died when he was 17
Fleming, Peggy	Mother pushy; when she was 13 her coach was killed in a plane crash
Foreman, George	Fatherless; ghetto poverty

Gehrig, Lou	Hostile family environment; poverty, only one of 4 kids who lived; racism as German immigrant
Grange, Red	Ill; told not to play sports; mother died
Griffith-Joyner, Flo	Parents divorced; 11 kids; poverty
Hogan, Ben	Father died when he was 9
Howe, Gordie	His father always put him down; 9 kids; poverty
Jackson, Bo	Fatherless; 10 kids; poverty
Jackson, Reggie	Mother left home; poverty; gambler father was his god
Joyner-Kersee, Jackie	Sudden death of her mother
Keino, Kip	Mother died young; absent father; beaten by relatives
Koufax, Sandy	Parents divorced when he was 3
Leonard, Sugar Ray	Parents incapacitated
Louganis, Greg	Adopted; ill as child; reading disability; abusive and pushy father
Malone, Karl	Father left; large family in poverty
Mantle, Mickey	Father and grandfather were athletes who trained him to be a pro; 6 kids in a two-room shack; abused by half-sister; a bed wetter until he joined the N. Y. Yankees
McLain, Denny	Father died young; no relationship with mother
Moses, Edwin	Dad died young; had "short complex" as child
Naismith, James	Both parents died young
Navratilova, Martina	Parents divorced; father's suicide
Nurmi, Paavo	Father died; poverty
Paige, Satchel	Sent to reform school at age 12
Pelé	Couldn't afford soccer shoes; wished to fulfill father's dreams
Powell, Mike	Father left family
Rigby, Cathy	Cheated death several times

Robinson, Jackie	Father left family
Russell, Bill	Parents divorced; mother died; poverty
Ruth, Babe	Parents rejected him; father murdered
Sayers, Gale	Parents separated; hungry; sometimes ate sparrows in the ghetto
Sosa, Sammy	Worked in streets to support widowed mother
Smythe, Conn	Parents separated; alcoholic mother died
Summerall, Pat	Club feet didn't prevent him from becoming NFL kicker
Thomas, Isiah	Poverty; father left family; crime neighborhood
Thompson, Daley	Father died young
Thorpe, Jim	Both parents died before he was 16; Native American racism
Trevino, Lee	Fatherless; poverty
Tyson, Mike	Fatherless; criminal since age 9; beaten by bullies
Williams, Ted	Parents rarely home; intense loner from childhood
Wills, Maury	Father always working; 13 kids; poverty; bed wetter until age 33

Note. The author does not contend that these are the 50 worst cases of adversity in athletes. I'm sure there are many examples left off this list.

CHAPTER 8

The Parents' Hall of Fame

"Most parents want to bring up a super-achiever; it's the North American dream."

Dr. Benjamin Spock, child psychologist

"Athletes, typically, are not consciously aware of why they push themselves," clinical psychologist Robert Grant says.

Also, the fundamental and most powerful of athletes' motivators come from their families. These influences constellate around feelings of worth in their parents' eyes. This also holds true with feelings of loveableness and desirability in respect to peers and lovers. Many athletes, unknown to themselves, are carrying within them the hidden messages of their childhoods. For example, depending on the structure of the family's system of relationships, the athlete might be trying to prove that he is a good child, adolescent or adult and therefore is worthy of respect, care, love and affection. He tries to prove his self-worth in the competitive arena. The athlete is terrified that he will be judged inadequate, worthless, or unimportant— a failure. This is the message certain significant individuals in his earlier years had conveyed to him both explicitly and implicitly.

Absent Parents

There are elite athletes from two-parent, seemingly well-adjusted families, such as Michael Jordan and Wayne Gretzky, but, as mentioned earlier, research of the backgrounds of 100 of the top athletes of all time revealed that 62 had a missing, abusive, or dead parent while another 30 had an authoritarian or unusually pushy parent.

In the 1995-96 season, research of the top 30 NBA players showed that 23 grew up without their natural father. Most of those were from the inner cities of America with complex and often debilitating socioeconomic problems. Karl Malone's father left the family in poverty when he was young, Glenn (Big Dog) Robinson was an illegitimate child, both of Penny Hardaway's parents gave him up as a tot, and Gary Payton's parents divorced while others like Shawn Kemp, Dennis Rodman, Damon Stoudamire, and Charles Barkley barely knew their fathers. Shaquille O'Neal was so moved that his natural father left early, then tried to come back into his life when he became a celebrity, he wrote and recorded a rap tune entitled "Biological Didn't Bother."

The high rate of father absence in the NBA seems to reflect an aspect of family life among poor people, many of them black, in the United States, relating partly to complex cultural, social, and economic conditions. A black child born into poverty has only a 1 in 5 chance of growing up with two parents until the age of 16, according to University of Wisconsin demographer Larry Bumpass. A father's absence tends to have more effect on the son when it is compounded with poverty (many NBA stars grew up poor) according to John Lewis McAdoo in his book *Fatherhood Today* (1988). "Many studies found a link between absence and delinquency and over-compensation problems and personality problems," he wrote. And yet the missing parents' syndrome seems to cross all socioeconomic, gender, and culture lines.

Sometimes the effect of an absent parent is quite subtle to detect, and other times it's out in the open. The mother of Desmond Howard left the family when he was 13. When Howard became a football player, he was said to play better in front of relatives, wanting to please them. Howard went on to win the Heisman Trophy and the 1997 Super Bowl MVP with the champion Green Bay Packers with his family in the stands.

Missing Fathers

"I see so many athletes, particularly males, who are looking for that wonderful, all-giving, all-caring, totally accepting father figure," said Bruce Ogilvie, who has interviewed tens of thousands of elite athletes. Ogilvie became a high achiever from a dysfunctional background, too, and is known as the father of modern sport psychology. His father left the family when he was young, and his mother was a "runaround" who was rarely home. "I grew up from age 10 pretty much living alone, but I went looking for a father figure to confirm me." Ogilvie took up football and wrestling and quickly became what he termed an overachiever. "I overtrained, overpracticed; I had an obsession to achieve my goals. I never wanted to lose my position on the team, so I played with terrible injuries. Part of that went back to confirm me as a man. All that male pursuit drives a lot of our athletes today."

The void left by missing fathers can be partly or totally filled by others, especially by the mother, but also by grandparents, uncles, cousins, teachers, and athletic coaches. Yet a missing father's shadow can have a profound effect, says Aminifu Harvey, associate professor of social work at the University of Maryland. "No matter how strong your mother is, a boy emulates his father, from going to the washroom and peeing like his father to hanging out with the guys at the park. He walks and talks like his father. Even if a stepfather or uncle is close to him, there is often still anger at the natural father for leaving."

Toronto sports researcher Varda Burstyn believes the missing father is one of the key motivators for elite athletes who try to fill the parental void by reaching for the top of the sports' world, which to them may represent a false societal view of masculinity. "Sports has been one of the most important institutions to take the place of, or augment, the missing familial father," she said. "It sets up heroes who are supposed to be masculine, but it's based on fantasy ideals, rather than what real men are like."

Damon Stoudamire of the Toronto Raptors, former NBA Rookie of the Year, said part of his fierce desire came from trying to become a better player than his father Willie, who starred at Portland (OR) State University, but didn't make the NBA, then left Damon's mother to find a job in the eastern U.S. because the family was poor. It's common for children to use sports to prove to others that they can be successful coming from the inner city without a father, said Bob Wade, who coached six players at Baltimore's Dunbar High School who went on to the NBA, including Houston Rockets' Sam Cassell and Charlotte Hornets' Muggsy Bogues. "I was their surrogate father and ruled with an iron fist," Wade said. "It can really leave a tremendous hole in a kid's life if he doesn't have one."

Many pro athletes have used their missing father as motivation, Harvey said. "Anger can make you win. If the father leaves, the boy can feel deserted and even responsible. He may want to unconsciously prove to the father that he was worthy to be his son and that by becoming a success, the father will come back."

Harvey added that people should not be misled by the many examples of athletes who have risen up from "challenged" childhoods to become successful athletically. There are, of course, thousands of gifted young athletes who never recover from disadvantaged childhoods because they don't have the opportunity or the same support network of family and coaches that the successful athletes have.

Pushy Parents

If children become great athletes or top achievers in other fields, it usually has a lot to do with their parental situation, said child psychologist Benjamin Spock, who won a gold medal with the United States eight-oared crew in the 1924 Olympics in Paris. "Most parents want to bring up a superachiever; it's the North American dream," he said." They want to get into Who's Who in America. The fire is lighted by the parent, but catches fire in the upbringing of the child who becomes out to prove himself." Spock said that the fuel for the athlete to get ahead during competitions is often adrenaline or related hormones.

Spock grew up with a missing father and a strict, even physically abusive mother, who made him feel ashamed of his efforts. "I became angry and rebellious against my mother; it was a neurotic response, but I guess it shaped my attitude towards raising children. I'm still trying to prove something by going into pediatrics and writing books about how to raise children."

"When we hear about boys who lost their father early in childhood, they often responded by becoming unusually mature," Spock added. "But it also takes a mother who had high ambitions. In psychological studies of successful people, you'll often find mothers who were very ambitious with high expectations for their children. A stage mother."

Child prodigies are made, not born, according to a British study which attributes exceptional ability at an early age to parental encouragement and exposure, rather than to genes or natural talents. According to the study's lead researcher, John Sloboda, PhD, a psychologist at the University of Keele in England, children's peak learning years are from four to seven when they are most receptive to instruction. It's not only the cultivation of a specific skill that matters during these years, he said, but also the establishment of the right habits, including discipline, attentiveness, and motivation.

In the case of many athletes who become superachievers, the parents are too pushy, which leads to insecurities in the athletes, according to Ted Turner, owner of baseball's Atlanta Braves, basketball's Atlanta Hawks, and the founder of CNN and the Goodwill Games. "Motivation for superachievers is a complex subject, but I think it goes back to some degree to a sense of insecurity. . . . that because they're insecure, they're always trying to achieve, trying hard to show they're good persons and that they're successful," he said. Turner should know something about psychology—he's been treated by six therapists for psychological and emotional problems he partly attributes to an achievement mania started by his pushy father, Ed.

Ed Turner, an advertising salesman, not only wished greatness for Ted, he willed it. After Ed's family lost its financial fortune in the Depression, Turner hoped his son could bring back the glory. He doted over the boy, showering him not only with gifts, but a harsh hand and corporal punishment. At age nine, the unhappy boy was whisked off to military school—"to intentionally make him insecure, because insecurity can produce hunger and force you to compete," said a relative. It worked because Ted became tenacious in sports and business. Besides his business accomplishments, Ted was captain of the winning U.S. side in the 1977 America's Cup yacht race. "I developed an unhealthy drive to achieve because I was so insecure," he said. "If I was losing in a race, I'd do anything to win, to the point of getting out of the boat and pushing." Halls of Fame should have wings for such parents:

© ALLSPORT/DAVID CANNON

Jack Nicklaus: "If I didn't win a tournament, I'd feel like a bum."

- Joe Montana's father quit his job to nurture his son's football talents.
- In 1997, Saeed Anwar hammered a record 194 runs in cricket for Pakistan against India, prompting his father Mohammad Anwar, himself a first-class cricketeer, to say: "I am proud of my son who smashed the world record. He has fulfilled my dreams."
- In the 1992 Olympics, injured British runner Derek Redmond was helped across the finish line by his father Jim, who said: "Well, we've started everything together. We'll finish this together."

What effect can such parental influence have on an athlete? "It can put another person on your back, give you the drive of two people," says Bruce Ogilvie, adding that effects of such involvement among athletes who never make the big-time are often detrimental.

Jack Nicklaus' father spent $35,000 on his son's golf lessons, provoking Jack to later say: "If I didn't win, I'd feel like a bum."

Baseball star Albert Belle may have received his intense motivation from his mother, Carrie, who claims she "brought him up to excel in everything. . . . He wants to be perfect." When he wasn't as a youngster, he threw bats and tantrums. "[LSU coach Skip]

Bertman believes that for all Belle's drive and intensity, there's a basic aspect of his personality that is not suited to the pressure of major league baseball, the pressure of expectations, the pressure to perform, the pressure to satisfy his mother. He rebels by being rude and disrespectful, even antisocial. The Belle who uses corked bats, Bertman believes, is the one overwhelmed by his need to succeed. Remove Albert from the world of baseball and he's Joey gain, pleasant and witty and smart. But with each home run, with every new success, Belle's profession becomes a more central part of his identity."

Children pushed into competitive sports early begin with the parents needs, then often develop their own needs, says Varda Burstyn. "Many parents have strong and healthy motivations for their children playing sports, but many have their own strong needs for their children to achieve. That just reinforces the sense that only by winning and besting others, hit, crunch, and burn is the way to get love."

Tiger–Standard Operating Procedure

While many athletes burn out or quit sports because of pushy parents, others use the push for incredible short- and long-term motivation, Spock said. The competitive sports jungle is full of fathers of tigers—men and women like Earl Woods. It was Earl Woods' plan to raise the greatest golfer who ever lived. A frustrated golfer himself, Earl didn't wait for his son to take up the game. Before he could walk, Tiger was taken to the family garage, strapped into a high chair by his father and shown how to swing a golf club.

A short time later, his father took him on the golf course. Before his fourth birthday, he shot 48 on a regulation nine-hole course. At age six, his father had him listening to subliminal tapes. What his dad tried to do, whenever possible, was cheat, distract, harass, and annoy him. When you spend 20 years in the military, train with the Green Berets, do two tours of 'Nam and one of Thailand, you learn a few things about psychological warfare. He'd drop a golf bag during the boy's backswing, roll a ball across the boy's line just before he putted. It was all a mission: to win, to withstand the pressure that lay ahead of him in tournaments. And it worked. Woods, named after his father's Vietnam combat partner, said he began to like the pressure of competition. "I like the feeling of trying my hardest under pressure. But it's so intense, it's hard to describe. It feels like a lion is tearing at my heart."

Tiger conquered the pressure, and his opponents. In amateur events, he was best in the crunch: he won three USGA junior titles all in extra holes or on the final hole. In the 1994 U.S. Amateur championship, he made the greatest comeback, overcoming a six-hole deficit to win. Then, in 1997, on his first full season on the PGA tour, Woods won the Masters handily and was the top money earner for the season.

Oppression

Many athletes seem to derive strong motivation from feeling oppressed because of their race, their culture, their gender, or even their size. "All my life, people have told me, 'You're too small, you're too small,'" said 5-foot-6 NHL forward Theo Fleury, an all-star throughout the 1990s with the Calgary Flames. One year he scored 51 goals, showing lots of emotion when he scored. His coach, Doug Risebrough, was always amazed how Fleury could play "over his head" with emotional play that he seemed to be able to control. "This is a sport that requires a lot of energy and enthusiasm and it allows guys like Theo to bring their game to another level. He doesn't feel comfortable unless he emotionally charges himself. . . . but you have to be careful because it can go from a positive to a negative. It can pull a player down." According to Risebrough, hockey was more than a game for Fleury. "The game represents a great platform of measuring yourself. I think he looks at it that way. But he enjoys it, too."

The opposite type of syndrome has been reported by many basketball players. Wilt Chamberlain said he tried harder because some people said it was easy for him to play the game at more than seven feet tall. "My drive stemmed from some inner need to prove I'm good, and smart, and not just big," he said. Wilt was big and smart enough to lead the NBA in scoring seven times and scored 100 points in a single game.

One of the most explosive examples of race motivation was Jesse Owens, a U.S. track star who badly wanted to prove that his Afro-American race could compete as well as, or better than, the host Nazis, a white supremacy party, in the 1936 Olympics in Berlin. "The German papers ran stories about how we were subhuman and wouldn't be any competition for Hitler's master race," Owens recalled. During the games, Hitler also snubbed Owens by leaving the stadium before one of his long-jump performances. "I was mad, hate-mad, and it made me feel wild," Owens said. "I was going to show him. I felt the energy surging into my legs and tingling in the muscles of my stomach as it never had before. I began my run, first almost in slow motion. . . ." Owens went on to win a record four gold medals in the Games.

But racial oppression may not be as strong as it used to be for American blacks, according to author and former psychoanalyst Varda Burstyn. "It was more so in the 1960s when there was a strong bond between civil leaders like Malcolm X and Martin Luther King and successful athletes of the day like Kareem Abdul Jabbar, Jim Brown, Muhammad Ali, and Jackie Robinson. The success of these black athletes became the embodiment of the right to equality of the black community. These super macho guys acted in the name of their communities. In the last 25 or 30 years, social movements have lost prominence and there's been a major shift to the right. Nobody is interested in Jesse Jackson anymore. And athletes like Michael Jordan haven't aspired to the needs of their communities and they won't address the racial issues. They identify with the oppressor rather than the oppressed. The black athlete has become a corporate warrior."

Another Olympic hero, weightlifter Naim Suleymanoglu of Turkey, became known as "The Pocket Hercules" and at 4-feet, 11-inches tall and 140 pounds, was "pound for pound the world's strongest man" after winning three gold medals at the 1996 Atlanta Olympics. "The people of Turkey want me to win, so I do it for them," said Suleymanoglu, who represented Turkish triumph over oppression as part of a minority in Bulgaria (in 1986, during a period of ruthless repression of that minority, he defected to Turkey).

"In the Olympic Games, particularly in track and field, the best performances come from either people from an oppressed society or oppressed segments of society," said former U.S. Olympic track coach Brooks Johnson. "There have been famous cases of black people who have been dominated and to some extent Jewish people. And people from the Iron Bloc did particularly well because they had a hunger that didn't exist in other places of affluence."

Some people bring to sports a drive that is nurtured in other areas of society. Monika Schloder represented West Germany in four sports and two Olympics and won an Olympic bronze medal. "One reason I was successful was I got into the habit of trying to prove myself," she said. Schloder, from a middle-class family, went to an elite prep high school in Germany, which would allow her to go to university, then become a Rhodes scholar. "I was suddenly surrounded by upper-class kids and they outcasted me, so I was constantly trying to prove myself in academics and sports." Schloder is now a sport sociologist at the University of Calgary.

Many Hall of Fame female athletes were given early motivation by trying to prove they were as good as the boys. Former long-distance runner Joan Benoit would get mad as a child when her two older brothers told her they didn't want her tagging along to games and events. "To them, girls were wimps . . . I resented this horrible treatment and tried to prove I was just as fast, just as tough, and as fearless as they were," she said. She became one of the greatest female long-distance runners in U.S. history.

Many female athletes got their original competitive fire trying to prove they were as good as the guys and now they've made strides into male-dominated sports like ice hockey, baseball, polo, and boxing, where Christy Martin became the first woman recognized by the World Boxing Council as its women's world lightweight champion. "Women are an oppressed gender, excluded from the best that society can offer," Burstyn said. "Since the second wave of feminism in the 1960s when women started entering male-dominated areas, they wanted the renumeration and the prestige. It's like the desire to show people, like the black people or the short people, that they can make an equal or better contribution."

"Women's involvement in sports is more complex than men's," Schloder said. "It has a social-psychological aspect; they try to maintain their femininity while at the same time showing male characteristics."

Sunny Hale, of Wellington, Florida, became one of the few women to compete in elite polo tournaments against men, keeping her motivation strong through chauvinistic attacks on her. "My aspiration has always been to be accepted by the upper-level players. . . .accepted because of my playing, not because they wanted the oddity of having a girl on their team," she said. Sunny's mother, Sue Sally Hale, was one of the first female polo players, but had to disguise herself as a man.

CHAPTER 9

Fueling the Fire

> "All my life, I've been under pressure."
>
> Wayne Gretzky

Along with home and neighborhood environments, the competitive sports world can be an important incubator for producing "insecure" athletes who develop a need to defend their self-esteem, says Steve Berglas, a psychologist at Harvard Medical School. "When an individual has a specific focus of competition from childhood forward, he is incredibly dependent on that competition; it can become the be all and end all of a man's self-esteem. He can become addicted to the adrenaline high," Berglas says. "It can become as natural as having one's favorite food."

Heavy doses of sports can turn an athlete's life into one long, daily confrontation, says Phil Jackson, coach of the NBA's most successful team of the 1990s, the Chicago Bulls. "Athletes in many sports, particularly basketball players from the playground, have been conditioned since they were children that every confrontation in a game is a test of their manhood," says Jackson, a student of the psychological and emotional sides of sports. "Win or die is the code; rousing the players' bloodlust is the method. Using force is a primitive instinct. I know it can work, but it can backfire. It's one of the things I want to try to change."

Psychological battles take place in the middle-class suburbs, too, in the air-conditioned gyms and the manicured playing fields, says former NBA player and broadcaster Doc Rivers. "You learn that in the competitive environment, it becomes warfare, survival of the fittest. It's about becoming overconfident, or too insecure." These daily confrontations can make athletes consciously tough and confident, although they are often driven by subconscious doubts fostered by the nature of sports, which is that you're only as good as your last performance.

Pressure and the Proving Game

The world of competitive sports can introduce a performer to worry, even fear, on a daily basis. Since it's generally regarded by most sport psychologists that pressure is self-imposed, the more ego, self-esteem and self-defense issues that athletes have, the more chance they will feel high pressure at a time when they're under the spotlight to perform. This may not be a healthy mental or emotional state and yet some athletes have used it for healthy productivity, at least in a professional sense. This is referred to as The Proving Game, by authors W. Tim Gallwey and Robert Kriegel in their book *Inner Skiing*. "Athletes get caught up in the proving game, an exercise that focuses wholly on self-image and distracts the athlete and inhibits the natural process of improvement," they wrote.

That's easier to avoid than it sounds, though, if you're an athlete like Kirk Gibson, who aspired to become the best in football and baseball. Growing up, Gibson's parents, a tax auditor and a schoolteacher, pushed him hard to excel in sports. "I've been an athlete my whole life, from day one," Gibson once said. "It was football, basketball, baseball, every single year of my life, every day of my life. Games and practices. I had to learn how to become tough. I had to practice how to become tough. Even in a nothing game you had to go all out. My parents were always there for me; they never missed a game throughout my career in any sport." Gibson says that this environment created a need for him to constantly prove himself, not only to his parents but also to his coaches, his teammates, and to his opponents. "Back in American Legion ball, I can remember wanting to be the one who'd win the game in the bottom of the ninth. It helps you define your identity. You learn you have to prove yourself over and over and the pressure makes you tougher. It makes you stronger. All my life, I waited for those moments where I have to prove myself. And I love the added pressure of admitting it."

Gibson proved himself enough to get a football scholarship to Michigan State University and professional baseball contracts with several teams. His biggest moment was slamming a home run to win a 1986 World Series game for the Los Angeles Dodgers against the Oakland A's despite being saddled with several injuries — as a huge television audience watched around the world. Gibson added that such moments can be prepared for by constantly practicing and playing under pressure. All the great athletes learn to become calm in a crisis and, in fact, use the pressure to their advantage. Magic Johnson became so accustomed to crisis situations in sports, after playing so many championship series with his pride on the line, he seemed totally at ease in a press conference in which he announced he had contracted the deadly HIV virus from a prolific sex life—a shocking admission from a superstar who fans thought was squeaky clean. There sat Magic, calm and collected, his words clear and sure, quite used to the pressure of the hot white lights and the glare of public scrutiny.

The best ones seem to relish the pressure, particularly with the outcome of a game in the balance. Some people call it possessing killer instinct. But is it instinct? Perhaps, as Brooks Johnson says, they have a *need* to win. Psychologist Alfie Kohn, a university lecturer and author of several psychology books including *No Contest: The Case Against Competition,* agrees: "Competitiveness is in reality a deficit-motivated trait," he says. "Being good at an activity is something we choose to do; outperforming others is experienced as something we *have* to do. Our self-esteem is at stake . . . competition is more a need than a desire." Cohn says that low self-esteem is what motivates many athletes. For many, competition feels like damage control. To lose is to have one's inadequacy exposed. It is a dreadful confirmation of precisely what was feared in the first place. One struggles to win, to be better than everybody else, in a desperate, vain effort to convince oneself of one's value.

And perhaps that need is developed, or at least enhanced, by constant confrontation, of constantly trying to prove oneself in competitive events. "No matter how many times they hear it, many talented or attractive people do not truly believe in their talent or attractiveness," Kohn says. "Their quest to be noticed, rewarded, acknowledged is endless, like pouring liquid into a container with a hole in the bottom. There is nothing surprising, therefore, about the fact that even some very capable individuals need to prove how much better they are than others."

Table 9.1 lists many examples where athletes have excelled after being challenged, in one way or another, to prove themselves.

Grace Under Pressure

In professional sports, some players are known to perform their best when the results are on the line. Jack Nicklaus, Michael Jordan, John Elway, and Reggie "Mr. October" Jackson come to mind. With athletes like these, their competitive fire is never extinguished even though they are showered with multimillion-dollar salaries, trophies, and corporate sponsors. They remain killers into their 30s and 40s when opponents are retiring to three-piece suits. In many cases, psychologists say, it's because the athletes have issues formed in their early years which, at least subconsciously, may remain unresolved. Those with killer instinct are best in the clutch. One of the most famous plays to end a football game was quarterback Doug Flutie's long, desperate pass, which has been tagged as the Hail Mary, in a dramatic win for his Boston College team in the 1984 Orange Bowl over the University of Miami. At 5-feet, 9-inches, Flutie should be too short to be a professional quarterback, a David in a world of Goliaths, and yet he became a legend in the Canadian Football League for winning games in the clutch. Where did he get this lust for pressure? Flutie grew up in a sports-oriented family and quickly developed a hatred to lose, partly from repeatedly losing to an older brother. The Flutie family had such influence and popularity in south Florida in football, baseball, and basketball that playing fields in the towns where the brothers grew up were named "The Flutie Athletic Complex." "My brothers and I all *had* to be the guy to get the ball or the base hit when the game was on the line. It started in Little League," Flutie says. "You get used to being in those high-pressure situations, and you get to know how to respond."

Flutie was the CFL's outstanding player six times and led his teams to three Grey Cup championships, but in 1998, he took a pay cut to go to the NFL with the Buffalo Bills—to try to prove wrong those people who said he wasn't good enough or tall enough to play in football's major league. The 36-year old Flutie immediately caused

Table 9.1 Out to Prove Themselves

Athlete	Event	Trigger/Result
Jack Nicklaus	1986 Masters	- Angry at media for saying he was too old to win • With nine holes to play, he came from five strokes back to win
Wilt Chamberlain	March 2, 1962, NBA games	- Angry at opponents for saying he was too slow and lacked stamina • Scored a record 100 points
Rennie Stennett	September 16, 1975, Major League Baseball game	- In his last visit to Chicago, had been hospitalized after getting hit in the head with a pitch • Had seven consecutive hits to set a record
Babe Ruth	October 1, 1932, World Series game	- Furious at opposing pitcher and fans for pelting him with fruit and insults • Pointed to the pitcher and belted a home run
Mike Powell	August 30, 1991, World Track and Field Championships	- Angry at media and track experts for underrating him • Broke the world long jump record
Roger Bannister	May 6, 1954, race in Oxford, England	- Running as a crusade to prove his highly-criticized method of training was the right one • The first man to run under four minutes in the mile
Billie Jean King	1975 Wimbledon tennis championship	- Angry from previous loss in which she felt she was cheated by the officials • Came from behind to defeat Chris Evert
Nancy Lopez	1985 LPGA championship	- Angry at officials for penalizing her • Came from behind to win the tournament
Jesse Owens	1936 Olympics Track and Field	- Was "hate-mad" at Adolf Hitler for snubbing him • Won a stunning four gold medals

(continued)

Table 9.1 *(continued)*

Athlete	Event	Trigger/Result
Brett Favre	1997 SuperBowl Game	- Angry after media said he was washed up due to painkiller addiction • Led packers to Super Bowl win
Darryl Sittler	February 7, 1976, NHL game	- The night before the team owner berated Sittler • Scored a record ten points
Babe Didrikson	1932 U.S. Track and Field Championships	- So emotional the night before, a doctor treated her for stomach problems • Broke four world records
Cassius Clay	February 25, 1964, heavyweight championship fight	- Angry at being the 6:1 under dog, his blood pressure was 200/100 • Scored a stunning upset of Sonny Liston
Kip Keino	1968 Olympics 1,500 meters	- Worried about letting his country down after collapsing with gall bladder infection; daughter born the same day • Won the gold medal
Elizabeth Manley	1988 Winter Olympics women's figure skating	- Upset she was given no chance to win, she used the cheers of the hometown crowd • Upset the favorites in the free skating competition
Pelé	1970 World Cup in Mexico	- Defending his country's pride after humiliating defeats • Led Brazil to the championship
Kirk Gibson	1988 World Series game	- Angry at self and media for letting his Los Angeles Dodgers down • Hit a ninth inning homer while crippled with injuries
Bruce Jenner	1976 Olympics decathalon	- Felt he was carrying his country on his back • Won the decathlon gold medal
Bonnie Blair	1992 Olympics speed skating	- Wanted to win for her dead father • Won the 500-meter gold medal

Table 9.1

Athlete	Event	Trigger/Result
Edwin Moses	1984 Olympics hurdles	- Wanted to win for his father who had recently died • Won the gold medal
Michael Jordan	1996 NBA finals	- Wanted to win for his murdered father • MVP as Chicago Bulls won championship
Jeff Blatnick	1984 Olympics wrestling	- Wanted to win for dead brother • Won gold medal
Sebastian Coe	1984 Olympic 1,500 meters	- Angry at British press for doubting him • Won gold medal with most remarkable finish in history
Joe Namath	1969 Super Bowl	- Angry at media for giving his New York Jets no chance to win • Led the most stunning upset in NFL history
Debbie Doom	1991 Pan American Games fastball	- Close friend and U.S. teammate Becky Duffin died of cancer • Pitched back-to-back perfect games
Bill Mosienko	1952 Stanley Cup championship	- Ranger's rookie goalie Lorne Anderson taunted him that he was too old • Scored three goals in 21 seconds
Alva Holloman	May 6, 1953, Major League Baseball game	- Angry at his St. Louis Browns manager for never letting him start a game • In his first start, pitched a no-hitter over Philadelphia
Mort and Walker Cooper	October 6, 1943, World Series game	- Their father died that day • As the pitcher and catcher duo they led St. Louis Cardinals to a win over the New York Yankees

a stir in the U.S. national media with outstanding performances in his first three games. He won an NFL Player of the Week award and, during the Bills victory at Indianapolis, sarcastically remarked to a teammate, "He's too short!" when the Colts quarterback Peyton Manning, who stands 6-feet, 5-inches tall, had several passes knocked down.

As he progressed in various leagues, the competitiveness of his coaches rubbed off on Flutie. One of his coaches was Don Matthews of the Toronto (CFL) Argonauts, a tough, swaggering, highly-motivated man who admits that when his team loses, he wakes up in the middle of the night in a cold sweat. "When we lose, I feel too embarrassed to go to the grocery store. I don't know if there's anyone who takes a loss more severely than I do. It hurts me," he once said. Matthews, who has coached more wins than anyone in the CFL regular season, says there are two things that motivate players and coaches: "The fear of defeat and the joy of winning. If the joy of winning ever becomes greater than the fear of defeat, that means I've accepted defeat."

Matthews says that players like Flutie can enhance their late-game heroics, but that they're probably born with a gene that allows them to win in the clutch. Flutie claims to react best when he gets challenged physically by opponents. When they foul him or step on his hands, he jumps up angrily and takes it out on them with his sharpened running and passing. Flutie also admits to being thin-skinned and says he plays harder when he hears criticism. At one point in his career, he took criticism so badly he stopped reading the sports pages. He has had no such problem since joining the NFL's Buffalo Bills. In 1998 he became the darling of the both the media and the tough New York fans after taking over the quarterback spot and leading the team to a string of upset victories to earn the NFL Comeback Player of the Year award.

The Killer Instinct

Performers like Flutie, Jordan, Gretzky, and Monica Seles seem to develop dual personalities—fierce "killers" during competition and calm, nice people once away from the stadium. When she reviews films and pictures of herself in tournaments, former tennis ace Chris Evert can't believe it's really her. "When I look back and see myself with that grim, fixed expression, I wonder, because that's not me," she once said.

Monika Schloder says it's more difficult for a woman to gain the killer instinct than it is for a man because women are not supposed

© ROBERT SKEOCH/THE PICTURE DESK

Too short for the NFL? Doug Flutie must feel he has answered that question convincingly since arriving in Buffalo in 1998.

to show anger or have temper tantrums. In her career as an international swimmer representing Germany, Schloder used competition-day tactics of rehearsal and visualization to elicit the emotional and physiological changes she'd need to defeat her opponents:

> I would lock myself away from everybody and in my mind and my emotions I'd feel the sensation of the water hitting

my skin, then I'd psyche myself up to treat the other swimmers as opposition forces, like it was good against evil, a fairytale thing. My eyes actually changed color, they took on a dark hue. I think it was hormonal. It was a positive anger and I felt myself become totally invincible. You couldn't beat me. If I didn't achieve this frame of mind, I didn't succeed.

U.S. swimmer Amy Van Dyken has also shown "changeling" qualities. When Jonty Skiller first began coaching her, he realized he was coaching two people. Out of the water, she was a giggling 13-year-old "who basically loves people," Skinner says. But the other Amy was a steely-eyed assassin "who loves to race." Van Dyken admits that as she grew up in the competitive swimming environment she learned to intimidate opponents by staring at them, spitting into their lanes, grunting, and clapping her hands—"if they are weak enough to let that get to them, that's their problem," she once said. Van Dyken went on to win three gold medals at the 1996 Olympics.

In part III on "soaring" athletes, we'll examine in more detail how winners use arousal and pressure to produce peak performance. Now, let's move on to discuss competition and the possible effects of intense competition on elite athletes.

Influence of Competition

According to Tara Scanlan, a UCLA sport psychologist, competitive sports can be beneficial to youths. "Sport can be used to teach a great number of desirable things: how to master skills and the satisfaction that follows; good general work habits and cooperation; how to break down racial and class prejudices; how to build respect for and responsibility toward other people," she says.

Rainer Martens, a former college football player, semipro baseball player and coach, and a pioneer sport psychologist, adds,

> There are 30 million children and probably as many adults who are sometimes involved in competitive sports. Some may be pushed into them by peer pressure and, thus, may experience more stress than they should and won't get the benefits they might. But it seems plain that most people compete at games voluntarily because it gives them

pleasure. Not for all and not all of the time, but often and for many people, sport is a major source of joy and therefore, on balance, is useful to them and to society.

The playground is often a key incubator for the best athletes, psychologist Robert W. Grant says.

> Moving to the streets or the playground is an important step for every child. . . . Through play, they begin to develop physically and mentally, and understand how people interact and get along. . . . The rules of the environment are duplicated in their playoff interactions. The rules of "ghetto ball" are pretty much the same as those of ghetto life; strength, style, effect, and intimidation are the rules of playground basketball. The court is a semisafe replica of the streets. Similarly, through play, children begin to rehearse and develop muscular, emotional, and psychological capacities.

"You learn survival in the ghetto playgrounds like you do on the streets," says John Shumate, former Notre Dame and NBA player, who grew up in Elizabeth, New Jersey, where an ominous sign was posted on an outdoor basketball court: *Don't Go On These Courts Unless You Are Hostile, Agile, and Mobile.* "Basketball gave me my motivation and drive, to go out and graduate from school, then from college." After his playing days were done, Shumate was motivated to get a head coaching job in college, then as an assistant in the NBA.

The Great One

Wayne Gretzky was raised on skates by his father, Walter, who had Wayne doing drills and maneuvering around pylons at three years old on their backyard rink in Brantford, Ontario. Wayne recalls that he loved to skate and play hockey by himself and with his friends day and night, but the pressure began when he started playing competitive hockey. He was almost always the best player, not only on his team but in the leagues he played in, right up from six years old through his teenage years. At the end of his "organized" first year, a six-year-old playing in a league of 10-year-olds, little Wayne was devastated because he didn't win a trophy at the year-end awards banquet. "I cried because everybody won a trophy but me. And my dad said something to me right then that I'll never forget: 'Wayne,

© ACTIVE IMAGES

Hockey's Wayne Gretzky is a nice guy who learned a killer instinct as a boy.

keep practicing and one day you're gonna have so many trophies, we're not gonna have room for them all.'"

Gretzky steadily improved and, at 10 years old, standing four-feet, four-inches tall, he scored 378 goals one season, but there was a lot of jealousy among parents of other teams.

"Once at a big tournament in my own arena in Brantford, I got booed when I was introduced. That's tough to take when you're 10 years old. . . . When I was 10, they were saying I'd be washed up at 12 . . . it became a good luck charm in our family. As long as people were saying I was doomed, we knew we were in good shape. Gretzky-bashing was popular in every sport I played as a kid—lacrosse, baseball, hockey, whatever. And it just got relentless. One time an opposing baseball coach came up to me before a game and said, 'You won't live to see Christmas, Gretzky.'" Gretzky added that "when you're a kid, all you feel is confused. And hurt. I think that part of my life shaped my personality . . . I learned that jealousy is the worst disease in life . . . I didn't want to get hurt anymore . . . hockey was no longer just fun."

Wayne Gretzky, the great one. Enough said.

At 14, Gretzky left home to play in Toronto. "Looking back on it, those years in Toronto were no way for a kid to live," he says. "I was awfully lonely, living with somebody else's family, coming home on weekends, trying to feel part of my own family by talking to them on the telephone. But what choice did I have? I didn't leave Brantford to go play better hockey. I left because the people drove me out. . . . When I think about it now, there is a lot of sadness in me still."

But Gretzky never stopped proving things to people, his professional coach in Edmonton, Glen Sather, says. His father's words about accumulating trophies came true: in the NHL, he has won 4 Stanley Cups, 10 scoring championships, 9 MVP awards, and 9 first-team all-star trophies. Of course, a lot of this came about through talent, but more of it from Gretzky's tremendous drive to succeed, which motivated him to improve his skills and resulted in some fabulous "zone" performances.

Competition Lessons in School

Schools with competitive teams seem to be valuable educators for elite athletes. In grammar school, children learn to play on a team and that winning is the primary concern, Grant added. "Sports become less fun but more exciting. The stakes become higher and so are the rewards." In high school, adolescents discover the greater prestige and attention given to athletes, he says. "Young adults begin to either pass or fall behind one another. Self-image, self-worth, and feelings of athletic competence are in transition during this age."

In their story in *The Clearing House,* authors C. Kenneth McEwin and Thomas S. Dickinson write that little is known about the long-term psychological effects of interscholastic sports competition. "Although many people claim that such participation promotes socialization skills and helps adolescents learn to cope successfully with stress, others question the readiness of young adolescents to become instant successes and failures on the playing field. Common sports practices, such as cutting would-be players from a team, can have negative effects on the psychological development of young adolescents; a student who is cut from a team, for example, is eliminated not only physically, but also psychologically. Those cut from teams often feel that they have not measured up to the expectations of those adults and peers whose judgments are so important to them."

Michael Jordan: "Challenge Me"

Michael Jordan has admitted that one of the burning motivators in his relatively stable childhood was getting cut from his high school team. In fact, as a youngster, Jordan didn't seem that motivated, but through playing games against others, he learned to become one of the most fierce competitors in sports history. In fact, his Chicago Bulls coach, Phil Jackson, says Jordan's fire would be something that science would like to duplicate, but probably will never be able to. "I see they're able to clone sheep now," Jackson once said. "It won't be long until someone tries to clone Michael Jordan, but the psychological and emotional components will be hard to duplicate. How do we duplicate what he has gone through to give him the competitive fire he's developed?"

The fourth of five children in a middle-class upbringing in Wilmington, NC, Jordan was a scrawny, big-eared child and lazy when it came to chores, according to his father, James. As a teenager, Michael was self-conscious but found some confidence in playing basketball, although that came grudgingly. During spirited backyard one-on-one confrontations with his older brother Larry, Michael learned to hustle and scrap and to hate losing. "Those backyard games really helped me become the player I am today," he said years later. "Larry would never give me any slack, never took it easy on me. He'd rather beat me up than have me beat him in a game. I learned a lot about being competitive from him." The lessons went on for some time—it was several years before Michael could beat Larry. "I felt if I could beat him, I could beat anybody." Winning became the driving force in his life. Jordan says his favorite childhood memory is winning a trophy, but not in basketball. "My favorite childhood memory, my greatest accomplishment, was when I got the MVP award when my Babe Ruth team won the state baseball championship," he says. "That was the first big thing I accomplished in my life."

But in his first year at Laney High School, Michael was cut from the team in favor of one of his friends. That brought Michael to tears. "I was pissed," he says. "I felt I was better. I wanted (the

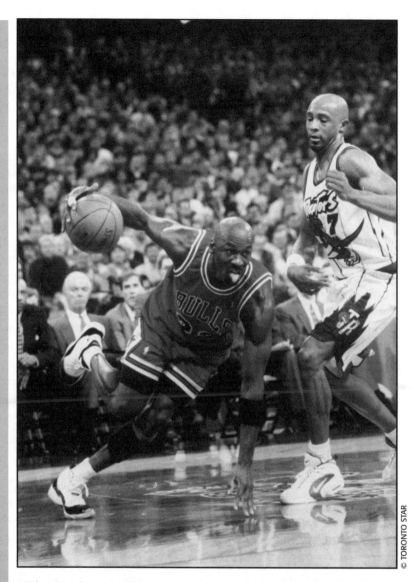

© TORONTO STAR

Michael Jordan raised his game against aggressive defenders like Alvin Robertson.

Laney team) to lose to prove to them that I could help them. To be successful, you have to be selfish, or you never achieve."

Jordan was so motivated, he worked hard on his game around the clock, and not only made the varsity team as a junior, but averaged 20 points per game. "What set him apart was his burning desire," says high school basketball scout Bob Gibbons. Much of that desire apparently was a desire to prove himself to others who thought he was inadequate and that carried on to college. Jordan chose North Carolina over other colleges who recruited him "because most of the people in Wilmington told him he couldn't play here," Carolina coach Dean Smith says. "And as we all know, he likes challenges." Jordan went on to win an NCAA title at North Carolina and became a star in the Pan-American and Olympic Games.

Hard to believe this man was cut from his high school basketball team—but if he hadn't been, he might not be quite the player he is today.

In the NBA, Jordan was supercompetitive and not only on the court, according to his coach Phil Jackson. "He's a very challenged person. And I'm sure that all of us who have coached him have realized that everything is competitive with Michael. He'll take it to the pool table, to the card table, and that's what makes him really great and terrific." Jackson could have added that Jordan is supercompetitive even in practices, in video games on his laptop computer, and even in conversations with people, where he often has to have to last word. "Michael wants to win badly in everything he does, from practice games to tiddly winks," says former Toronto Raptors coach Darrell Walker, who banged heads in practices with Jordan when he was with the Bulls. "If you challenge him, he can be a very vindictive person."

Too Much Winning

Many coaches stress winning over most other things, which often leaves losing players feeling inadequate, McEwin and Dickinson say. "Also related to the psychological development of young adolescents is the prevalence of the win at all costs attitude. . . . The way that sports programs are set up ensures that at least 50 percent of all players in team sports will be 'losers' in every game. At the end of the season, 80 percent of participants will be 'losers.'"

"The process (of becoming a modern warrior) starts in the schoolyard," sport psychologist Tom Tutko claims. The kids who are best in sports are generally the most popular and those who perform poorly are often scorned. Repeatedly being the last one picked when kids choose up sides can leave lifelong emotional scars; there is always the feeling when you play you are somehow being tested, being judged as a person as well as a player."

Is it any wonder, then, that a "survivor" from this system like Jordan feels he must win at everything, from cards to golf to video games? Psychological pressure and win-at-all costs attitudes are the downfall of many athletes, says Robert Grant. Grant says there are basically two groups of highly competitive athletes—the majority who often fall by the wayside and the minority who thrive, at least professionally.

According to psychologist Alfie Kohn, several hundred studies have shown that serious competition can give athletes deep insecurities and self-esteem problems. "Your value is defined by what you've done and who you've beaten," he says. "Competition leads children to envy winners, to dismiss losers, and to be suspicious of just about everyone. Such mindsets can leave the athlete with an emotional hole that's hard to fill for the rest of his or her life, an unsatisfied hunger, says Varda Burstyn, a former psychotherapist . Burstyn says that while some athletes reap benefits from sports, it can give an athlete a false, empty sense of what love is. "It becomes dangerous when winning and losing is too important. In order to be loved, you have to be better than everyone else. That's a very profound element of our sport culture."

The Professional Incubator

As he grew physically, psychologically and emotionally in the highly competitive sports world, Michael Jordan changed. He admitted in 1996 that playoff wars against the rough-and-tumble Detroit Pistons, who beat the Bulls for two championships in 1988-90, turned him into a killer. "The Pistons taught me a hard lesson. They changed the whole game of winning. It was, go to all extents to win. . . . Let's be downright dirty and win. I didn't want to be perceived that way, the sort of individual you hate; yet I wanted to have the same sort of success, I wanted those competitive drives. I wanted to succeed, if you could do it in a nice way. I learned from Detroit that in order to win you have to be willing to attack someone all-out on the court." After a bitter loss in Game 7 of the 1990 Eastern Conference finals, the Bulls' third straight playoff defeat to Detroit, Jordan decided he had to do "whatever it took." That night, he sat in the team bus and cried. "I was crying and steaming," he recalled. "I was saying, 'Hey, I'm out there busting my butt and nobody else is doing the same thing. These guys are kicking our butts, taking our heart, taking our pride.' I made up my mind right then and there it would never happen again. That was the summer I first started lifting weights. If I was going to take some of this beating, I was also going to start dishing out some of it. I got tired of them dominating me physically." For five of the next seven seasons, Jordan and the Bulls won the championship.

If he was a late bloomer in the "aggressive warrior" mode, Jordan is not alone. Track stars Donovan Bailey, Michael Johnson, and others may have blossomed in their late teens or 20s. It's naïve to think that only childhood experiences have a dramatic impact on a person's psyche and attitude, says Michael Rutter, MD, professor of child psychiatry at the Institute of Psychiatry (in the UK), considered one of the world's leading academic child psychiatrists. "Childhood experiences can be very influential to a person and last a lifetime, but so can experiences in adolescence and even adulthood be important to a person's psychological and emotional development," he says. The experiences can be especially influential if they are intense, like those in competitive sports.

Sometimes an elite athlete will suddenly become aggressive or highly aroused in his teens or his 20s if latent "childhood defense mechanisms" suddenly kick in, says former psychoanalyst Maurice Vanderpol. "Sometimes they're dormant and kick in late, particularly in adolescence, when different parts of our character becomes functional. They may not even be evident in high school or even into our 20s and 30s."

Sport psychologist Bob Rotella says it can be an advantage for an athlete to be a late bloomer. "Look at Jordan and [Larry] Bird, you see so many late bloomers like that, who got a hunger from the sports world early in their careers, then when their bodies filled in, they took off. Then they had the desire *and* the body."

The pressure to win becomes more intense when elite athletes are introduced to professional coaches, Robert Grant says. "Young adults are looking for role models to pattern their growth after. If they are aspiring athletes, their coaches have a tremendous amount of power and influence over their athletic careers and overall feelings of self-worth, confidence, and identity, especially if they have most of their self-esteem wrapped up in athletic success." (And, of course, an athlete's ability to win becomes all-important in the quest for college athletic scholarships and professional contracts.)

The World's Fastest Man

The elite sports world can transform gentlemanly performers into nasty warriors, Varda Burstyn says.

> It's hard for a gentleman to survive in the sports' world because of what he has to do to himself to become the best. ...It's not impossible, but it's difficult. To get to the top, you have to become as manic as those already there. Any system, if you spend a lot of time in it, whether it's sports or politics, you generally have to adopt its values. The systems have their own structure and heart and soul. To get up the ladder requires you to compromise and chances are that when you get there, you're not the same person as you were before. The psychological pressure is a transforming experience."

Burstyn cites the case of Donovan Bailey, the 1996 Olympic 100-meter champion and world record holder. "When he won the Olympic gold medal, I saw him as being a kind of a gentleman, a Canadian in all the best ways, but then he became boastful and arrogant," she says.

Bailey was a late bloomer in competitive sports. His parents divorced when he was young and, after emigrating from Jamaica, he grew up in the middle-class suburb of Oakville, Ontario with his father and stepmother. Before he became a serious track warrior in 1993, he worked as a marketing investment consultant and owned his own business, then he began to view track as a business.

Dan Pffaf, Louisiana State University track coach who has coached many world-class athletes, including Bailey, believes that elite athletes become warriors because of intuitive ability that is nurtured and honed by competitive sports, where there are primarily just winners and losers. "They thrive in a (combative) environment. They know how to take the adrenaline and channel it. They feed off the fear."

Pffaf prepares his athletes like they are going to war, often sequestering them in private villas for special mental and physical training before an important competition to get them ready for a fight, much like an army. "Why was sport invented?" Pffaf says. "Go back to the ancient Greeks. Throwing spears and discus and running. What was the marathon all about? Messengers during the war. Physical culture is indelibly linked to military endeavor. We can't run from its militaristic history. In track and field, the goal is to win. That implies conflict. The average spectator doesn't go to see a dead heat. How hollow was the 150 (meter against Michael Johnson)? It wasn't a complete battle. What was the gladiators stuff all about? One and the same."

Bailey agreed with his coach. "It really is like preparing for war. It's very essential for us to focus and try to make as little mistakes as possible. Because if you do make any little mistakes, it's over for you. You're going to be going home. So, essentially, if it's war and you lose, you're dead." Is it any coincidence, then, that at the moment of truth in a sporting event, athletes often go into an "arousal" mode for self-defense during the "battle?"

Pffaf believes that athletes such as Bailey have sharp animal tendencies for striking out and devouring opponents and also tendencies of entertainers before an important performance. "I think every great actor will admit there's butterflies before a performance," Pfaff says. "It's what you do with those butterflies. Do you turn them into positive energy or do you let it be negative energy? Obviously, Donovan has the ability to turn the pre-stage anxiety into very positive forces."

Bailey says he takes losing personally and uses it to get revenge. "If I run a race and I get beat, I get angry and I internalize it. I'm always looking forward to the next race, kind of like storing my energy right from that moment." Bailey says his best performances often come when opponents make a race personal. In a sport sometimes involving huge egos and cruel mind games, protecting one's pride is a big motivator, he says. Foes often insult one another through the media. Some examples:

• Michael Johnson says part of what drove him to become a record-breaking runner was the criticism that Carl Lewis leveled at him and also losing to Lewis in races. "It would bother me for weeks if I lost to him," Johnson says. Another Johnson quote: "Every guy I compete against, when I line up and get in the blocks, I hate them all."

• In 1997, American Maurice Greene and Bailey hooked up in the finals of the world championship 100 meters in Athens, but not before trading personal insults. As he upset Bailey for the gold medal, Greene stuck his tongue out at the Canadian while crossing the finish line. Bailey was ungracious in defeat, telling the media Greene had a lack of education and insulting Greene's religion.

"Shame and pride are two constants that underlie many professionals and Olympic athletes and their experiences," Burstyn says. "Too much competition can do that, too much winning and losing. Shame comes from a sense that you have failed in some way and it leads to a feeling of unworthiness. The achievement of pride is opposite of shame. You stand straight up and feel good about yourself. Sports is a place people go to find that sense of pride, but there's a healthy pride and then there's a narcissistic arrogance. In searching for a sense of self, athletes have to have strong pride, but arrogant narcissism often becomes the reality. But at least underlying this motivation is a desire to take pride and feel good about one's origin and to prove something to a society that shames you."

PART III

Soaring Athletes

In the previous chapters, we raised the issue of athletes' environments and how they may affect their psyche, their long-term motivation, their "emotional drive." We examined the possibility that their insecurities and desires (or needs) to prove themselves sometimes are a driving force that motivate them to train hard, develop their skills, and defeat opponents over and over again. Proving themselves serves as a defense of their ego.

Out of that, other questions pop up: on the short-term, what things trigger powerful mind-body forces which act as additives to performance? How do athletes provoke and control this arousal? In this segment, we'll look at "triggers" which elite athletes use to spark that extra effort, especially under pressure in the moment of truth, and their methods of harnessing the pressure. Here are some of the triggers we'll look at:

- Intrinsic triggers: With an apparent need to prove themselves, athletes use opponents, crowds, and media as catalysts.

- Extrinsic triggers: Money, awards, doing it for teammates, relatives, or country.

Often, it is hard to distinguish between intrinsic and extrinsic motivations. For example, an athlete may use the lure of a big cash contract (extrinsic) to try harder, but perhaps the underlying motivation is intrinsic because he wants the big contract to soothe his ego, to show he's "worth more" than his opponents.

Finding the optimal levels of arousal and concentration can be individual endeavors for an athlete. In chapter 10, I'll look at how athletes raise their hormone levels through anger and fear. In chapter 11, I'll discuss how they use calming techniques prior to competition to bring themselves down when they get over-aroused, which follows, in chapter 12, with a look at concentration and visualization techniques. In chapter 13, the focus shifts to athletes during the heat of competition and how they can change their mind-body chemicals for the moment of truth.

CHAPTER 10

New Tricks of an Old Trade

> "I try to make pressure and tension work for me. I want the adrenaline to be flowing. There's nothing wrong with being charged up, if it's controlled."
>
> Golfer Hale Irwin

The anticipation of competition is usually enough to get an athlete "psyched." But many elite athletes need to get higher to produce an extra spark to beat top foes or break records. They use a variety of triggers to reach Mount Arousal. Coaches know the value of getting teams up, especially in explosion sports. "A good coach goes into a (football) locker room at half-time and, if his team is behind, knows how to get the adrenaline up in his players to get the job done," said Robert Eliot, former director of the Institute of Stress Medicine International in Denver. "But if you raise the players too high, then they start dropping the ball, playing like Keystone Cops."

Pressure Boost

Pressure is a blessing for those who know how to control it, says Patrick J. Cohn, PhD, a golf psychologist. "Pressure increases your motivation to practice, boosts your concentration to help you hit a difficult shot, and

131

supplies extra energy or adrenaline for a long drive. Pressure becomes a problem only when you don't cope with it and it takes you out of your optimal emotional zone. Excitement and increased arousal helps you to play better, except when it reaches a point where you become over-aroused, and then your play worsens." "Pressure," Mark McGwire said near the end of his record-setting homerun season of 1998, "is knowing that every eye in America is watching you."

In pressure games, coaches usually don't have to do as much. They know the pressure will automatically trigger arousal and, if anything, they have to bring the players down to help them keep control. The best athletes love pressure because they know that in the past it has improved the performance of their mind-body and they've seen how it has made others "choke." Years ago, fans applauded Boston Red Sox slugger Ted Williams because he elected to play the final double-header of the season, even though a poor day might have dropped his average below the magic .400 mark. But Williams knew he could make pressure work for him and, indeed, he went six for eight in the two games, raising his average to .406.

Nothing is more pressure-packed than the Olympics, says Jim Reardon, a psychologist from Columbus, Ohio, who has worked with U.S. decathletes.

> At the Olympics, everything is magnified four times because they only come around once every four years. In the 1996 Olympics, American runner Michael Johnson welcomed all the various personal and corporate pressures that came upon him in the 1996 Olympics. Behind the gold shoes, Nike and Coca-Cola sponsors, and Superman confidence was a mortal with a pumping heart, a well-tuned fight-or-flight system and, apparently, psychological and emotional needs.

"I crave the pressure," Johnson said. "The higher the stakes, the better I am. The big races put me in the zone, where I'm more focused and aggressive." Johnson had lots to prove to the track world, and to himself, after missing out on an individual gold medal in the 1992 Olympics in Barcelona. "I have always been *afraid* of ending my career without having won an individual gold medal," he said.

Johnson admitted it took some time for him to realize that pressure can be good for an athlete. "If there is one thing that will really take you to another level of performance—to the plateau where your victories are measured in the blink of milliseconds—it might be the ability to embrace pressure, to understand it, to draw it in, to make it your own and use it to your advantage," he said. "I know that probably sounds nuts. We've been trained to think of pressure as the enemy, the unfair burden that holds us down."

In Atlanta, Johnson finally won the gold in his first of two races, the 400 meters, which increased the pressure for the 200 meters a few days later because no Olympic male had ever won both the 200 and 400 in the same Games. To make things worse, Carl Lewis, whom Johnson had seen as a rival to media attention, won his ninth gold medal in the long jump. In the 200-meter semi-finals, Johnson lost to his chief rival, Frankie Fredericks of Namibia, but both qualified for the finals. So Johnson, who had also lost an earlier race to Fredericks, used an emotional trigger as he lined up in the starting blocks for the 200-meter Olympic finals—he envisioned himself as the underdog, then he let the cheers of 80,000 American fans well up inside him. As he readied for the starting gun, Johnson had several things in his mind, he later recalled: "There was pressure from the 80,000 people there who expect you to win, not to mention having the Olympic schedule changed for you, and all the years of magazine covers, photo shoots, people calling, people calling to try to take off the pressure but just making more pressure, and the fact that Frankie and Ato Bolden (of Trinidad and Tobago) had been running really, really well. I thought if I didn't win this, a lot of things were going to be said that I would not want to hear."

Johnson said he let all this pressure build and then, a split second before the starter's gun went off, a very clear thought came to him: "The 200 is the one I want, this is the reason I'm here." It was the perfect final thought and "it dumped a whole other ton of pressure into the mix. It was like one of my competitors coming up and hitting me." Just before the gun sounded, a tremor throbbed through the body of runner No. 2370—but it was possibly a subconscious reaction because Johnson said later he was focused only on listening for the starter's pistol. All of Johnson's mental, physical and emotional resources fired as the race starter: He reacted to the pistol in .16 of a second and shot down the curved track at 25 miles per hour—faster than the speed limit allowed cars on streets surrounding the Olympic Stadium. Fredericks led early, but, with the crowd chanting "Michael! Michael!" Johnson overtook him after 80 meters, chest puffed

Michael Johnson welcomes pressure to get him in the "zone."

© ALLSPORT/MIKE POWELL

forward, back arched beautifully—"Running faster than I have in my life."

Sports Illustrated would write of the stretch drive: Johnson's "effort was engraved on his face. His gold chain sawed back and forth across the straining cords of his neck as he drew two, three, four meters ahead of Fredericks. The great crowd stood as one, calling him on. He hit the line, looked left at the clock and for an instant his expression was, as he later put it, 'Where the hell did *that* come from?'" His record time was 19.32 seconds, a time experts believed would not be possible for years. Fredericks, who admitted he hated pressure, finished a full four meters behind. And forgotten in the bedlam were tendon injuries that would keep Johnson out of the 400 relay a few days later. One last comment from Johnson: "I like the pressure. I was afraid out there tonight. But I like to be afraid." Fear? We know that fear can debilitate performance. But, when used properly, as a defense, it can help.

The Trash Talk Trigger

Few things can arouse a player like the sight of an opponent up-close and personal. If you had the luxury of sitting at courtside during the 1996-97 NBA season, you may have seen games being played within games: Michael Jordan of the Chicago Bulls getting mad at Gary Payton of the Seattle SuperSonics, Charles Barkley of the Houston Rockets blowing off steam at the New York Knicks' Charles Oakley, and rookie Marcus Camby of the Toronto Raptors daring to taunt veteran Karl Malone of the Utah Jazz. These seemingly childish shouting and sometimes shoving matches can be good for business. NBA stars know that when they're ticked off, they can raise their emotions and often the levels of their game.

Many players use "trash talk" to try to raise their game and shoot down their opponents. "We don't try to hurt one another," Hall of Fame NBA center Kareem Abdul-Jabbar said. "We just try to hurt each other's feelings." Jabbar's opponents were sometimes distracted and thrown off their games by this show of disrespect, but the great ones thrive on being "dissed." "Go ahead, disrespect me, I want you to," Michael Jordan said in a television commercial. Remember from chapter 5 how Jordan punished opposing players and coaches who didn't treat him as the god of hoops that he is?

In a 1996 NFL game, receiver Shannon Sharpe of the Denver Broncos, with his team smashing the host New England Patriots 34-8, teased Patriots' fans by shouting into a red phone behind the Denver bench: "Mr. President, send in the National Guard, please. We need as many men as you can spare because we are killing the Patriots. They need emergency help." Sharpe's routine was caught on videotape by NFL Films and secured by New England coach Bill Parcells, who fashioned it into a psychological weapon. Parcells showed the film to his team repeatedly in the coming weeks and, thusly motivated, they won six of seven games to go all the way to the Super Bowl past Denver. Prior to their meeting in the 1994 Wimbledon tennis tournament, Jana Novotna "dissed" opponent Martina Navratilova in the London media, saying she was too slow to win again. "I think this year is much too much for Martina," she said. "Her will is there, but the body just can't do it anymore." It was a feeling shared by many tennis players at that time and that apparently upset the 37-year-old Navratilova, who was ending her reign as the queen of the sport. She went on to upset Novotna 5-7, 6-0, 6-1 to advance to the semi-finals.

This type of reaction is a type of self-defense, according to exercise physiologist Jack Raglin. "It's anger sort of directed as an instrument," he says. "These are threats made to their self-esteem and athletes have a very strong self focus. They're used to performing well and a large part of their self-concept is bound up in sport competency. When threats are made to that, it would make sense that (the athletes) would want to prove them wrong."

In ice hockey, disrespect preceded the greatest single-game performance ever. On Feb. 6, 1976, owner Harold Ballard of the Toronto Maple Leafs berated his all-star center, Darryl Sittler, in the media: "If only we had a center . . . it could be a time bomb." That bomb went off the next night as Sittler exploded for 10 points.

Michael Jordan has this "dissing" revenge down to a science. He wields a grudge like a stiletto. Often he doesn't wait for the game to begin to get mad at a foe. Air Freud has the Bulls' public relations staff scour newspapers for quotes in which opponents question his superiority, then he works himself into a lather for the next time they meet.

Jordan learned some of his tricks from Larry Bird of the Boston Celtics. When the two locked horns, Bird would often taunt Jordan, who was six years younger, bragging to Jordan how he was going to beat him with his moves or his deadly outside shot. And it would come to pass as Bird would psyche himself into scoring against MJ, one of the league's best defenders. Bird knew the "trash talking" would make Jordan play more intensely on defense the next time down the court and would force Bird to raise the level of his offensive play even more. Of course, it became a two-way street with Jordan telling Bird under his breath that he was going to score at the other end of the court and thus, by defending their egos, two titans were able to raise the bar in a brilliant game of psychological and emotional stress, er, chess.

Of course, other NBA players have used Bird and Jordan as their own motivational tools, like John Starks of the New York Knicks. Upon hearing of Jordan's short retirement in 1993, Starks said: "I'm going to miss him. He brought out the best in me." Or, perhaps more correctly, he brought out the *warrior* in him.

Jordan admits to fabricating stories to trick himself into an angry state against opponents, but that doesn't surprise sport psychologist Bruce Ogilvie, who said that a former NFL defensive end, whom he wouldn't name, would get himself motivated by pretending an opponent had raped his wife. (As discussed earlier in this book, the mind body arousal system sometimes has a hard time distinguishing between fact and fantasy if the athlete can get himself "psyched.")

Fueled by the Crowd

Many athletes admit that a desire to prove something to others is a great trigger. Sports pages regularly carry stories of players who perform better than average when they face a team that has traded them or cut them. In 1997, pitching great Roger Clemens felt betrayed by the Boston Red Sox, for whom he had toiled for 13 years. After a mediocre season in 1996, he felt he was forced out of Boston by general manager Dan Duquette, who felt he was washed up, and joined the Toronto Blue Jays on a mission to prove he still had what it takes. Clemens revived his career, winning 21 games and the Cy Young Award. When the Blue Jays visited Boston's Fenway Park, he struck out 16 batters to stifle his old team. "If someone tells me that I can't do something, it becomes more of a challenge," Clemens said of his mindset. "In high school, I was always considered a good pitcher, but I was never considered the best. The thing was, I felt I was the best. When people who don't have any idea what they're talking about say something bad about me, tell me that I'll fail, it just adds

Roger Clemens: "Everybody wants to win, but it burns much deeper in me. . . ." In Boston and Toronto, the five-time Cy Young Award winner has enjoyed the kind of career that fantasies are made of. He hopes to finish his career with the New York Yankees.

fuel to my fire. Everybody wants to win, but it burns much deeper in me than it does in other people. That's my edge. It's like, 'I'll show you.'"

Tony Gwynn of the San Diego Padres is never satisfied with his performance, even though he's won eight National League batting titles: "There were always coaches who said that I couldn't do something. I couldn't throw. I couldn't hit with power. I couldn't run.

I couldn't field my position. I think that's one of the reasons I've been successful, because they can measure everything you do on the field, but they cannot measure what's inside you and what drives you. It's easy to cheat yourself and do just enough to get by, but that's what everybody can do, just enough to get by. But those who want to be successful and maintain that level of success have got to push a little bit harder and do a little bit more."

Golfer Jack Nicklaus finds that defending himself against embarrassment is a big motivator. "My urge for self-improvement has very little to do with winning, and nothing at all to do with making money or other materialistic factors," he said. "I've always believed that performance takes care of those things. Anytime that there's a cooling off in this impulse to improve, one emotion above all others will get a good blaze going again. It's *embarrassment*. I am very easily embarrassed by myself. No single emotion is more responsible for what I've achieved."

Sometimes a noisy crowd can motivate the visitors, such as Reggie Miller, of the NBA's Indiana Pacers, who enjoys perceiving himself as the enemy and often shoots better in road games. But research suggests that athletes in explosion sports perform better when in front of a big home crowd, although they may perform worse at home and have a tendency to choke in more finely-tuned sports such as baseball. A noisy crowd can offer the love and support for a home team—such as the 78,000 NFL fans at Arrowhead Stadium who raise the sound level to nearly 120 decibels, comparable to a jet taking off, in supporting their Kansas City Chiefs. For individual performances, an enthusiastic crowd can motivate miracles. Champion figure skater Elvis Stojko is a master of concentration, but he sometimes allows the noise of the crowd to spark him to athletic moves like a quadruple toe loop and triple toe loop combination. "In many different situations, (the crowd) has helped me out," he said. "They get you going. There's such a significant relationship there . . . you pull them in with eye contact."

U.S. tennis player MaliVai Washington would rather have people screaming for him. He credited a noisy crowd of 17,000 for a tennis victory over Slovakia's Jan Kroslak in the 1996 Olympics: "When I hit the forehand winner down the line in the tiebreak to go up 4-2, I don't know if I've ever heard an uproar that big. The average tennis crowd thinks it's supposed to be quiet and at certain times, clap. You don't chant, you don't have cowbells. Today, you had the 'USA, USA' chant and you had more like a soccer crowd. . . When you get that crowd on your side, the other guy's feeling the pressure and your adrenaline is going. That's one of the intangibles that sometimes makes the difference."

Some athletes feed off negative comments coming from the audience. In an LPGA tournament in 1992, Dottie Mochrie was challenging for the lead when she left a putt short. "Loser!" a fan shouted at her. "It was some man," Mochrie recalled. "That'll get you fired up in a hurry." It did, too. Two holes later, on the first playoff hole, Mochrie was declared the champion.

Pick the Right Time

Biochemists say it's hard to sustain anger for a long period, that athletes should pick and choose when they get psyched during competition. Former Olympic canoe gold medalist Larry Cain of Canada seems to know this. He advises athletes to save their arousal for the right time during competition. "At international competitions, usually I'm incredibly bored through everything until I come to the final," he said. "You don't waste any time psyching up on the unimportant stuff. You are saving it all for the final, the big race." Cain said that he sometimes fabricated things in his mind to get a good start to a big race.

> I try to develop a little bit of anger in order to have more explosiveness on the starting line. I pick an individual (opponent) and say 'I'm going to beat this guy.' At times, there's intense hate. I would still get along with him, but I won't talk to him or have a beer with him because he's the enemy. It's a gimmick. . . . I picture losing as an embarrassment. I hate being embarrassed. If I lose, it's almost like I'm after revenge.

But even during a race, it's important to find the optimal level of arousal, where you can be hyped and yet still in control, added Cain, who got too aroused for a race in Germany. "I got too explosive, too nuts. I went out too fast and ran out of gas at the end and finished fourth."

Guy Ogden, a former international runner and now a specialist in the treatment of sports injuries in London, England, said athletes can heighten the adrenaline response prior to competition "by doing a kind of mental war dance. Ideally, a ritual of preparation should be well-established in minor competition so that each item of the countdown is recognized and triggers a further boost to confirm the approaching demand . . . it is not economic to sustain this for too long." Ogden advises elite runners not to talk to anyone, not even their coach, at least 10 minutes before the event. "Get yourself in order mentally . . . I need 45 minutes to facilitate a fully heightened adrenal response." He recommends using music to increase the hype or provide a calm when necessary.

Indiana Pacer's clutch shooter Reggie Miller thrives on catcalls and boos from an antagonistic crowd: "I shoot a lot better."

The Tricky Triggers of Motivation

Not surprisingly, considering the thousands of different personalities you'll find in the sports world, athletes reach motivation via many different avenues. We have all known what it feels like to want to impress our friends and family. Perhaps not all of us have experienced a tragedy that moved us to boost our performance—and not many of us, I imagine, have had million dollar carrots dangled in front of us to spur us on to excellence.

Winning for the Gipper

It's nice to know that not all strong motivations are self-centered. Athletes have produced remarkable feats while motivated to do them for their teammates, family, or their country. As examples: in 1996, the Las Vegas Stars of the Pacific Coast (baseball) League dedicated their winning streak to first place in memory of their teammate Mike Sharperson, killed in a car crash. Mired in a terrible 1997 slump, Toronto Blue Jays Joe Carter was so angry at the dismissal of his manager and friend, Cito Gaston, he wore Gaston's number on his back and clouted a homer to beat Baltimore. Bulgarian soccer star Hristo Stoichkov deliberately made himself angry during matches to motivate his teammates. "When they see that I'm angry and that I'm being really aggressive, my teammates catch a bit of that from me and they play more intensely," he said.

Other athletes are motivated by greats who have gone before them, like basketball's Larry Bird, who before games looked up at hockey player Bobby Orr's Number 4 sweater, retired in the rafters at the Boston Garden; former IBF world middleweight boxing champion Roy Jones Jr., who watched tapes of boxing legends before his bouts; and Roger Clemens, who enjoys playing at Yankee Stadium, Fenway Park, and Tigers Stadium, where he gets chills looking at the names of all-time greats on the outfield walls.

Family Factors

As we've mentioned, many athletes are motivated by the presence of relatives in the audience. For some, having mom or dad watching from close proximity adds pressure that causes choking, but for many others the presence of family is a significant motivating factor.

But family members don't necessarily have to be close by to influence an athlete's performance. Sometimes misfortune for someone in the family can spur an athlete on. For instance, Belarus gymnast Vitaly Scherbo had no plans to defend his six Olympic titles in Atlanta until his critically injured wife, Irina, began her recovery from a near-fatal car crash. After the worst season of his pro career, NFL quarterback Neil O'Donnell had a big game to lead the New York Jets to a 41-3 victory in the 1997 season opener—dedicated to his sister-in-law who had delivered a stillborn baby. "It was on my mind constantly. I was going to win this for her." Gary Hall, Jr., swimming for his grandfather whom he believed had been falsely imprisoned, won the gold medal for the U.S. 400-meter medley relay team with a record last lap in the 1996 Olympics.

Tragedy Trigger

Sometimes a tragedy sparks peak performance. Princess Diana's 1997 car crash inspired emotional performances in at least four athletes: in tennis, Greg Rusedksi won the U.S. Open; golfer Greg Norman wore black for an under-par performance in the Canadian Open ("Emotionally, this was the most powerful morning I've ever had in my entire life"); David Coulthard won the Italian Grand Prix; and England won a World Cup qualifying soccer match 4–0 over Moldova.

Personal Ties

Some athletes are motivated by patriotism or other strong links they feel to an organization or group. Getting psyched up to compete alongside or in the name of fellow countrymen is common, especially during the Olympics. In 1968, Kip Keino of Kenya was asked by Olympic officials not to compete in the 1,500 meters because he had collapsed in an earlier event from a gall bladder infection. "I would rather die on the track, fighting for my country, than on a hospital bed," Keino announced. He then went out and beat American Jim Ryun for the gold medal.

Then there is the powerful motivation of winning for your race, as Jesse Owens did in the 1936 Olympics and as Dana Rosenblatt did to win the New England middleweight boxing title in 1993 to inspire his

Jewish people, the Star of David emblazoned on his trunks. "I want to be a role model for Jewish kids," he said. "I didn't have a Jewish role model when I was growing up."

$$ Motivation $$

Many psychologists believe that in the long run lucrative contracts are not significant motivators for today's athletes. With salaries skyrocketing, it may be that modern athletes do not have the motivational edge of their predecessors. Players can become millionaires right out of college (or even high school) in many professional sports. Yet, ironically, the motivating factor for many of them is not the cash itself but the belief that other players are making more money than they are —or so believes Glen Sather, general manager of the NHL's Edmonton Oilers. Off the ice, Wayne Gretzky has an aw-shucks, down-to-earth demeanor, but he's sometimes driven if he feels dissed over contract negotiations. Says Sather, "One time, Wayne read an article in *Sporting News* that he was the bottom paid of the NHL's elite guys, and it really pissed him off. You should have seen him play."

Sather, who coached the Oilers to four Stanley Cup championships in the 1980s, knows the power of greenbacks. In one crucial game, the Oilers were in danger of losing the playoffs, so in the dressing room between the second and third periods, Sather trudged into the room lugging an equipment bag. To the surprise of his players, Sather untied the bag and dumped the contents onto the floor—$100,000 cash. "That's the bonus money you'll lose if you lose this game," he told them. The Oilers skated out and pummeled the opposition. "It got their eyes rolling. . . . That money meant a lot in those days (the 80s)," Sather recalls. "But today [the escalating salaries] has nothing to do with money. It's a matter of pride. They read that somebody is making more money than they are, and they get caught up in it. It's getting worse. They all want to be the guy with the biggest stick on the block. It's about power and control, and guys use it for motivation. They'll show them who deserves the most."

Tricks to Boost Arousal

While each athlete is different (at least in small ways) in his or her methods of trying to attain peak arousal, many share common beliefs about what works for them and what doesn't. Some try artificial means, such as caffeine or other stimulants or music to boost their arousal state.

The Caffeine High

Some athletes use stimulants to get "up." This is not a diet book, but one stimulant we'll mention because it is used quite often is coffee or caffeine products. Caffeine is on the list of the International Olympic Committee's banned substances because it's a powerful central nervous system stimulant and can be harmful if taken in large doses. In 1988, Steve Haig, a former Olympic gold medalist, tested positive for caffeine (pills) in the U.S. Olympic trials and was disqualified. But in many sports and leagues, caffeine is legal. Deion Sanders sometimes drinks coffee on the sidelines of football games. Former linebacker Brian Bosworth claimed he took the pill equivalent of 40 cups of coffee before a game. Caffeine has also boosted below-average professional athletes, like Acie Earl, who once scored 40 points after drinking several cups of coffee and several caffeine-laced carbonated soft drinks before the game. (A revenge factor may also have contributed to Earl getting "up" for the contest, which was against the Boston Celtics, who had released him the previous season.)

Music and the Mind

As external stimulants go, athletes love music. Precompetition music is used as an upper, a downer, or to provide an even keel for an athlete's performance. Songs like "Chariots of Fire," "Eye of the Tiger," and the theme from the movie *Rocky* have been used by athletes and teams to fire them up before a contest. The Chicago Bulls use the song "Sirius" as they go through their warm-ups. Chris Duplanty, goaltender for the U.S. water polo team in the 1996 Olympics, says he gets chills whenever he hears John Williams' Olympic music. Tom Petranoff, former world record holder in javelin, played the song "This Is It" in his head at the crucial point in his competition to pump himself up and help him concentrate. And the New York Yankees Paul O'Neil plays Rolling Stones music before a game.

Boxers like Muhammad Ali have motivated themselves, or calmed themselves, through prebout rock'n' roll. Los Angeles Lakers legend Magic Johnson used to turn up the sound system in his Ferrari full blast as he drove to the Great Western Forum for a basketball game. Former New York Giants' linebacker Harry Carson listened to organ music in church before games. And entire teams have plugged into it, like the Brazilian national soccer club, which uses salsa for pregame rhythm. In the 1970s, the Philadelphia Flyers got a nightly boost from singer Kate Smith's "God Bless America," which had them playing dizzying hockey at the Spectrum.

Yet many athletes ignore their favorite music as a precompetition additive that could get them into the right frame of mind, focus, and hormonal balance. For all of its fabulous potential, music has been an underappreciated sporting weapon until recent times. Boxing great Sugar Ray Robinson said he could have become better in the 1950s had he found a way to use music: "In the minutes before I boxed, I searched for the rhythm . . . in some matches there were bands playing between bouts and that music would be blaring as I came into the ring. I always wished they would have continued to play while I was boxing. I think I would've boxed better."

This type of rhythm can spill over after a match has ended. Defender Mike Reid of the Cincinnati Bengals wrote his best music and played his best concert piano immediately after his NFL games.

Athletes should choose music they enjoy hearing, says Esther Haskvitz, assistant professor of physical therapy at Springfield (Massachusetts) College, who claims it helps concentration and motivation and increases an athlete's exhaustion threshold. Heavy rock music is particularly good for athletes who have minor injuries because it masks pain, according to Roberta Wigle, music therapist at the University of Michigan Medical College. And it's been proven to raise an athlete's brain levels of natural drugs endorphin and serotonin, as well as self-esteem and confidence, in both professional and amateur athletes. On his way to winning the Ontario Amateur Golf Championship in 1998, Michael Hospodar used the rock tune "Moneytalks" by AC/DC to motivate himself when he'd hit a bad shot. "When I stumble, I take a deep breath and replay that song in my head, to get aggressive, to get my blood flowing," he said.

Perhaps the best place to look for its success is at events that have music incorporated as part of the act, such as figure skating. American skating champion Dorothy Hamill used music to turn her fears into strength and victory for the 1976 Olympic gold medal: "My knees were trembling . . . I felt enormous pressure, but then I let the music be the walls I climbed inside, and I shut everything else out. I focused my mind into a tunnel and looked to the other end where the light was shining. As soon as I started, I possessed endless strength." In the 1988 Olympics, Canada's Elizabeth Manley provided a more electrifying effort than favored rivals Katerina Witt and Debbie Thomas by enlisting not only her music but the hometown crowd in Calgary as her ally. Manley's coach pleaded with her to ignore the crowd, but she refused.

> When the music started, I felt as though I were riding on the wings of the crowd's ovation. I was inspired—I felt wonderful. I approached the triple lutz without hesitation, and when I hit it right, I let out a yell of delight . . . I was possessed. I felt I was actually flying, and I didn't miss a single [move]."

According to clinical psychiatrist Anthony Storr of Oxford, England, and author of *Music and the Mind,* fast music is less effective for sports and activities that feature spontaneous creativity and thinking and more effective for sports with repetitive moves, such as bowling, as illustrated by the case of Troy Ockerman.

Troy's Perfect Trey

After he bowled an unprecedented three straight perfect games in Corunna, Michigan, in 1993, Troy Ockerman credited heavy metal music, along with a need to prove himself, with his success. "Who would suspect that arousal of this kind could be used to motivate a bowler?" exercise physiologist Jack Raglin said. "But it happens, and it shows that athletes can get hyped up even for these type of sports."

Here is Ockerman's story. (His comments appear in italics.) Before his historic night of bowling, at home on an electric guitar, Ockerman thumped out a heavy metal song he'd composed himself—a fast-paced, hard-driving song without a title, similar to the soundtrack from an action movie. *Before a match, I like to get my adrenaline levels up. I try and get really hyped.* Then, as he drove his car to the bowling alley, he listened to a tape he'd made of the song until the beat was playing automatically in his head . . . *thump, thump, thump.* Little did Ockerman, a 24-year-old amateur bowler, realize he was on his way to a feat unparalleled in the history of the sport. But perhaps subconsciously he did. Over and over again in his mind and in his practice, he had prepared himself for this wonderful night.

At the Riverbend Bowl, his motivation intensified when he looked up on the bulletin board for the scores of the tournament: it showed that Wayne Bunce was the King of the Hill for the month. He was better than Wayne Bunce, he told himself, but he kept finishing second to Bunce in tournaments. He got mad. *Deep down, I knew I was better. I kept telling myself, I'm tired of finishing second. I'm better than him.* But he'd have to go beyond himself to prove it to all their bowling colleagues in Corunna. But he knew he couldn't get too pumped up. Whenever that happened, he'd throw the ball too hard down the alley and it would roll off target. So he kept in tune with the rhythm of the music in his head . . . *thump, thump, thump,* rather than *thump, THUMP, thump, THUMP.* He had to be like Bruce Willis in *Die Hard:* be ready for anything, but don't smash through the condo window until you have to.

It was tempting not to go wild. All his life, the diminutive Ockerman had lots to prove to others physically; he stood only five-feet, four-inches tall. In school, he'd been too puny to play football. An only child, he'd chosen individual sports where he had only himself to rely on. As a teenager, he'd rushed to the aid of two friends who got jumped in a fight outside a bar. Now everybody called him Taz, short for Tasmanian Devil. *The devil is short and thick, like me, with a big mouth and feisty.*

There were other things to prove that night—that he could beat two lefthanders whom he was scheduled to face before Bunce. Lefthanders worried Ockerman because they generally scored better because of oil conditions on the Riverbend alley. Before the bowling matches started, Ockerman went through a ritual designed to get him into a "zone" for the night. He kept listening to the soundtrack music he'd programmed into his head. It's a trick that other athletes have used with great success.

At the bowling lanes, Troy Ockerman used his music and an appreciative crowd to his advantage, as well as his ritual of visualization. Using his mind with his eyes closed, he programmed his body for the actions it would need to bowl three games: he visualized himself walking straight down the alley with the ball in his right hand, keeping his body low while dropping his eyes to a spot two feet ahead of him, going slowly into the backswing and, after five quick steps, projecting the ball to arrows on the floor leading to the 10 pins. In fact, he went further than visualizing what he would do—he "felt" it all before it happened. *I feel my walk, feel my arm, feel my release. I program the physical memory, the feelings I'm going to have. Some nights I have poor concentration, but the pregame mental programming seems to overcome it.*

Taz had a chance to prove himself, prove his killer instinct, early in the first of three matches: his opponent Jerry Schulze started poorly with a split. Quickly, Ockerman rolled two consecutive strikes. Then a couple more. *Each time I saw the pins tumble in my mind before I threw the next ball.* Pretty soon the first game was over and Schulze had bowled very well, a 258. Taz shot 42 pins better. He'd bowled a perfect game—300 out of a possible 300 points.

Troy's next opponent was Jim Porter, who was in first place in the tournament. *Something else to prove, I thought.* Porter was to discover that Troy had enveloped himself in a Super Zone. Totally tuned into what he had to do, he was aware of what the ball would do for him even before he rolled it. And, after his mental visualization, he liked to do it fast. One second standing at the line. Five quick steps. High arm swing. Power and speed. Lots of spin. Urethane ball, go with God. *People have tried to slow me down over the years, but it's a natural pace for me.* Between shots, he deliberately didn't concentrate. *I don't want to lose the adrenaline, so I keep myself moving—sipping a Diet Coke, tapping my feet to the music in my head, running back and forth talking to people, and joking with them.* He looked around to find that other bowlers were congregating around his alley. When the second game started and he continued to throw strikes, the crowd began cheering for him. *I felt another adrenaline surge. Physically I got stronger, my steps were faster, and there was more revolution on the ball. It got more powerful as it hit the pocket. I had to be careful I didn't get too strong and fall out of my rhythm.* Throughout his life, Troy has performed better while riding the crest of emotion. *Under pressure, I tend to get myself pumped up for things. I think I'm more aggressive because I'm small.*

Porter scored 237, well above his average, but it wasn't nearly enough to derail Taz whose second consecutive 300 had now drawn quite a crowd of spectators. Next up was Wayne Bunce, the king of the bloody hill. If he thought he was going up against Ockerman's usual 216 average, he had another think coming. *After my two perfect games, I had him totally psyched. He had no chance.*

It was all rhythm the rest of the way, to the beat of the electric guitar playing in his head. Troy stood at the line with his ball in his hand and brimmed with confidence, with the feeling, the knowledge that everything was the same as it had been the last time he'd stood at the line and thrown a strike, that he was inside a magical bubble. *I didn't really understand what was happening; I was focusing so much, I was almost out of it. Mentally, everything was dead. I didn't hear the crowd much anymore. It was like a tunnel vision, a flow. Everything was flowing the same way it had before. My timing was perfect. My arm swing was a flow. My confidence increased and strengthened the rhythm, the flow, the tempo.*

While mentally things seemed numb, physically Taz was more aware of what was happening in his game then he ever was. *I felt lightheaded. . . . All I had to do was set the ball down on the alley and my body was perfectly programmed to do all the rest. Sometimes I get physically fatigued, but as long as I'm mentally up, I can perform well.* His sensitivity to his powerful hormones continued and at times he turned white, friends recall.

Meanwhile, Wayne Bunce was destroyed. Ockerman yelled "Yes!" as the final pin fell into the gutter, and his colleagues went wild, lifted him onto their shoulders, and carried him around the alley, sheet white as all the blood drained from his face—which physiologists say is a fight-or-flight symptom.

Thirty-four of his 36 shots that night hit the pocket of pins perfectly. Two were a little "high," yet all the pins fell victim. Three straight perfect games. Who knows what amazing forces came together that night, but Ockerman apparently tapped into four key areas that sports psychologists cite as instrumental toward achieving peak performance:

- He "programmed" his body with a muscle memory to repeat his bowling swing.
- He created a "bogeyman" force in his mind, a need to prove something to somebody.
- He raised his hormone levels with precompetition music.
- He created a flow with total focus on the task during competition.

CHAPTER 11

Relaxing and Focusing

"A lot of people thought I was praying, but actually I was trying to get focused. Maybe that's what prayer is."

Diver Greg Louganis

Sometimes athletes get "pumped up" enough naturally and don't need mind games or heavy metal music. Sometimes they have to "come down" to meet their optimal arousal level or their optimal mindset prior to competition. Again, it all depends on the type of athlete or the type of sport or the type of situation.

In general though, sport psychologists tend to talk their client athletes into staying relaxed and focused. "I have never worked with a great athlete, be it a world champion or an Olympic gold medalist, who never got nervous before a big match or event. They all do. The big difference between these champions and most of us is that they have learned how to stay cool and focused when the pressure is on," said Shane Murphy, PhD, former chief sport psychologist for the U.S. Olympic Committee.

They don't panic when they get nervous, and they use specific strategies to keep their nerves under control. Despite the stress they're under, they know how to achieve at a very high level. I call the skill they use "keeping cool." ... Gold medals are not won by chance and Olympic athletes are fully prepared for the pressure they'll encounter at the Olympics. In fact, many of them use their anxiety in a constructive way to push themselves to even greater heights.

"All this rah-rah stuff is generally bad. Nine times out of 10, the arousal technique generates pressure and performance suffers," said Robert Nideffer, a clinical psychologist and teacher at San Diego State University, who has worked extensively with athletes. Locker room pep talks, he finds, only add to anxieties about winning. Players who do well do so despite this goading rather than because of it.

Tom Tutko agrees, but adds that the calming techniques are probably better for amateur athletes:

This isn't to say that a charismatic or dynamic coach can't inspire a team to an extraordinary effort; it's just that, applied to most of us, the method usually has a reverse effect.

Most recreational players don't need to be pushed to try harder. They are already trying too hard as it is. Thus, there is little in the traditional approach to sports to help us to understand and deal effectively with the psychological part of the experience. We are left to improvise and muddle through.

We've discussed ways that music can help a bowler like Troy Ockerman get psyched up and, conversely, ways it can act as a tranquilizer or a security blanket for other athletes like Harry Carson and Dorothy Hamill. Besides music, there are at least five other strategies many elite athletes use for coming down:

- Relaxation and meditation
- Focus and visualization techniques
- Breathing techniques
- Relaxation cues
- Humor

Relaxation and Meditation

Athletes must relax in order to avoid tension which can lead to choking, said psychology author Dan Millman.

> Stress happens when the mind resists what is . . . athletes commonly resist the natural processes by trying. The word itself implies a weakness in the face of challenge. The moment we try, we are already tense; trying, therefore, is a primary cause of error. In more natural actions, we omit the try. When competitors feel they are under pressure and begin to try, they often fall apart. . . . Inner athletes have a sense of letting it happen without any sense of strain. This may seem like idealistic fantasy, but numerous descriptions of the lives and duels of martial arts masters testify to the existence of this kind of grace under pressure. The higher the stakes, the more calm, clear, and relaxed these masters become.

According to Kevin Elko and Debbie Yohman, elite gymnasts can find the zone of peak performance only by first relaxing every part of their body. "Most people seldom experience this state because their thoughts, especially the judgmental ones, get in the way," they wrote in *USA Gymnastics Online*. "For some, it might be the thought that they're too slow, uncoordinated, or weak. Others might start thinking about that bit of criticism their coach threw at them earlier in the day. These thoughts have GOT to go, or the zone will be impossible to find." They recommend that athletes sit quietly in a quiet place and listen to their own breathing, allowing their minds to go quiet. "The mind that is blank can perform in the zone." Again, relaxing is an individual thing and many athletes carry out their own relaxation techniques.

Leif Robert Diamant and Richard M. Baker are members of the Community Holistic Health Center in Carrboro, NC. In their book *Mind-Body Maturity*, they wrote that relaxation can co-exist with arousal, as long as it comes first: "If psyching up is a means of creating optimal arousal of mind-body resources, relaxation is the most effective foundation of psyching up. Relaxation involves the releasing of any unnecessary tension, tightness, or concerns. Relaxation means the muscles do nothing and the mind, effortlessly, does as little as possible. Relaxation means heart rate, blood pressure, and respiration slow down. Relaxing (to make loose again) often is accompanied by slower brain wave activity and heightened endorphin production. Relaxing allows the athlete to develop awareness of his or her muscles and thought processes in subtle and beneficial ways." Relaxing is also a way of recharging in the middle of an athletic event, they said.

Some performers incorporate meditation with arousal and report that is it a good way to enhance a feeling of "flow" in their competitive performance. Parry O'Brien, one of the greatest shot-putters ever, used yoga in the 1950s, long before sport psychology. He said yoga taught him concentration and the Hindu principle of "ayurveda" in which he acquired serenity. He listened to Tibetan bells, Balinese and Afro-Cuban drumming to achieve a warrior's frenzy, then went into self-hypnosis. "I'd record pep talks to myself. I'd put the tape player under my bed, get into a sleepy state and let it all sink into my subconscious," he said.

Getting to the Twilight Zone

Sometimes, when calming and concentration techniques merge with an athlete's high arousal (is this what we should be calling an optimal experience?), a slow-motion effect is reported, and the action seems to slow way down—a sort of tachypsychia. Full-blown tachypsychia (defined in chapter 3) may be the most difficult of the arousal zone states to summon. At its height, it's certainly the most fleeting. Maybe that's why, when many athletes are asked how they get there, they just shrug their shoulders like basketball player Reggie Miller and say, "You don't come to the zone, the zone comes to you." But there is evidence to suggest otherwise. Like other positive facets of the psycho/adrenaline system, it seems to kick in at optimal arousal—the point at which the athlete has reached harmony of the mind-body-hormonal triangle. That's the state the Japanese call "ki" and the Tibetans "lunggom." It's directly related to intense concentration, visualization, and perhaps hypnosis. "We may be able to harness it," says John Krystal, associate professor of medicine at Yale University. "It's similar to inducing a trance and it's under the control of the adrenaline system." To get to tachypsychia, the athlete may need to reach the highest "workable" level of the mind-body alarm system. Whereas extra speed and strength kick in during a two- or a three-alarm reaction, tachypsychia seems to require a four- or five. When an athlete who has reached optimal concentration is suddenly faced with a crisis stage of competition—bingo—the dopamine and noradrenaline arrive to give momentum to a situation that's already there, some biochemists believe. These wonder hormones seem to always attach themselves to the direction of momentum the athlete is headed. (Those chemicals were found in large quantity in a study of British racing drivers who were concentrating hard and achieving good results.) Of course, when they're pumped into the blood of a competitor who is concentrating poorly or is anxious or fearful, the opposite—choke and poor performance—can occur.

As in other peak performances, anger is often a key quotient, as long as it is channeled optimally, and with confidence. When he's playing poorly, Doug Flutie—now in the NFL after years of great success in the CFL—gets mad at himself and takes command of a game. That's when tachypsychia often appears. In a 1994 CFL game, he got mad at an opponent who stepped on his arm. "After that, the whole game in front of me slowed down for a while and my concentration became superior," he recalls. "Suddenly I had more time to react to what the defense was doing and my adrenaline levels seemed way up, but I didn't let them get out of hand." Flutie added that he saves those emotional bursts for the latter stages of a game. "I can't hold that concentration level for 60 minutes. I wish I could bottle it, though." Such moments not only give Flutie more energy, but more desire to win, he added. "It keeps your morale up, knowing you have the ability to bring on those powers."

Tachypsychia doesn't last long—from a few seconds at it's most intense to a few minutes in a more watered-down form. The great athletes know how to strive for it at the turning point of a match. And remember—it's important not to confuse various types of peak performance zones. This short-term state seems only vaguely related to long-term zones, such as Joe DiMaggio's 56-game hitting streak. In between are many other mind-body "flow" states, lasting a whole game or through several competitions.

Former tennis great and Olympic women's coach Billie Jean King calls tachypsychia the perfect emotion. She tries to bring it on as often as possible by focus, relaxation, and using cue words such as "Go!" during the turning point of a competition. She explains:

> If a match gets close, I slow down my rituals. If I bounce the ball twice before serving, I'll bounce it slowly, or repeat the ritual, bouncing it four times, exaggerating. I make absolutely sure I have total clarity, acuteness, focus. I try to visualize where I'm going to hit my serve . . . it's an exercise in total commitment -technical and visual. I go through all this before I start. Then I feel the adrenaline flowing (like many athletes, she may be misinformed about the type of hormone she refers to, but the spirit of her words seems accurate), and I know the moment has come. 'Go!' I say to myself, and I commit myself. You're totally involved in the moment.

When King synchronizes such moments, the ball starts to look bigger to her and slows down as it comes at her off her opponent's racket.

Some athletes are born with a big advantage: their hormonal and concentration systems are set up differently, says cardiologist Arnold Fox. They are allowed to take in greater detail, and perhaps are offered more room in time, because their visual and hormonal systems are different, and / or are better developed. It's been said that Ted Williams could see the seams on a 100-mph fastball, although part of that was his intense concentration of pitchers' habits while he was sitting in the on-deck circle.

"We know that people who are able to 'flow' have a greater ability than others to screen out irrelevant information," says Mihaly Csikszentmihalyi. "It could be the way their brain is put together, but I think it's something that people can learn through technique."

Focus and Visualization Techniques

"The performance becomes almost holy; spiritual awakening seems to take place. The individual becomes swept up in the action around her; she almost floats through the performance, drawing on forces she has never been aware of."

Former women's basketball star Patsy Neal

As discussed earlier, there seem to be several types of performance zones, and some may be interconnected, like arousal and flow. Flow doesn't involve anger or defense or ego, Mihaly Csikszentmihalyi says, but it can result from an athletic competition if the athlete uses the experience not to conquer an opponent and subsequently make himself feel better but to stretch his skills to meet the challenge provided by the skills of an opponent. "Competition improves experience only as long as attention is focused primarily on the activity itself. If extrinsic goals— such as beating the opponent, wanting to impress an audience, or obtaining a big professional contract—are what one is concerned about, then competition is likely to become a distraction, rather than an incentive to focus consciousness on what is happening."

John Douillard, who teaches professional, recreational, and international athletes and coaches about flow techniques, believes it's difficult to achieve the state while a person is in high arousal states, particularly the radical fight or flight. Rather, he said, flow is more related to Eastern philosophies such as Tao and Zen. "In ancient cultures, exercise was a piece of a much larger puzzle," he said. "The original Kung Fu masters, for example, spent hours not to master the art of breaking bricks but to unleash their full human potential, to achieve what they called enlightenment."

In a doctoral dissertation at the University of North Carolina, Susan Jackson used the notion of flow to explore the experience of 28 world-class athletes and found that all her subjects agreed that flow state was significant in their pursuits and even peak performances. Of the characteristics of flow, they said, the most relevant were concentration, the merging of action and awareness, a feeling of mastery and enjoyment of activity for its own sake.

Feelings of flow are apt to occur in non-competitive situations, says Marlin M. Mackenzie, EdD, an athletic counselor.

> I'm sure you have experienced at least one run during which you felt as if you were one with the mountain, free of pressure and tension, skiing with effortless control, and having tons of fun. Many people refer for this kind of state as the zone. One of my clients described her zone as a Zen state: ". . . a light, ghostly feeling, as if the wind could go straight through me instead of slowing me down. Light, like you don't feel you're touching the snow . . . I don't think I left a mark even though I know I did." Another client describes the zone as feeling weightlessness and experiencing an auditory resonance reproduced as a vibration through his body. (Skier) Jerry Beilinson describes his

zone poetically: "I captured the feeling of grace in movement, which brings my mind and body together with the quiet wilderness. It's like falling in a controlled way, a smooth, graceful way of moving very fast, faster than I can under my own power. It feels like a dolphin swimming. Skiing brings about a feeling of liberation from the ordinary feelings of my body. . . . Skiing is like dancing, which allows me to express my emotions through the way I ski.

Former international cyclist Davis Phinney said he could achieve a type of flow in competition with a focusing technique he called the "grin factor." During an intense finish to a race, a smile would crease his face and a feeling of exhilaration would take over. "I started calling this feeling the grin factor," he said. "It isn't exactly a scientific measuring device, but it is an accurate gauge of how much fun something is. Think of ripping down a fast descent, going faster than you previously dared, on the edge but in control, and at the bottom you punch a fist in the air and shout. Or you're spinning along in a paceline where everyone rides in sync, the miles fly by and when the group pulls in at the customary water stop, everyone beams and starts talking at once." Phinney said the grin factor became more important to him when his competitive days were over. Then, he said, the feeling became more subtle. "Maybe you're rolling along by yourself on a road you've ridden many times, but on this ride you notice everything: the color of the sky, the scent in the air, the feel of your tires on the pavement. It's what I love about cycling, and it's possible only through focus."

Csikszentmihalyi has said that athletes cannot summon themselves into the state of flow. "Even the greatest athletes cannot achieve it at will," he said.

You must understand that flow does not begin in the mind; it comes from physical or mental performance. You can't make it happen, but you can invite flow by preparing for greater challenges, removing distractions, and learning to focus. It helps to establish a routine. There almost has to be a physical ritual to achieve flow. Some athletes have a certain way of practicing, a certain way of tying their shoes before a contest—it is not merely superstition. It allows them to focus."

A certain amount of skill is necessary to get into flow, Csikszentmihalyi added. If the challenge is too great for the athlete's expertise, discouragement can set in.

Willie Unsoeld, the first American to reach the summit of Mount Everest, agreed that athletes must master fundamentals of their sport before they can reach flow and other states, but they also need some risk or challenge to increase arousal. "The right amount of risk throws you into a state of total concentration where there is nothing but the moment. You feel as if you have more time and more strength to accomplish things than you ever thought possible. But before you take that risk, you've got to master the fundamentals and become competent in the technical aspects of what it is you are doing."

During such altered states of intense concentration, the brain goes through profound changes, said Brad Hatfield, who conducted studies at the University of Maryland. Hatfield outfitted skilled marksmen with tiny electrodes that measure the brain's electrical activity and monitored their minds as they shot at targets. He discovered that just before a shooter pulled the trigger, the left side of their brain erupted in a burst of alpha waves, which are indicative of a very relaxed state. Similar results have been found in golfers, archers, and basketball players shooting foul shots. Hatfield's work suggests that during peak performance, the mind relaxes its analytical side and allows the right side to control the body. The result is a flow-like state that many people report while they are deeply engaged in an activity. There is evidence that athletes can learn to control these brain waves to improve performance, said sports researcher Dan Landers, who conducted experiments with archers at Arizona State University.

But often athletes have no control over flow or other zones, says sport psychologist Alan S. Goldberg. "Unfortunately, peak performance and the zone are not always waiting for you when you suit up," he says. "All too often you go out to play with great expectations and find that your mind and body are totally out of sync that day. . . . It's as if the connection between your brain and muscles has short-circuited." When the connection is made, according to Goldberg, athletes find

> that almost mystical experience that make the sacrifices
> and long, painful hours of training all worthwhile. There's
> nothing more personally satisfying than having everything

effortlessly come together for you. Your muscles instantly respond as programmed with powerful, fluid movements. Your senses are heightened and precise as you react perfectly to every situation without conscious thought or effort. For that brief moment, you are in harmony with the universe, and the gods of peak performance are smiling on you.

Athletes who enter flow may be able to overcome pain, as well as distraction, according to Michael Murphy and Rhea A. White in their book *In the Zone*. They say that many athletes can turn pain into strength and joy, similar to the way that some mystics and religious devotees embrace pain with intense concentration. Murphy wrote: "In Zen Buddhism, there are periods of practice that last for weeks, during which a monk might sit in meditation for 16 hours a day or more. The pain and distraction that arise during these sessions are overwhelming, but depths of knowing, joy, and freedom emerge from the experience . . . sport and religious practice both embrace ordeal in the service of illumination and freedom. By consciously transforming pain into delight, the athlete begins to awaken to the inner presence of which the world is not the master. Distance runners are notorious for the pain they go through. Champion miler Herb Elliot said that his coach, Percy Cerutty, helped him to world records "not so much by improving my technique, but by releasing in my mind and soul a power that I only vaguely thought existed. Thrust against pain." (That description seems to be a combination of the "flow" and "painless" zones, but perhaps there is a link.)

Breathing

Proper breathing is an athlete's bridge among mind, body, and emotions, Dan Millman says. "To understand your emotional state and to gain mastery over emotions, it's essential that you begin to observe and gain conscious control over your breathing."

Breath awareness and discipline were central to the teachers of the most ancient spiritual traditions. Yogis, Zen masters, and martial artists have all placed great emphasis on breathing properly. The one unifying link between mind and body is the breath. Meditation deals with the mind but could also be called a physical relaxation exercise.

Relaxation exercises, in turn, deal with the body but could also be called meditation exercises. Both body and mind are intimately related to the emotions through awareness of breath. The various approaches to well-being demonstrate the intimate relationship of the three centers: physical, mental, and emotional. Meditation practices center around insight and release of thought. As thoughts are released, emotions flow naturally, and the body relaxes. As the body relaxes, the mind tends to become quiet as well, and the emotions open up.

It may not sound as romantic as it seems, according to John Douillard, who recommends a type of *snoring* before competition to combat anxiety, fear, and worry. "The pressure of race-day stress for an athlete is unparalleled; the intensity of waiting for the start of the event can be overwhelming." He recommends that a runner sit down before a race and make snoring sounds while inhaling and exhaling.

You will find that to make that sound while inhaling, you will constrict your throat in the same way as when you exhale, but you will have to breathe with considerably less force. This is particularly true in the beginning, when you are first finding out where in the throat it is most comfortable to make the sound . . . (this technique) is usually done while comfortably seated, for about 5 to 10 minutes per sitting.

Sport psychologist James Loehr advises athletes to make relaxation techniques part of their training. "Your goal is to learn how to slow down brain wave activity on command. Most concentration and competition problems stem from excessive neurological arousal (brain wave patterns are too fast). Pressure, nerves, fear, anger, and frustration serve to increase EEG (a brain frequency). Breath control training, meditation, yoga, listening to specially prepared relaxation audiotapes and progressive relaxation exercises can all be used for this purpose."

Loehr added that progressive relaxation exercises have become popular with athletes. This simply involves systematically tensing and relaxing specific muscle groups. Voluntary relaxation of muscles is paired with the cue to relax. Decreasing muscle tension is generally accompanied by decreasing brain wave frequency. EEG research clearly shows that the more you practice slowing down brain waves, the better you get at it.

Poor breathing causes hyper-ventilation, Tom Tutko said. "It is no coincidence that the term for being overwhelmed by emotional pressure in sports is to choke—you are literally choking yourself," he said. "Fright, horror and anxiety take your breath away. . . . Release from tension means freedom to breathe. You are back in control; the world no longer closes in on you."

Olympic champion sprinter Donovan Bailey says there is a strong link between anxiety in sports and in real life. He said he used the same breathing technique he used during 100 meter races to save his life in an automobile accident. In 1997, his Mercedes went out of control on black ice, flipped over and burst into flames. Although the car was destroyed, Bailey was uninjured, which he attributed to taking a deep breath just before the crash impact—just as he was used to doing at the starting line of races. "When I had the accident, I was totally relaxed, totally at ease," he said. "I had about a second and a half to think before impact and I saw the pole. If I braced, I would have died or been paralyzed. I took a deep breath and relaxed like I was at the starting line at the Olympics and there's all that chaos around . . .I landed on my neck upside down with my head against the crushed roof, but I think what I do for a living actually helped me out in terms of saving my life."

Relaxation Cues

Elite athletes have a variety of cues or code words they use to bring about relaxation. Jackie Stewart, who won 27 Formula One races and three world driving championships, would deflate an imaginary beach ball to take away heightened emotions while British golfer Tony Jacklin relieved distress with a slight wiggle of his hips just before taking his club back. "It's just a little quiver like a jelly on a plate," he said. "This relaxes me sufficiently to get the club started back smoothly and fluently."

These techniques must be perfected and used over and over again in practice, Tom Tutko said. "Learn a relaxation technique. . . . Pitchers tug at their caps before the throw. Golfers waggle their clubs after teeing up. Basketball players breathe deeply before making the free throw. Just about all athletes, in fact, have some ritual to relax themselves, to relieve tension. . . . Relaxation is necessary, then, to break the emotional snowballing effect caused by negative emotions such as anxiety and anger, which divert your play. Indeed, relaxing your body not only stops the snowballing, it reverses it; as your body relaxes, it has a calming effect on your mind and anxieties subside."

Shane Murphy, author of *The Achievement Zone,* said that during the 1992 Olympic Games, whitewater paddler Joe Jacobi suffered an acute attack of butterflies after he and his partner completed their first run down a treacherous course. In the nearly three hours they waited for the second run, two other teams beat their time and Jacobi had to calm himself with a technique he had practiced. "I held each breath for several seconds and said the words 'Relax. Recharge. Ready.' to myself on each breath," Jacobi said. "I did that dozens of times between the two runs. Then we went out and warmed up and visualized ourselves going down the course." Their final run was faster and gave Jacobi and his partner, Scott Strasbaugh, the gold medal.

Robert Nideffer says that arousal can be controlled by controlling what you attend to. "If athletes think intently about their skills rather than the possible outcome of a match, they will automatically calm down and their arousal has a good chance to be funneled into that skill," he said. "Cues act as triggers to calm us down, to get our attention back on the task at hand. If you can learn what those triggers are, you can gain control over arousal by controlling what you attend to. Good method actors do this when they cry on cue.... The ball coming at you would be a process cue," he says. "(Such cues) are stimuli that trigger very complex, yet automatic, motor responses. Quite often, these cues are emotionally neutral. As an athlete gets caught up in the process cues, and in the process of performing, arousal automatically adjusts to a more optimal level." But if an athlete thinks about winning rather than the process of what it takes to win, arousal may be increased too much, Nideffer says. He adds, however, that "outcome" cues relating to winning can be useful in practice, to motivate an athlete to train hard, or prior to a performance, to get the athlete aroused. But during performance, such "outcome" cues can be distracting.

Humor

Humor is a common tool used by athletes to break tension, especially in a tension-packed game like golf, where Lee Trevino, Chi Chi Rodriguez, and Fuzzy Zoeller seem to break all the rules of focus and concentration by often joking with fans between shots. Steve Jones credited his ability to laugh all day to winning a tight battle against Greg Norman for the 1997 Canadian Open golf championship. "It helped me relax between shots. Then I made some of the best pressure putts in my life."

If an athlete is feeling down, laughter can produce endorphins and raise the level of mood, psychologists say. In the third set of the 1996 Wimbledon women's final, after almost three hours of tension in a match against Aranxta Sanchez Vicario, Steffi Graf started giggling, partly because she heard the crowd chanting her name. Graf went on to win the championship. Such funny tactics tend to relax a competitor when tension starts interfering with performance, Loehr said. "When you think silly thoughts and start to have fun again, you regain control and get back to your skill level," says Loehr, who advises athletes to loosen up their teammates with laughter when arousal levels get too high.

"Humor is a good sign that we have a balanced perspective," Dan Millman said. "After all, no matter how magnificent our athletic aspirations or achievements, we remain eternally tiny specks in the great universe; missing a putt or double-faulting a serve is hardly going to shake up the cosmos." Of course, that may be hard to digest for many athletes who consider their profession their entire cosmos.

Some athletes use props to help them relax, like diver Greg Louganis who carried a teddy bear around with him prior to big meets. But in the crunch, like prior to his gold medal dive in the 1988 Olympics, Louganis relied on thoughts of his mother. "Whenever I was in a real tough situation—and this was the toughest situation of my diving career that I'd ever been in—the one thing I always told myself was that no matter what happened, my mother was still going to love me. In that moment, I had an image of my mother sitting at home, watching me on TV. Even if I did a bomb of a dive, she would still say, 'Oh, wasn't that a pretty splash?' That image made me smile and helped me to relax."

Effects of Alcohol

Just as a few athletes use caffeine to get up, a few use a moderate amount of alcohol to come down. Club golf pro John Irwin said a few beers put him into a relaxed state just before he scored a record 10 consecutive birdies at the St. Catherines Golf and Country Club on June 11, 1984. But it didn't dull his concentration. He recalled: "On certain holes, I might've been surrounded by water, but I didn't see the water. I was totally concentrated on where my shot would land."

Former British darts champion Sid Waddell said he thrived on the tension of the big match and yet he used beer as a relaxant to get into "the zone." "It's the big occasion that brings out the best in me," he said. "I say to myself 'I'll kill this. And I do. I thrive on tension. You need urgency, yes, but if you get too uptight, you will never do yourself justice. I find I only get in my groove after three or four pints of beer."

While he admits that alcohol in moderate quantities may have relaxing effects on a small minority of athletes, Tom Tutko doesn't recommend alcohol use before or during performance. "Don't spend too much time experimenting with alcohol as a way to boost your performance," he advises. "Despite the exceptions, there's a much better chance that alcohol will harm performance rather than improve it."

CHAPTER 12

Staying in the Twilight Zone

> "Playing in the zone creates a mixture of positive emotions and these emotions are helpful to attaining peak performance. Feeling energized but calm, pumped up but in control, and intense but relaxed are emotions that are conducive to peak performance."
>
> Golf psychologist
> Patrick J. Cohn, PhD

Whether athletes are "getting up" or "coming down," they must maintain mental and emotional control otherwise their performance could suffer. The way to grasp and maintain control, experts say, is through concentration and visualization (or imagery). In the next two chapters, we'll examine how athletes summon such mental control in various stages:

- In training
- Just prior to competition
- During competition
- During a key moment of competition

Training With Fear

For many modern athletes, who use "visualization" and other mental and emotional techniques, getting control of a pressure situation starts in practice. "People handle pressure when they have been prepared and groomed to handle it, rarely before," says sport psychologist Robert W. Grant.

"Athletes don't always know instinctively how to perform at their best in competitive situations," Shane Murphy says. "They have to spend as much time practicing their competitive mental skills as they do their physical skills."

Many coaches believe the best way to conquer pressure is to get used to facing it in battle. According to sport psychologist Bob Rotella, one major reason that Mark McGwire beat Sammy Sosa 70-66 in the record-breaking home-run season of 1998 was that McGwire had previous experience dealing with the homer race (and its intense media scrutiny) in 1997 when he hit 58 homers, just three shy of Roger Maris' record.

Athletes need to get used to the intense hormonal feelings they get during high arousal, said Mike Lashuk, assistant dean of physical education at the University of Calgary. "If the athlete is not used to the adrenaline rush, it creates fear," he said. "You can pee your pants or throw up." Sport psychology consultant Alan S. Goldberg said athletes must get used to their fears in training. "When confronted with fear, most people become overwhelmed and use the F.E.A.R. strategy they learned in childhood: Forget Everything and Run," he said. "To defeat your fears, however, you must learn to move toward rather than away from them. . . . To beat fear, you must force yourself to get up and do the thing that you're most afraid of, over and over again." Goldberg recommends a "chunking down" technique in which athletes attack their fears a little bit at a time in practice by pretending they're facing distractions during a performance, such as being in front of a big crowd.

Many athletes have learned that in order to be ready for the stress and anxiety—the arousal—of competition, they must simulate those feelings during training sessions. This can mean arousing one's emotions by simulating game conditions or by "visualizing" what might happen, or what an athlete would *want* to happen during a performance. Simulating game conditions is sometimes accomplished by bringing in spectators, referees, or judges, or by playing tape recordings of crowd noise over the public address system. Some elite coaches, like Indiana University men's basketball coach Bobby Knight, deliberately intimidate players in practice so that they will not be intimidated by opposing players or fans during a game (although these tactics have been criticized by some coaches).

"Emotional responses, like muscles, need time and stimulation to grow," says James Loehr. "Successful athletes practice with intensity and emotions to get used to the feelings of arousal and to train their biochemical responses."

We'll see later that many experts believe athletes need to focus only on the present and their performance (rather than potential outcome); otherwise, they might get distracted by anxiety. Ironically, many of the same experts say that athletes can and should focus on the future and upon the potential outcome during practice in order to create more tension. Then, of course, they must learn to defuse that tension by focusing on the present and on performance in order to try to meld arousal with "flow." If that sounds a little complicated, it is. But welcome to the world of elite athletics. "Practicing in front of an audience or a video camera helps," said psychologist Roy Baumeister, PhD. Then, when the game begins, he suggests focusing on an opponent or another external cue. "Concentrate on the ski slope, the ball—anything other than yourself."

Sport psychologist Rainer Martens, well-known for his research at the University of Illinois on competitiveness, said athletes can learn to become more competitive and less distracted by mastering the physical techniques of their sport.

> It is really rather simple. . . . The trick is to concentrate on mastering specific techniques—positioning the feet, gripping the ball, whatever—until the individual is comfortable with them. This obviously helps mechanically, but it is also the best way to reduce stress and the problems it can cause. If people can focus on mastering specific acts that involve things they can control, they will be less inclined to be distracted by things over which they have no control. Being self-centered in this way helps to reduce anxiety about what opponents are doing, which is the source of most of what is threatening about competition.

Using Imagery

A survey of 1,200 track and field athletes, qualifiers for the U.S. Olympic trials in 43 events, was conducted by psychologists Stephen Ungerleider and Jacqueline Golding. Of the 633 who responded, 83 percent said they practiced some form of imagery, visualization or mental practice prior to a big event. The survey found that older and better-educated athletes tended to use mental practice more.

Visualization has been used for decades, but it's only recently that athletes in North America have broadened it to include other senses, and now the emotions, although it's been practiced for decades in nations of the former Eastern Bloc. Grigori Raiport, past president of the Russian Success Method Training Center, suggested in an issue of *The Sports Psychologist* that while the body has its limits, the mind's potential is vast. He said: "Russians analyzed the nature of athletic inspiration and discovered that it consists of three components: physical, emotion, and mental thoughts. The Russian method is designed to train athletes to reproduce those thoughts and feelings at will, using auto-conditioning. This technique allows athletes to choose their optimal mood for a competition, be it joy, happiness, or anger. Even such a negative emotion as sorrow can be used constructively." It's both positive "thinking" and positive "feeling," he added.

Steve Backley of England, who won gold medals in the javelin in the Commonwealth Games and the European Championships, hears the "music' of his feet during imagery sessions. In practice, a videotape was made of his javelin throws and a beeping noise was inserted every time his foot made contact with the ground as he made his approach to throw the javelin. He watched and listened to the tape over and over again, then, just prior to competition, he would recreate the "beeping" noise in his mind to visualize himself making the throw. "This is the music I need to re-enact such a performance," said Backley, author of *The Winning Mind*. "I know this series of beeps like I know my favorite pop record."

Psychologist Maxwell Maltz, PhD, revealed that lower parts of the brain and central nervous system cannot distinguish between something that has been vividly imagined and something that actually has happened. Maltz found that when an athlete did such "visualization" of a routine, all of the nerves involved in making the muscle move are also electrically stimulated, although at a lower level than normal. If athletes accept this, they can rehearse their competition under semi-realistic conditions . . . before they compete. It makes the athlete feel more comfortable under the pressure of actual competition because he has the "feeling" he's already been there.

Imagery is a deeply focussed rehearsal that uses all the senses to create a 3-D experience in the athlete's mind. The athlete imagines an event as though he is seeing himself going through the motions to a successful conclusion while also hearing the sounds, smelling the grass, feeling the touch of his instrument, perhaps even tasting the salt of his own sweat and even feeling the arousal he would experience at the height of the pressure. Sometimes it also includes an athlete's memories from a successful event.

"Imagery is very helpful in preparing for peak performance and it is actually the emotions in the imaged scene that seems to make the process most effective," said Bob Phillips, PhD, director of the Golf Psychology Training Center in Norcross, Georgia. He said that research shows that athletes who focused on the strong emotions involved with the actual performance were much more successful than those who only focused on the images of successful performance. "The best way to accomplish this higher level of emotion is to be sure that you step into the image," he said. "If you simply see yourself doing the action you are not really practicing the swing or putt (in golf) and consequently you are not involved with the feeling as deeply as you could be. Make sure you are aware of what you see, hear, and smell in the scene."

Elite athletes use their own forms of visualization and imagery, according to Julie Anthony, PhD, a former tennis pro and now a clinical psychologist at the Aspen Tennis Center in Colorado. "They have their own techniques and they choose not to put titles or clinical labels on them," she said. For example, speed skater Dan Jansen, a gold medal winner in the 1994 Winter Olympics, only visualized his 1,000- meter race when he retreated into a place in his mind he called a "war room" complete with an imaginary big-screen television, sofa, and stereo.

Martha Farah, PhD, professor at the University of Pennsylvania in Philadelphia, said that "mental capacities such as memory, perception, imagery, language and thought processes are rooted in complex structures in the brain." Her research suggests that imagery is not part of language symbols but is the chemistry of the visual system. Using the technology of computerized axial tomography (CAT) and positron-emission tomography (PET), Farah and other neuropsychologists who examine brain-damaged patients have found that the brain uses the same pathways for seeing as it does for imaging.

Focus is largely disciplining yourself to keep attention on what's important. The great ones practice it. Martial arts guru Bruce Lee had a nifty little trick. Each day, while going through his normal routines, perhaps on his way to a studio or mailing a letter, he'd suddenly stop what he was doing and concentrate very intensely on something completely unrelated to what he was doing: perhaps a butterfly which had just landed on a leaf or a postman delivering a letter to a home. For a few seconds he would completely lose himself in this, absorbing everything about the butterfly or the postman. Then, presto, he'd snap out of it and resume his daily chores. "This helped to hone my focusing abilities for the time when I would need them in competition," he said.

A good drill for teams, coaches say, is having a coach suddenly stop a ballhandling drill to have all the players focus on an airplane flying overhead. When the plane goes out of sight, the coach can ask the players everything they noticed about it, and its habits in the air. And then, presto, back to the ball drill. Then, 15 minutes later, the players should attach themselves to something else completely unrelated, holding their attention for a longer period as they increase their attention span.

Getting Game Day Under Control

On the day of competition, some athletes need to focus imagery around one aspect that could make the difference. In the 1950s, American hurdler Harrison Dillard, winner of four Olympic gold medals, would concentrate before the race on the steps he would make to leap over each hurdle in order to avoid knocking them down. This had been his weakness and a frustration in prior races.

Former Canadian skating champion Brian Orser (silver medallist in the Battle of the Brians of the 1988 Winter Olympics) said he practiced imagery that was "more of feel than visualization. I get this internal feeling prior to my skate, sort of program my whole body, what it's going to feel, the nerves, the emotions. It's hard to explain. You have to experience it. I can even get a feeling for an entire program. I can get myself so psyched-up in practice, it can lead to a perfect performance. . .I go for the feeling. I never think in technical terms." Orser was the first skater to pull off a triple axel during competition and he was successful because he felt the emotions of the jump the night before, laying in bed. "I felt myself going through the jump and even feeding off the energy of the crowd and I felt so good afterward, I couldn't wait to get out on the ice the next day." During physical practice, Orser often got too pumped up with adrenaline and "jumped out of my shirt," so in mental imagery, he imagined himself slowing down his heartbeat and getting just the right amount of psyche into the jump. On competition day, Orser said he didn't go into the emotional imagery too soon. "I don't like it to happen too soon. When the skater before me is on, that is when I get hyped. I feel my routine, bringing the adrenaline needs to a head."

According to Stephen Ungerleider's 1996 book *Mental Training for Peak Performance,* the images that successful U.S. Olympians recalled tended to be associated with strong emotions. "When javelin throwers prepare their approach for the javelin throw, for example, there is a sense of power and tension. This emotion pumps up the individual so that he can prepare the mind and body to throw the javelin. Only one in 10 athletes explained that their images did not conjure up strong emotions."

The Ritual

While we may chuckle at the seemingly-silly rituals and superstitions of athletes on the day of competition, there's often method to the madness, experts say. A couple of examples:

• San Francisco 49ers great receiver Jerry Rice is almost manic in his attention to detail in the locker room, trying on different socks and pants until they are just right.

• Baseball's Wade Boggs followed a strict pre-game schedule when he played with the Boston Red Sox: arriving for a night game at Fenway Park at 3:15 p.m., hitting ground balls at 4:00, drinking water at 4:17, loosening up for batting practice at 5:17, and base-running at 5:35. Once the game started, he was careful not to step on the chalk lines going on or coming off the field. You may have noticed, his ritual revolved around his favorite numbers: seven and 17.

• Wayne Gretzky of the New York Rangers always plays with the right side of his jersey tucked behind his hip pad, while Peter Bondra of the Washington Capitals numbers his sticks one through five for use during a game but keeps using the same stick if he scores with it.

Some athletes don't even know why they go through these routines, but psychologists believe it's mainly for one or more of three reasons:

1. To ease fear and provide a sense of control over a forthcoming event

2. To provide a sense of comfort, some external sign they may do well again

3. To get centered and avoid distractions

Often they use the rituals to get themselves "centered" before the event, such as putting their equipment on the same way every time, or listening to their favorite music. Rice's diligence to detail before the game is done to carry over into the action, according to Joel Kirsch, PhD, a former sport psychologist and now with the American Sports Institute. "He pays attention to those things because out on the field he also needs to pay attention closely—reading opposing defenses and reacting immediately to changes. So he prepares himself mentally, in a meticulous, diligent way. He has a long, methodical buildup."

"We all have certain trinkets or signs we've learned to associate with good performances," said Michael Sachs, associate professor of physical education at Temple University and past president of the Association for the Advancement of Applied Sport Psychology. "They provide a sense of comfort, some external sign that we may do well again."

Not all athletes are sold on such rituals, however, such as former great distance runner Frank Shorter, who said: "I thought it better never to find myself in the middle of an important race wondering if I'd gone through the sequence of superstitions correctly."

Task Vision—Concentration Without Thinking

"Probably the best way to train them is to take them all to a nudist colony and tell them not to see anything."

Dick Selcer, Detroit Lions defensive back coach,
on how to teach a cornerback not to look over his shoulder for the ball,
but to concentrate only on the receiver.

In a way, Dave Hanson's night at the New Frontier Lanes in Tacoma, Washington, on December 23, 1991, was absurd. He bowled incredible consecutive scores of 278, 300, and 300 while running around the bowling alley doing his nightly chores as an employee. Shouldn't it be hard enough to knock down 878 out of a possible 900 pins without checking in other people's bowling shoes and fixing machines between shots? However, we may be able to learn something from his feat. Athletes report greater success under arousal when they are concentrating so well (or are so relaxed) on their performance, or their task, they are unaware of things happening in the outside world. It becomes like a *task vision*. Perhaps while they are in this task vision, their programming kicks in — not only their training and skills, but the hormonal programming which is allowed to reach close to optimal levels.

Back to Dave the Employee. Another oddity on his stunning night was that he'd had little to eat all day, no breakfast and just a sandwich for lunch. But he did drink six cups of Folger's coffee over his four-hour performance (from 6:30–10:30 PM), plus an espresso. Caffeine has been known to boost short-term performance. "I always drink a lot of coffee," Hanson said. Hanson's other explanations for his feat were that it was two days before Christmas and he's always in a good mood before Christmas. And his son, David Walter, had been born two months earlier. Hanson wasn't even supposed to play that night in the Tacoma handicap league, but the New Frontier Card Room Team needed an extra player to fill out a roster that included Dave's father, Walter, and his co-worker Mike Muller. Although Dave had a nifty 220 average, he explained that he probably wouldn't be able to contribute much that night because during the action he had to see to his usual functions of working behind the front desk and picking up loose pins from other bowlers' shots.

Yet, Hanson sort of looked forward to playing that night, because it was a lower league than he was accustomed to and because his close friends were watching. "I wanted to show that I was better than them. I wanted to show some talent and to shoot a 300 . . . I wasn't thinking about it. I think it was subconscious. My subconscious took over. I wasn't consciously aware of what was going on. I'd grab my ball and just throw." Prior to each shot, Hanson would visualize his shots going down the alley and knocking down all the pins. "I concentrated on the mark without thinking about my footwork or arm swing . . . and I did not think negatively. I always try to stay positive." Hanson's "mark" or aiming point was a discoloration on the pine board about 27 feet past the throw line. Between many shots, Hanson was called to his duties: running down a nearby lane and cleaning the gutter of a wayward pin, and running into the back to fix the pin placement machine, but the distractions never hurt his form or results when he returned for his next shot. "I could forget about all the other problems by focusing on each shot," he said." I got the ball back in my hands and really concentrated."

As the successful shots started piling up, Hanson said the discoloration mark in the pine board where he was aiming got bigger and bigger. "It seemed like my target became larger and larger as the night went on. My arm swing became more free; I had more room for error because the mark was getting bigger."

In the 10th frame of his third and last game of the night after missing a handful of pins, somebody mentioned that Hanson needed the next strike to break the Washington state record of 866 for a three-game set. Uh-oh. Suddenly, Hanson stopped to think: "I could be the state record holder! I pressured myself with that next shot," he said. "I was thinking about making it." His shot missed his "mark" on the pine board and was off to the right of the pocket, but the pins fell. Another strike! With his last two balls, the pressure was off and Hanson returned to his subconscious world and threw two more strikes for a final three-game total of 878.

Hanson was an amateur when he tossed the 878, but the following year he turned pro, joining a regional pro tour in the northwestern U.S. He found it hard to get back into "the zone" of that holiday evening. "I just can't get there again," he said in 1996. "I guess I'm trying to concentrate too hard."

Besides the age-old distractions of trying too hard and worry, there may be more distractions than ever before for athletes, both long and short-term: complacency due to big contracts, agents, free agency, corporate sponsors, and increasing media scrutiny. Some of the traditional distractions:

- fear (especially of failing)
- ego
- self-consciousness
- conscious thought processes
- winning and losing
- pain and fatigue

The distraction of winning and losing can be the most debilitating of all, psychologists say, because it can lead to most of the other distractions. Those who focus only on the performance may perform better when their arousal hormones kick in. Task vision is seeing only what you need to see when performing an athletic feat. It is removing from your little world all unwanted and unnecessary distractions to give your full attention to the moment. Many athletes imagine everything on the outside of the task to be blurry and insignificant, while everything on the inside is crystal clear. They create an air-filled bubble. On the outside, they have no control and in fact, no interest; on the inside they feel powerful because they have already developed the skills to control their fate, to deal with any problems or situations that pop up. And yet, an athlete may have to broaden his task vision to include what his opponents are doing, what the coach is yelling, and sometimes even what the referee might rule. According to former runner Sebastian Coe, two-time gold Olympic medallist in the 800 and 1,500 meter races, athletes "have to have an awareness of opposing runners, sensing how other people are breathing, whether they're breathing hard and whether their feet are coming down heavily — that way you respond to a break." In that regard, Coe was always aware of his opponents' shadows on the track.

Deep concentration and confidence in oneself and abilities take the athlete to a state where there is no conscious awareness of the task, but plenty of unconscious awareness. The Japanese refer to it as "mushin" or "no mind." After much practice of motor skills and concentration, the athlete lets his mind go, separates himself from the task. "Consciousness gets in the way," said Karl Newell, a kinesiologist at the University of Illinois. "If a pianist starts worrying about where his fingers go while he's playing, it will change the performance."

Sometimes things happen beyond an athlete's control. Nancy Lopez never won the U.S. Open but has finished second three times and she says she could have beaten Hollis Stacy in 1977 if her pants' zipper hadn't broken on the first hole. "I spent the whole day worrying that someone would see my underwear," Lopez said.

Of all of the "zone" experiences he's studied over the years, especially with pro ball players, Grand Prix race drivers, and world-class mountain climbers, Bruce Ogilvie says there is one thing in common: the athletes reported a state of focus so deep that they felt they were having an out-of-body experience where they lost track of time and seemed to be an observer of the event. They found a state of relaxation despite the commotion around them and going on inside them. They live in the present, without worry of what has gone before or what the outcome of their match may be, thinking only about one thing at a time. It's what Bruce Lee, a master at focused power, called having a "tight mind." It is also a feeling of great satisfaction to know that you are giving total dedication to the effort. It becomes almost a spiritual experience. NFL quarterback Joe Montana, who led the San Francisco 49ers to four Super Bowl titles, lived in the present so much, especially in the fourth quarter of games, he'd often forget what plays he'd called just two or three downs earlier.

Some experts and researchers say we can learn focusing techniques by watching children. "Kids are masters at living in the present, creating magic out of the ordinary...adults often try to learn how to concentrate, "said former athlete and ski instructor Thomas Crum, author of book *The Magic of Conflict*. "Kids get totally consumed, they are centered . . . we have never lost the child in us . . . when we give ourselves permission to be completely in the present."

Mitch Smith, a psychotherapist who specializes in helping athletes to use their minds to achieve peak performance, recommends hypnosis to get athletes into the right competitive state in order to overcome pressure. "The problem with being in the zone is that for most athletes, entering into states of absorption is a spontaneous or chance experience," he said. "Athletes need to understand that our ability to enter into states of absorption and to maintain them is increased when the ability is nurtured. A therapist with advanced training in the use of clinical hypnosis can train and condition an athlete to be able to enter into a hypnotic trance systematically or with a simple cue. Most athletes are surprised at how they can begin to enter and maintain their zones of absorption more easily during performances as a result of practicing with their ability." Smith trains athletes to respond to post-hypnotic suggestion or cues, including one to manage anxiety and to adjust arousal levels.

Task vision doesn't need to be applied throughout the course of a sporting event; in fact, it may be impossible and counter-productive to hold such intense focus for two hours. Look at some golfers who've tried to stay in this zone for four complete rounds and their wheels fell off. Rather, it may be better to shift in and out of intense concentration, like Lee Trevino does or bowler Dave Hanson. This task vision is so important for arousal moments because hormones such as dopamine and noradrenaline accelerate the direction in which an athlete is headed, said Keith Franklin, a professor of neurobiology at McGill University in Montreal. If he's headed in a positive, highly-focused direction, that will increase. But if he's distracted and anxious, the hormones will increase those states, too. When we talk about momentum in a sporting match, this is part of the equation—one athlete is often headed in one direction and an opponent in another. The rich get richer and the poor get poorer.

"Putting your mind somewhere else" can also conquer pain, said Bruce Lee, who would often practice until his knuckles were bleeding and raw, yet felt no pain. "Without mind there cannot be pain. It can become mind over matter," he said.

Confidence

Athletes say they've got a much better chance of controlling pressure situations when they are confident and use positive thinking. "The biggest thing is to have the belief that you can win every tournament going in," said golfer Tiger Woods. "A lot of guys don't have that. (Jack) Nicklaus had it. He felt he was going to beat everybody . . . Under pressure, you win with your mind."

It's a common trait among not only athletes but all human beings to worry about situations, says Richard Earle, director of the National Institute of Stress in Canada and a former weightlifter. Studies show that people have about 66,000 thoughts every day. "And 70-80 percent of those thoughts are negative," Earle says. "It's the people who think positively about stressful events who are the most successful."

Doubt has been studied less than anxiety and fear, according to W. Timothy Gallwey, a golf coach, author, and peak performance teacher with major corporations. "Doubt and fear are definitely friends, perhaps even relatives, but they are not twins," he said. "We often experience fear in the presence of a real or imagined threat—that is, when we are vulnerable to harm or imagine we are . . . but we do not feel anxiety if we do not first doubt our ability to sink (a putt). If we can lessen our self-doubt, our fear automatically wanes."

"Self-doubt interferes with performance," says Lawrence L. Kerns, a Barrington, Illinois, physician affiliated with the Columbia-Woodland Hospital who specializes in behavioral and mind-body medicine and author of *The Conscious Athlete*. "That sense of supreme confidence serves athletes well." Adds Andrew Lovy, chairman of the psychiatric department at Columbia Olympia Fields Osteopathic Hospital in Olympia Fields, Illinois:

Once athletes have that confidence, they don't feel the pressure of the game. They consider that this is the epitome of what they've practiced for. This is the reason they've developed their skills...The physical mastery of a skill, the practice, has to come first. Without that, it's all desire. And there are a lot of wannabes out there who haven't paid their dues.

But those who have paid their dues approach stressful situations with bravado. "All I know is that when I'm batting, I believe I'm the best batsman in the world, that bowlers are second class, that I'm in total control," said ricketeer Desmond Haynes. "If I feel negative at any point, I stop the bowler and make him wait for me, just to reassert that control."

While on his way to winning the gold medal in the Olympic decathlon in 1976, American Bruce Jenner said: "I started to feel there was nothing I couldn't do if I had to. It was a feeling of awesome power, except that I was in awe of myself. . . . I was rising above myself, doing things I had no right to be doing."

CHAPTER 13

Altering Your Chemistry

Much of this book is about the mind-body chemicals of athletes and how their hormones work for and against them, depending on their mental and emotional attitudes. In this chapter, we'll look at one of the most dramatic issues: How they alter their mindset and consequently their chemical makeup in a split second to make all the difference between winning and losing.

When they feel doubt, distraction or nervousness during competition, the great ones transform the situation into a positive, says psychologist Stephen Ungerleider. "Great athletes such as tennis star Steffi Graf, Olympic swimmer and multiple gold medal winner Janet Evans, and pole vaulter Sergei Bubka always carry a visual image, a cognitive cue, and a source of extra energy," Ungerleider says. "They know that they can call up an image, trigger a word or phrase and get that extra breath when they need it. These are the same athletes who convert negative experiences such as anger, frustration, and aggression to positive moments of arousal with extra oxygen and energy at the finish. These are the winners!" With every emotion, there is a chemical reaction that responds physiologically, he says.

Biochemists and neurobiologists agree with him. They say that when an athlete is feeling too nervous or too anxious, it likely means that too much adrenaline or cortisol is pumping through his system. Adrenaline and cortisol tend to be pumped out in large portions when the athlete feels fear. If a body becomes flooded with it, tension is not far away and that usually means a seizure of athletic skills. Adrenaline tends to be useful more as a defensive hormone. The trick, scientists say, is to change the body chemistry to a blend of more pro-active hormones, perhaps a combination of adrenaline and noradrenaline, as well as chemical neurotransmitters such as dopamine, serotonin, and others, which are more aggressive.

While it's next to impossible to study these "game day" responses in a laboratory, a number of biochemists, athletes, sport psychologists and coaches interviewed for this book believe an athlete can change the body chemistry by turning his feelings of anxiety or fear to other feelings—excitement, challenge, or even anger. But then those feelings of excitement, challenge, or anger must be immediately channeled *dispassionately* into the skill or routine the athlete is performing. The method that athletes use for this "quick switch" differs from person to person—some intently focus on the act, others completely relax, while others go into the no-think mode. In any event, the purpose is to let the nervous energy be channeled into the skill, not to aim it at the opponent.

Many psychologists believe that anxiety is a form of fear. So, for now, let's refer to the feeling of anxiety as fear. And let's review their advice and some of the variations: fear to challenge to skill; fear to excitement to skill; or fear to anger to dispassionate skill. So, theoretically, in hormonal terms that could mean: adrenaline (fear) to noradrenaline (anger) to dopamine and other hormones.

Turning Fear to Anger

If we accept that an athlete's pre-competition nervousness is a primitive mind-body reaction to challenge, then perhaps we should first look at its biological basis.

As discussed in earlier chapters, nervousness is the mind-body's way of readying us for possible physical harm. This primitive system has remained virtually the same for millions of years and should stay intact for another 100,000 or so, experts say. Its original "skills" intended for fight or flight were fighting and running. Hence, the term "fight or flight." Those were the original animal responses. But, as human beings we have evolved as part animal, part thinker. We've complicated our arousal system in the way we react to life. Little do we need to respond to physical threats any more. Instead, we respond when our self-esteem or ego are threatened. The arousal system still responds to threats, but now they're more sophisticated and they involve thinking. But the animal fight or flight response didn't involve much thinking. You were threatened with physical harm, your arousal engine kicked in, and you fought like a lion or you ran like a deer. Now when our arousal nerves kick in, we often think too much, worry too much. In modern times is it possible we "choke" more than our ancient ancestors did in the moment of truth because there are more distractions, because we think too much?

Another potential problem is the skills the arousal system are used for have changed dramatically. Sure, in running events and fighting events those skills are still heavily used, but not so much in other sports, which may require subtle motor skills such as golf, figure skating, baseball hitting, and archery. And yet, the most successful athletes in all types of sports seem to not only cope with their arousal systems, but to use them as powerful additives to performance— their trump card. Maybe the most successful athletes have learned to make their arousal response "natural" to their particular skill through trial and error, and much practice, both in training and in game situations.

Professionals in other fields have learned to turn their arousal response into good performance in a skill, such as police officers using guns to protect themselves and to protect society. Massad Ayoob, a police captain in New Hampshire, is a fear expert. Ayoob, who has written numerous books on self-defense, teaches police officers to survive life-threatening situations by changing their outlook within a split second. When a gun-toting officer is threatened by a suspect, the fear that an officer feels can cause him to seize up, or at least defend himself in a less effective manner than normal. Or it can sharpen his reflexes and skills. "Just as there is good cholesterol and bad cholesterol, so too is there good fear that galvanizes an appropriate response and bad fear that paralyzes its victim," he said. "Fear can be a positive stimulus, creating what Bradley Steiner brilliantly called 'fear energy'. . . letting the fear turn briefly to anger helps that critical transmogrification. But, because under the law a man in the grip of anger loses the critical defense of reasonableness, the anger must then be immediately channeled into a focus on dispassionately performing the indicated response. There's got to be a flow." In other words, Ayoob advises people caught in threatening situations to immediately recognize their nervousness as fear, then quickly get angry, then just as quickly turn that anger into the act or the skill required to get out of the situation. For a police officer, that would mean putting all the energy and focus into operating his gun. Added Ayoob: "The focus is not on, 'I'll kill you for trying to kill me!' The focus is on the job at hand: now is the time for Front Sight, Press [a gun term]."

Using Nervousness to Boost Performance

It's been discussed at length in this book that many athletes use controlled anger as a motivator, but much of the time it is subconscious, or for pre-competition use. Many athletes and sport psychologists prefer to look on their successful formula not as turning fear to anger to dispassionate response but from *nervousness to challenge to performance.* (Anxiety is another popular word that comes up, but it may be a moot point.) "Those who fail do so because they can't translate normal anxiety into positive performance," said Andrew Lovy. "They translate anxiety into fear, which leads to panic, which kicks in too much adrenaline and all of a sudden they're shooting off-target."

"Pressure is coming down the last hole at tour school, knowing you have to make par to make the cut," said PGA tour player Trevor Dodds. "I turned it into a challenge and it has made the world of difference because I pulled off a shot that is really, really difficult by turning a threat into a challenge."

Ayoob believes that athletes in crisis points of a match use a method similar to the one he teaches police. "They don't fear physical danger, but maybe it's fear of failure," he said. "They learn to turn it into positive response." Remember Jim Brown's football quote: "Fear is a gift from God, for survival."

Former track coach Brooks Johnson believes the best athletes learn to change fear and other "negative" emotions into potent forces. "Some people are able to take the negative feelings they have and convert them into energy," he said. "It creates this sort of electricity and they take it and focus it on their event. Bill Russell got so nervous before [NBA] games, he'd lose his lunch [throw up], then he'd go out and turn that nervousness into a marvelous performance. It's yin and yang, an awesome pressure. . . . All the great ones have the ability to do this. You cannot get to a certain level without this mentality. Everybody at that level is similar. Yes, it's on the border of being unhealthy, but it's required as much as their skills and training."

Back to anger for a moment. Anger mobilizes more fighting energy to an athlete when he or she needs it most, says sport psychologist James Loehr.

> Nervousness and fear make you more helpless and passive and you can't get close to your performance potential. In the fight-or-flight response, fear is designed to help you run away from a threat, but in sports that never works. Some athletes blow fear away by getting angry or more aggressive. That changes the biochemical pathways in the adrenal glands. If you look on a situation as too much of a threat, you produce too much cortisol, but when you look on things as a challenge, with spirit and fight, it activates the adrenal medulla system to produce adrenaline and noradrenaline.

Loehr is president and CEO of Sport Science Inc., a research and training facility in Orlando, Florida, which trains athletes, FBI, and police swat teams with the same techniques in response to pressure situations. In sports, Michael Jordan uses this "nervousness-to-challenge-to aggressiveness" technique effectively, Loehr says. "He knows that emotions mean mind-body chemistry. He's become almost a Zen master in his ability to control hidden emotions, breathing, and heart rate." Loehr adds that, in his prime, tennis player John McEnroe was successful by venting anger towards officials, opponents, and fans, to take the advantage away from his own nervousness. "After an outburst, (McEnroe) would become quiet and go through a set of rituals to bring his concentration back. It worked for him, but his rage for perfection was too much over his career. It ruined his enjoyment of the game and for him tennis became too much of a war. Anger can work for you at times, but I don't recommend it."

Rick Smith, golf coach for the 1993 U.S. Open champion Lee Janzen, advises golfers to mentally become more aggressive when

© MICHELL B. RIEBEL/ACTIVE IMAGES

John McEnroe was widely criticized for venting his anger at officials.

faced with adversity. "Take your anger to a place where it toughens you," he says.

> Certain people can't do it. They're already thinking about their failure. You have to look forward to the task in front of you. It's like a mudder, playing golf in the rain. It might be a lousy day, but this guy says "Great, because I know everybody else will be complaining." You take it as a

positive and say "This is my opportunity." It's just that some people are better at it than others. A great player is one who doesn't mind when everybody else is complaining.

While many athletes create tremendous long-term "emotional drive" by taking this personally, removing ego at the right time can reap rewards. In a NBA playoff game in the 1970s, guard Walt Frazier of the New York Knicks was punched in the face by an opponent, but strangely, the foul was called on Frazier. But instead of exploding, Frazier turned his intensity into his basketball skills. In fact, the expression on his face didn't change. He simply called for the ball and sank seven straight shots to win the game—"an amazing display of productive anger," according to writer John Leo.

How They Do It

What are the keys to an athlete changing the arousal feelings to positive results? Psychologists point to three main areas:

1. An athlete's focus on performance rather than results
2. Confidence
3. No thinking to the point of surrendering to skills

Athletes have a better chance to be successful during a crisis point in a match if they are not focused on the results of their performance, according to Nideffer. In a previous chapter, Nideffer said that an effective way to get into "neutral" in a performance is to use "cues" during high stress—thoughts that focus on execution of a skill or strategy, rather than the potential results of a performance. "The ball coming at you would be a process cue," he said. "[Such cues] are stimuli that trigger very complex, yet automatic, motor responses. Quite often, these cues are emotionally neutral. As an athlete gets caught up in the process cues, and in the process of performing, arousal automatically adjusts to a more optimal level." But if an athlete thinks about winning rather than the process of what it takes to win, arousal may be increased too much, Nideffer says.

Jack Nicklaus says it's important for athletes to make an effort to understand their fears, to recognize that it can be either an ally or a foe. "Many times when fear starts to hit me, my best chance of overcoming it lies in facing it squarely and examining it rationally," he says. "Here's what I say to myself: 'OK, what are you frightened of? You've obviously played well or you wouldn't be here. You're still playing well overall. You're always telling yourself you get your biggest kicks out of the challenges of golf. Well, go ahead and enjoy yourself. Play each shot one at a time and meet the challenge.'"

Confidence is the key link to overcome or channel nervousness, said Dan Millman. Athletes can get a better result from their arousal just by slightly changing their attitude from a negative to a positive, he said. "If your mind is filled with negative images or ideas—'I'd better do well or it will be humiliating; my parents (girlfriend, boyfriend, teammates) are depending on me—I can't mess up; I hope I don't break my neck'—then you will experience the jitters as fear, weakness, or even paralysis. If you work on positive images—'Now is my chance to come through in a real pinch; my parents (girlfriend, boyfriend, teammates) are going to be proud of me; wow, look at that enthusiastic audience'—then you'll experience these nerves as excitement and anticipation."

Surrendering and Relaxing

The "dispassionate response" stage is achieved often by athletes suddenly relaxing and letting their athletic programming, along with the pumping hormones, do the work. If we accept the second stage as the third part of a three-stage rocket, the third stage is all-important — the gearing-down to dispassionate response, or channeling the action to the sports' skill. Some athletes may seem to relax to get into this final stage, but Ayoob believes it may only be a mental or conscious relaxation. "It's the suspension of other emotions and perceptions because you become so focused on the task at hand. But if you were hooked up to a cardiac test, you'd find that you weren't physiologically calm."

On his way to 109 singles titles and 5 number one world rankings, tennis legend Jimmy Connors was able to turn his emotional passion into effective physical response during crucial parts of a contest — and yet he was able to keep his mental state undistracted and still in control. Often he got mad at himself to go into this state, but sometimes it came after a controversial call by an official. "I'll direct my anger to influence my play," he said. "I'll use it to lift my game. I'm angry, but I'm taking advantage of it. That attitude has won a lot of matches for me. Whether I've just hit a great shot or become fired up after a bad call, my mind seems to go on automatic pilot as my emotions surge."

Athletes who "surrender" to their performance to the point they are totally immersed in it have a better chance to trigger superior mind-body resources, according to Kathy Sexton-Radek, PhD, of Elmhurst College in Illinois. She gave vision tests to and queried 41 members of NCAA Division I college sports teams and found that those who were "intrinsically motivated"—who lost themselves in their performance without worrying about the results—had sharper vision and quicker reaction times than those who played with a trophy or a championship in mind.

Slow, deep breathing is an effective way to relax and help change the mind-body chemistry, Millman said. "The three primary emotional obstructions—anger, sorrow and fear — are each characterized by an imbalance in breathing. Anger is reflected by weak inhalation and forceful, exaggerated exhalation. Sorrow (as in sobbing) is characterized by spasmodic, fitful inhalation and weak exhalation. Fear can result in very little breathing at all." Millman advises athletes to breathe slowly and deeply with shoulders relaxed, mouth closed.

Actors and Athletes

James Loehr likens athletes to actors in that they can change their emotions, and subsequently their performance, through practice. "Elite athletes have learned to move their emotional chemistry to the directions they want just like actors," he says.

> Both professions have the same skills. Michael Jordan and (former tennis great) Chris Evert have been two of the great actors and actresses of their time in sports. They learned to act out their confidence and fighting spirit, to trigger positive emotions and chemistry, no matter what the situation in a game. At times they have felt nervous, but they never showed it. In a crisis, Jordan follows out the same emotional script with such precision time and time again and that's why he succeeds so often.

Like great actors, great athletes can move their emotional chemistry around to the desired direction.

Strange Happenings at Noon: The Author's Story

Altered mental and emotional states and amazing arousal zone performances are not the exclusive domain of elite athletes. I've experienced at least a dozen as an amateur athlete in basketball, soccer, baseball, golf, and track and field. In 1994 and 1995 at YMCA pickup games, I experienced flawless shooting performances in which I was so much immersed in a "zone" that I saw two different versions of the basketball and the basketball net: after the ball left my hand, I saw it go into the net twice—the first time shortly before it did, and then I would see it go in a second time. It was like there was a split screen in which I could see both the real ball and another ball slightly ahead of it. And, during those two afternoons of intense concentration, none of my shots missed. I'd guess I was at least 10 for 10 in each performance.

Throughout my amateur career in leagues and pickup games, I've also (through arousal) induced physical strength and speed at least 25 percent above what I'd normally be able to produce. Most of my career, I've weighed a skinny 143 pounds, but have been able to bring younger, stronger men to their knees through arousal techniques.

In 30 years of playing in pickup games and in organized men's community leagues, I've used myself and my friends as lab animals to study the use of noradrenaline and other hormones in physical situations. Sometimes I just sat on the bench and watched them. It was like a nutty laboratory with all those 175-pound rats scurrying around, half of them without shirts: Dave the lawyer, Billy the truck driver and Harry the psychotherapist, with thinning hair down to his shoulders, all had unique skills, not only physically, but mentally and emotionally. To become better players, we started sharing observations and information about one another:

- In pressure situations, none of us performed the same as we did without pressure. We either scored more, or we scored poorer.
- We sometimes used our own personal panic-threshold buttons to evoke top performances.
- Some players in their 30s and 40s could do as much physically as they had done in their teens because they had developed their hormone systems.
- The high-octane noon-hour competitions often drained our anxieties, allowing us to return to work more relaxed and efficient.
- When the outcome of the game became too important, arousal levels spilled over and arguments, even fights, occurred.
- During seemingly obscure moments in the break of action, answers to problems in our lives would suddenly become clear. This didn't happen every day, but when it did it left a lasting impression.

The most exciting finding was my split-screen experience. In order to understand my particular powers, you'll need to know some background. I don't know if I'm any different than anyone else as a human animal: I'm sensitive, particularly to my body chemicals, my metabolism is fairly fast and I look kind of wimpy. When I see myself in the mirror on my way to the shower in the YMCA change room, I see a stickman. In some ways my wife Jennifer is stronger than I am. I guess that's why I look away when I see myself in the mirror near the shower. But through determination and controlled anger, I've been able to perform what was not expected of me through short and long-term command of my body-alarm system.

I'm not sure where this ability comes from, but I suspect that much of it has been a subconscious need to prove myself. To know the way I think, you should know something about my background. I emigrated to Canada from England when I was five and before I was 15 I moved with my parents more than 20 times. I was close to my mother, but she was very ill through my adolescence, and my electrician father was a good man, but we didn't have much in common. I wanted his attention, but he rarely gave it. Perhaps he *couldn't* give it. In any event, my heroes became sports figures— Bobby Hull, Hank Aaron, and Arnold Palmer. In school, I didn't have a lot of confidence, especially in sports because I was smaller and skinnier than the other kids. Some of them laughed at my body when we played skins vs. shirts in gym class. I played inter-school sports at a small school after grade 11, but I was rather passive and didn't start using my arousal system until I was 22. It happened in 1971 in a basketball tournament in Grantham, Pennsylvania, in which I was playing for a Buffalo club team made up of former and current American college players. I had played only at a Canadian high school with 75 students and physically I didn't belong on the same court with them. But anger and determination allowed me weapons to compete at their level. In the championship game, our coach decided not to use me in favor of a taller, more aggressive player. Sitting on the bench as the contest wore on, I started a slow burn. I was particularly miffed because I was the team's off-court manager and had made all the arrangements for games that season. Finally, with about five minutes remaining and our team down by 15 points, I went in. Single-handedly I turned that game around. The opposing team must have thought I was a demon unleashed. I played the game of my life, driving through the talented home team almost at will, scoring at a rapid pace and generally controlling the action so much, our team completely wiped out the deficit and went ahead. It was easy to see the opponents as the enemy because I'd never met any of them before. The holes in their defense seemed much broader than normal and I could dart in and out before they closed up. It seemed like a combination of others moving in slow motion and me in overdrive. Pain I'd had from back spasms and a mild groin pull disappeared and I felt completely liberated from aggravations and worry. Going 100 mph, I felt strangely at ease, vaulted like a rocket into orbit, leaving my fears and insecurities behind. It felt lovely to be taking big risks. The opposition didn't know how to stop me; in fact, they became afraid, an athletic kind of afraid. When you see that insecurity in an opponent's eyes, you go for the jugular. I had never felt so physically powerful and in control of a situation since the day I stopped bedwetting at age 11. My confidence level was enormously high. In a few minutes, I scored 14 points and had untold assists, rebounds, and blocked shots. I even jumped above the rim, something I'd never done before. It sounds dramatic to say that a basketball game changed my life, but in a way, it did. Suddenly, I was aware I had powers beyond that bag of bones in the mirror. I became a much better player, knowing I could call on extra resources for an important moment in a game. And it spilled over into my professional life, too. For 6 or 7 years I'd been an average reporter, then in the next dozen years I won 11 national and international writing awards.

I don't use five-alarm fight or flight much anymore (perhaps because part of my self-esteem is not so much wrapped up in a basketball performance?), and I'm not recommending that amateurs provoke their anger night after night; that's an ethical question. But I see nothing wrong with triggering hormones in competitive situations to give yourself an edge. If it's a competition, there will always be some pride and self-esteem on the line and a natural desire to win.

Anyway, I started studying the mind-body's arousal system in 1988. While I found it to be an automatic defensive response, I wondered if there were ways to use it *consciously*, or at least to program the subconscious. I would lay awake at night, going over the things I had learned about my research that day and go to sleep hoping that I could trigger something in my subconscious to help myself in pressure situations to get optimal use of my adrenaline system. Then in the daytime, my arousal system would kick in during the pickup basketball games at the YMCA.

The split screen sensations appeared on two afternoons in the middle of games with sweat pouring from my brow. But they were not triggered through conscious thought. Somehow, the taste of sweaty salt was a trigger to send me to the next level; that, plus my "bogeyman." Some of my mates turned tougher when women were watching them from above on the exercise balcony, but for me, my opponents gave me the incentive to excel.

On both afternoons, I felt I had something to prove against an opponent. He was Dale Getty, 15 years younger than me. He was the epitome of an all-league jock; he'd been a quarterback of a university football team and an international caliber basketball player. He was muscular, talented, and extroverted, the image I'd had of "macho" when I was a teenager and none of those things myself; maybe that's why my idols were Arnold Palmer and Bobby Hull. Off the court, nice guy Dale and I got along well together, but I always got pumped up more against him. The concentration on my shot was always sharper when Dale was covering me.

One afternoon, I felt the power surge early. It's hard to describe, but I was quicker, springier, and tougher than normal, like my feet were unshackled from gravity. It was like I'd traded my bag of bones in for a new, improved version. Everything I touched seemed connected—there was great flow to the action whenever I was near the ball, like a dance on the varnished floor. I had no feeling of elbows, knees, or joints in my body, just elastic. Whenever I got that feeling of *no feeling*, I used a cue word to vault me to the next flight stage. "Now!" I'd say to myself, as if I was slamming my foot to an imaginary accelerator. At that point my mind would stop making conscious decisions for my body. The hell with it; whatever happened happened. And my concentration became almost supernatural. Macho Dale was helpless to stop me. He got that insecure look I've seen many times, although I didn't look into his face often. You couldn't launch your bogeyman against an opponent if you were friendly with him in the field of battle. You played dispassionately, trying to aim your energies at the task at hand and not the middle-aged guy across from you; your aggression also carried less guilt that way. In organized leagues, I knew players who intentionally didn't learn their opponents' names for the same reason.

While I was shooting in the zone, I would see the flight trajectory of the ball before it actually left my right hand. Then I would see the ball go into the basket twice—the first time about one-quarter of a second before it actually did. But this was not pre-conceived visualization—more of a precognition less than a second before it happened. And this occurred on several shots on both those days. The crazy thing was it felt totally natural, although prior to this I had never experienced it before. I'd shoot, then I'd see two balls, one right behind the other. Both of them swished. Never did I "see" the ball leave my hand and then have it end up missing the basket. In fact, I don't remember missing any shots in those two zone afternoons, although I probably missed one or two. Another thing, I don't remember any conscious thought while I was on a roll. I was plugged into something so smooth and so connected with everything else, I knew the results would be positive. I wasn't playing; I was feeling. There was little or no strategy. It was all action, or reaction. I was so immersed in the zone, I didn't stop to think: Hey, look what I just saw! I was too busy keeping the momentum going. There was no conscious attempt to aim at the basket. I just faced the target and threw the ball up and it was caught in an invisible giant vacuum cleaner and sucked into the basket. That's how big the metal hoop seemed to me. As I cut down on my peripheral vision and shrunk the gym down to only the things I needed to see (task vision), the target got bigger. Sounds simple, eh? It was, and it wasn't.

PART IV

Crashing and Burning Athletes

Until now most of this book has focused on the productive use of two strong drive forces in the lives of elite athletes: their long-term drive and their game-day arousal. In this section, we'll discuss the dangers these two strong motivators can bring, both on and off the playing fields.

Chapter 14 looks at the dreaded phenomenon of how and why athletes choke, and how there may be more pressure on them these days (and there are also more solutions available for them to overcome it). The chapter also looks at how high arousal can give a performer a distorted view of the action. In chapter 15, arousal turns ugly with cases of angry athletes losing control during competition, from boxer Mike Tyson to baseballer Robbie Alomar to auto racer A.J. Foyt. How athletes can become addicted to their sports, to gambling, and even to their hormones, is discussed in chapter 16.

CHAPTER 14

Choking Revisited

"My nerves just kept getting the better of me."

Golfer Gary Cowan

In this day and age, there may be more chances for athletes to become overaroused, to feel more pressure and anxiety—to "choke"—than ever before. And yet, ironically, there may be more information and strategies available for them to not only avoid choking, but to thrive on additional pressure.

"There is more pressure today and more at stake, without a doubt, with all the million-dollar salaries, being in the spotlight with all the media attention, and the fan interest," said psychologist Stanley Teitelbaum, PhD. "In the foreseeable future, I can see this increasing, leading to more pressure and anxiety because the fans love it. They're demanding more and more from performance and attendance keeps getting greater." On the night before the championship game of the 1998 World Cup of soccer, Brazil's Ronaldo, twice named the best soccer player in the world, suffered what doctors termed a type of convulsive fit brought on by emotional stress related to the big match. In Brazil, soccer is considered more of a religion than a sport and pressures from high stakes corporate sponsors may have also played on the 21-year-old Ronaldo's mind. The next day, Ronaldo and his team were upset 3-0 by France as 1.7 billion people watched on television.

Life in the Pressure Cooker

Any added pressure on an athlete can result in a better or poorer performance, Teitelbaum added. "The best ones make the pressure work for them, but many others get close to the brass ring and self-destruct."

Just ask U.S. decathlete Dan O'Brien. In 1992, O'Brien seemed a lock to make the U.S. Olympic team. He was the reigning world champion in the grueling 2-day, 10-event test of speed, power and endurance which produces the "world's greatest athlete," and, in fact, was the favorite to win the gold medal at the Barcelona Olympics. Some track observers called him the next Jim Thorpe and Reebok TV commercials made him somewhat of a household name in America. But in the U.S. trials, O'Brien's timing was thrown off by an unusual pit setup in the pole vault competition and in his first two jumps, he didn't clear the bar at a relatively easy 15 feet, nine inches. He needed to clear that height on his third jump in order to stay alive in the overall decathlon, but when he thought about what would happen if he missed, O'Brien started to panic. He recalled: "I thought, 'I'm down to my last jump. My whole decathlon is on the line.' I thought about the commercials, and I told myself, 'Oh, God. I don't want to look bad.' I ran over to my coaches in a panic and said, 'What do I do? What do I do?'"

O'Brien tried to calm his emotions, but he couldn't shake his anxiety. On his third and final jump, he failed to clear the bar again ... and did not make the Olympic team. Then the muscle-bound man broke down and cried. "There had been such high expectations from everybody. I felt as if I'd let the whole world down."

Even athletes who succeed most of the time under pressure have choked in their careers. In the 1936 World Series, Lou Gehrig froze at third base and didn't score on a single by a teammate. Ted Williams hit just .250 in his only World Series, and Barry Bonds, one of the best players of his era with a lifetime .288 average going into 1998, was just

16 of 80 (.200) in the playoffs. In golf, choking is called the "yips" and they are what keep many talented players from getting onto the tour, according to Canadian veteran Gary Cowan, who repeatedly failed to qualify for the U.S. PGA senior tour "because my nerves just kept getting the better of me." Golfers are compassionate to their opponents' choking because they know they are susceptible to becoming a victim themselves.

Boxer Evander Holyfield said that athletes often choke because (unlike Michael Jordan, Nancy Lopez, and John McEnroe) they can't control their emotions. "Once you get angry, your body starts doing things you don't want it to do," he said.

Overcoming choking is a psychological skill learned in practice during pressure-packed performances, according to Bob Weinberg, former president of the Association of Applied Sport Psychology and North American Society for the Psychology of Sport and Physical Activity. "(Tennis star) Ivan Lendl was prone to choking early in his career until he finally bested John McEnroe in the 1985 U.S. Open," Weinberg said. "After that, he became tough to beat under pressure [after losing in the finals from 1982-84, Lendl won three straight Opens]. Some athletes seem more gifted under pressure than others, but it's something that can be developed."

Dan O'Brien: Learning to Breathe Again

His unexpected "choke" at the 1992 U.S. trials was a wake-up call for O'Brien. In the next four years, he dedicated himself to learning how to react when hit by an anxiety attack and he listened intently to the advice of sport psychologists such as Jim Reardon. "My failure in '92 caught me totally by surprise; I didn't feel it building up. It was a total shock. I decided to be better prepared for '96." The first thing O'Brien did was to realize that having fears and anxieties are normal among elite athletes facing pressure situations, that he didn't have to be a non-feeling superman. Then, in training, O'Brien deliberately provoked anxiety by watching video tapes of his embarrassing failure of the 1992 pole vault, then immediately went out and vaulted." Reardon wanted his client to watch the tapes not to analyze technical mistakes he had made but to re-live, and then de-mystify the stunning experience. "I wanted to build up my anxiety and create a situation of total stress, so I could get used to that sensation," O'Brien said. "You can cross over [anxiety] barriers, but it has to take place in training."

© VICTAH SAILER

Dan O'Brien: "I wanted to build up my anxiety and create a situation of total stress, so I could get used to that sensation."

But it wasn't easy to overcome. "Every pole vault since 1992 was nerve-racking for me," O'Brien said. "I got increased heart rate and sweaty palms; I really had to force myself to relax and do things correctly." In the four years after Barcelona, he won all eight decathlons he entered, including his second and third world championships. Besides the pole vault, just one of 10 events in the decathlon, O'Brien also toughened himself for the pain of the nine others, especially the 1,500-meter run, by pushing his body past the breaking point in practice.

When the long-awaited 1996 Olympics arrived in Atlanta, O'Brien had perfected his relaxation techniques to bring him to an optimal stage of arousal for his various decathlon events with deep breathing to lower his heart rate. "You have to be aggressive to make the pole vault work and yet you have to be relaxed and keep your wits about you," he said. (In other events, O'Brien used more arousal in the "explosion" events of long jump and shot put, but less in the discus "where you need to be explosive but have to stay within boundaries when you throw to keep your posture straight.")

He also removed much of the distress from the pole vault event by training in the Olympic Stadium well in advance of the U.S. trials which had defeated him in 1992. "He was on the same runway, in the same stadium, in front of a large crowd," said Reardon, who deliberately increased O'Brien's stress by trying to distract him while he was training. "We tried to remove some of the trauma because that's what Dan experienced in '92. For trauma victims, anniversaries are always difficult; they trigger fear and anxiety."

Another key that allowed O'Brien to avoid choking in Atlanta was that he learned to block out all external forces, particularly worries that he would lose corporate sponsors and let other people down, and put all the onus on himself. If he failed again, the only person he would answer to was himself. "I had to put my performance entirely on myself and be ready to blame myself and not others if I failed again. I took some of the importance out of it by saying to myself this wasn't for the gold medal, but for my personal pride. I couldn't care what others thought any more. I only cared about what I thought of myself. We have to learn how to deal with our egos." During his performances in Atlanta, he went into a form of task vision in which he concentrated only on the present. "I took one jump, one throw, one run at a time. I tried to *become* each event." O'Brien went on to win the gold medal in Atlanta with an Olympic record for the decathlon of 8,824 points.

Like Dan O'Brien, golfer Greg Norman is trying to become more aware of what makes him choke in major championships. What he's learning is that, as has been outlined by many psychologists in this book, athletes often choke because they don't turn nervousness or anxiety into dispassionate "performance" response, but rather are too aware of self, the scoreboard, or opponents. Norman has blown so many leads in major tournaments (like in the 1996 Masters when he saw a six-shot lead evaporate as his approach shots kept going over the green), to choke in golf is known in some circles as "pulling a Norman." What's frustrating is he plays great the rest of the time and is the PGA tour's all-time money winner. "Greg is incredibly talented with an enormously strong drive to succeed," said sport psychologist Noel Blundell, who works with athletes in a wide range of sports from golf to tennis to windsurfing. "With that extreme need to achieve, he has a tendency to get distressed. It manifests itself in a breakdown of rhythm, timing, and concentration." Norman has admitted that he may think too much during the buildup to the Masters each year.

Training the Mental Side

At times, Norman seems to have been in denial about his choking and is very defensive with the media about it. After his collapse at the Masters, he said: "All these hiccups I have, they must be for a reason. All this is just a test. I just don't know what the test is yet." But he's taken steps to get a handle on the mental side of his game, huddling with sport psychologists and positive thinking gurus like Anthony Robbins. From them, he has learned 48 different strategies, including a type of visualization in which he pulls a chain in his mind as if to flush negative thoughts down an imaginary toilet. "What I took out of my session with Tony was a reminder of who I am and how good I am," Norman said. "Sometimes you forget all the little things you've done." Little things? Like winning more than 70 tournaments!

Norman has used anger as an extra club in his bag. In the 1995 NEC World Series of Golf, Norman nearly quit after the first day of competition when he claimed that playing partner Mark McCumber cheated by "tapping down" the green on his putting line, a charge that McCumber denied. "I could have bench pressed 500 pounds, I was that mad," said Norman, who channeled that intensity into the rest of the tournament to rebound from an opening day 73 and come from behind and win the championship. The incident seemed to have the opposite effect on McCumber, who shot 68 opening day, but ballooned to 76 the next day and finished 14 shots behind Norman.

Another golfer, Davis Love III, once considered the best golfer not to have won a major title, looks on choking as something you learn to defeat and once you do, you have more success in pressure situations. "I'm glad to be rid of it," he said after finally losing the label of choker and winning the 1997 PGA championship. "I'm looking forward to taking this and running with it and turning it into a lot more chances."

Some athletes are aware of their choking, but it only adds to worry, more anxiety, poor performance, and perhaps injuries like cramps. At the 1997 world track and field championships in Athens, sprinter Ato Boldon, of Trinidad and Tobago, was considered the favorite in the 100 meters and put more pressure on himself by boasting he would win. But he finished fifth after his thighs cramped. "Do I have finalitis?" he said to reporters after the race. "Why is it every time I get into a world final, I cannot finish the race properly?" Then, after a good cry, he competed in the 200-meter finals and won the gold medal, his first major title.

Slumping

Another form of choking, but more of the long-term variety, is when athletes go into a slump. A main reason for a slump's enduring nature seems to be related to an athlete's psyche, when his mind and body are out of sync, when the "head gets in the way of body and muscle memory," according to Alan S. Goldberg, EdD, a sport psychology consultant and author of *Sports Slump Busting* (Human Kinetics, 1997).

Increasing Pressure on Young Athletes

At the amateur level, there may be more youths choking today than ever before because of the potential financial rewards if they can become a professional athlete, says Newmarket, Ontario, tennis pro Dave Cooper, who teaches players of all ages. "There's too much pressure to win, to go unrealistically for the brass ring," he said. "A lot of kids are playing to win as a relief, to keep their parents at bay, or their coaches or friends. They feel they're letting someone down if they lose, so a lot of the enjoyment has gone out of sports." Fewer amateurs would choke if they were taught to feel good about themselves, win or lose, Cooper said. Athletes sometimes have lower self-esteem if they are from a smaller town, he added. "We'll have tennis players who suddenly realize, 'Hey, wait a sec, I'm from Newmarket and my opponent is from Toronto. I have no business being here.' Then their game falls apart and they lose."

Cooper teaches his students to learn from their choking, to look back and see at what point of a match it happened and why it happened. "They find out that they'd been playing too aggressively, or more often than not too tentatively. They were playing not to lose. Then I suggest to them the next time that situation comes up, they reverse the way they acted so that their brain learns to counteract those old feelings they had."

Younger, less emotionally mature athletes are more susceptible to choking than older athletes, said Steven Hendlin, PhD, who has a sports psychology practice in Irvine, CA, in which he helps golfers improve their game. "There are only a handful of people like Carl Lewis who know how to translate the intensity of extreme performance pressure to succeed and who can use that moment to help them come through," Hendlin said. "That is the difference in the emotional maturity of Lewis and (younger athletes). Lewis likes the attention of the crowd and people cheering—he rides on it. But the more jacked up the feeling in (the young athletes), the easier it is for them to make a mistake."

Fear of Danger

Some sports, such as boxing, football, and skiing, offer physical danger to the athlete, which trumps up a special kind of fear and anxiety—perhaps closer to the "natural" age-old response of fight or flight, in which a person goes through numerous physiological changes in order to try to survive physically. Dan O'Brien admits that he is sometimes physically afraid of the pain that will come in the 1,500 meters, the final event of the punishing 10-event decathlon. Marlin M. MacKenzie, EdD, a counselor for professional and amateur athletes, said that in competitive skiing, performers can fear getting injured or even killed. "Fear is initiated either by the thought or act of losing balance and control," he said. "The paradox of skiing well without undue fear is deliberately to go with gravity. In other words, skiing consists of falling upright, not in a heap, down the mountain . . . when fear creeps in, the willingness to become part of gravity wanes; as a result, performance deteriorates."

Greg Louganis experienced a series of anxieties in the 1988 Olympics, including the fear of serious or fatal injury. In a preliminary dive in the 10-meter springboard competition, Louganis smashed his head on the board, only the second time in 180,000 dives it had happened to him. A few minutes later, after his head had been sewn up with four stitches, he climbed back up on the board for a second dive, not only fearing for his safety but worried that blood contaminated from his secret AIDS virus had dripped into the pool. Louganis patted his heart and pulled off a near-flawless dive with no splash. "Controlling my fear gave me a goal," he said. Later, Louganis used the "dive of death," a reverse two-and-a-half pike that had killed a Soviet diver, to win the gold medal.

Throughout his life, Louganis had learned not to give in to pressure and problems; as a child he had been taunted because he was adopted, homosexual, dyslexic, and the product of an interracial marriage. He said that throughout his diving career, he used several things to calm himself before big events—to listen to classical music, carry his teddy bear "Gar" to the pool with him, and to remember that his mother loved him.

The Dangers of Altered States

Psychologists say that high arousal often brings about altered states as the mind-body prepares itself to deal with a threat. Psyched-up athletes have reported strange sensations such as a form of tachypsychia, in which plays seem to happen in slow motion as the mind-body speeds up its metabolism and sometimes absorbs more detail to give the athlete more time to respond to a situation.

But this and other experiences can distort an athlete's perception to things going on around him or her. During high stress, an athlete may experience (provided by Massad Ayoob):

• Tunnel Vision: Visual focus can zoom in as a baseball infielder desperately tries to catch a Texas League blooper and block out images of a teammate barreling in to catch the same fly. Crunch.

• Distance Distortion: Using the same baseball scenario, with the concentrated image of a ball filling the frame in the intense player's mind, the mind can create a very real optical illusion of a larger ball image. Sometimes the ratio reaches a 3 to 1 margin, and the distances around the ball can become distorted.

• Auditory Exclusion: This is tunnel vision of the ears. What the cortex of the brain deems irrelevant may be ignored. A player intensely focused on a play may not hear teammates or coaches.

• Cognitive Dissonance: A series of events in a controversial play may be remembered out of sequence. Trivial happenings during a match may assume exaggerated importance in a player's memory while some major aspects may be blotted out.

• Denial Response: An athlete may not realize he committed a serious mistake or violation in the heat of battle.

These altered states, of course, do not occur on every play, but knowledge that they *may* occur can be crucial to a coach or athlete when trying to reconstruct what happened after a crucial loss or a fight or controversy. Baseball player Roger Clemens was called a liar for his version of an incident with umpire Terry Cooney in the most important game of the 1990 season for Clemens' Boston Red Sox. Clemens, who was under enormous pressure to win the game for the Sox, was ejected after allegedly swearing at Cooney and threatening him, yet after the game, Clemens said he wasn't aware that he'd been abusive and didn't realize he'd been ejected. Could it be that athletes and officials who engage in heated confrontations get so worked up, they go into these distortions and later look like liars when they can't remember what happened? It's entirely possible, according to stress expert Massad Ayoob, who has investigated many such confrontations in police work.

"Athletes sometimes have arousal levels so high, they allow their emotions to cloud their cognitions and thought processes and they may not think clearly," said Montreal sport psychologist Wayne Halliwell. "A narrowed attention span is like looking through a straw and it can be very detrimental," said Gary Wells, a psychologist and researcher at Iowa State University. "Under arousal or stress, the tension narrows; things that are central in [an athlete's] line of vision may be encoded deeply, but peripheral matters are shut out."

When skiers are sent into high arousal through fear, they can create problems for themselves, says Marlin M. MacKenzie.

> When scared, skiers invariably experience a sense of urgency to do something quickly, and they experience what seems to be an unusually rapid passage of time. Their perception of external reality is frequently restricted to tightly focused awareness of a "danger" immediately ahead that looms much larger than it

normally is. Their internal screen is dominated by repeated meta pictures of imagined "doom," such as hitting a tree, slamming into the billy bags, or tumbling forward over their skis. Sometimes they remember scenes of others who have fallen on the trail or racecourse ahead of them. Or they relive past accidents in their minds. They re-experience the pain and hear again the voices of the medical personnel who treated them. No wonder they lose control or have second thoughts about going down a tough new trail. No wonder they feel weak, break into a cold sweat, become covered with goose bumps, and get dizzy. Their fearful thoughts activate the autonomic nervous system and put them into a lousy state that precipitates even more doubt and fear.

At the opposite end of the arousal spectrum, some athletes can go into trances that can put them at risk. Seven-time NASCAR national champion Dale Earnhardt sometimes goes into states before a high-charged car race that are so sedated, he falls asleep at the wheel. "It's not unusual for Dale to doze off before a race or under red-flag conditions," said Don Hawk, president of Dale Earnhardt, Inc. But it has almost cost him. In 1997 at the Southern 500, Earnhardt fell asleep at the wheel and his car crashed into a wall, putting him out of the race. He quickly recovered after tests at hospital. Joseph Healy, a neurologist at McLeod Regional Medical Center in Florence, SC, believes that Earnhardt had entered some sort of altered consciousness.

"Athletes must recognize and understand pain," James Loehr says. "They must be tuned into their bodies and their feelings because they can get so focused that their pain becomes very distant and subdued. The smart athletes sometimes take a chance by playing to risk a tissue injury, but not structure damage. You've got to make sure something is not seriously wrong; you can't just be macho about it."

Another dangerous distortion can be an athlete's short-term feeling of power and invincibility while aroused. He may feel this power and energy will last throughout a competition, but, in fact, it may burn out along with the adrenaline and other short-term hormones.

CHAPTER 15

Intensity Overload

"I wanted to knock everyone out. Tony just got in the way."

Boxer Vinny Pazienza after decking the referee

World-class athletes, despite their discipline and years of training, can be just a short fuse away from losing control. When they are pumped up for a pressure match, psychologists say, they are liable to fly over the optimal level of arousal and soar out of control, doing things they may later regret. When they lose it, it's often because they allow aggressive hormones such as testosterone and adrenaline to overflow in their mind-body systems, says Redford Williams, a professor of psychiatry and psychology at Duke University. These are the same rocket fuels that allow them to perform amazing feats, he said. Three cases from 1997:

- Boxer Mike Tyson was disqualified for biting part of Evander Holyfield's ear off in their heavyweight championship fight.
- Dennis Rodman, of the NBA's Chicago Bulls, kicked a photographer under a basket during a game. He had to pay an out-of-court settlement to the victim and was suspended by the league for

one of his many violent incidents, which included head-butting a referee.

- Former auto racer A. J. Foyt got violent as a racing owner. Angered after losing a protest at the Indianapolis 500, Foyt slapped winner Arie Luyendyk in the back of the head and shoved him to the ground.

"It's hard to say what causes a Mike Tyson or a Dennis Rodman to lose control under stressful game circumstances," said Williams, author of the book *Anger Kills*. In order to examine what makes top athletes snap, we must look at basic human behavior and basic human ego issues, he said. People may be prone to such anger outbursts more than we think, he added. "In a more abstract mode, most of us are able to inhibit or curtail these impulses that cause us to do things in the heat of a moment that will be dangerous. However, even perfectly normal guys and gals under certain conditions can lose it, too. Away from the sports fields, people's egos compete on the highways. There's road rage where drivers have duels on the highway over their egos, but I suspect it happens more to people who have a hostile personality type, whether they're athletes or not," Williams said.

Nature of the Beast?

The aggressive nature of many sports, such as boxing, football, and ice hockey, leaves athletes on the brink of arousal, of losing control of their emotions, even of committing violence.

"We have a very violent, emotional game and things are going to happen," said Brian O'Neill, former executive vice-president of the National Hockey League. The NHL had such a problem with fighting and bench clearing brawls (2.1 fights per game in the 1986-87 season), it had to change rules to clamp down on offenders. It seemed to work as the number of fights dropped to below one per game by 1996-97. "The way I see it, fighting is not a big part of the game. It really is an incidental part," NHL Commissioner Gary Bettman said. "This is a sport where players are hitting—and hitting is encouraged—where players are moving 30 miles an hour with a stick in their hands. The game is played on edge with a lot of emotion and every now and then you'll see a fight flare."

Many coaches encourage their players to be pugilistic. In 1997, coach Mike Murphy of the Toronto Maple Leafs said he had been wrong to discourage fighting in the team's preseason training camp. "I should have made training camp a brawl fest," he said. "Next year, I will. If I'm here next year, get your cameras because there'll be a brawl every scrimmage. I said [the previous September] I didn't want fighting. Next time, there'll be fighting. I'll get every goon out of the OHL (junior league). I'll get every goon alive." And yet, in that same year, Murphy's president and general manager, Ken Dryden, called for the NHL to discuss the possibility of banning fighting so that players who fight would be tossed from the game. Dryden said the old argument that fighting is a release for players who would otherwise injure one another with their sticks doesn't ring true. "That's not what the psychologists and anthropologists say," he said. "They say violence breeds violence."

Said Tie Domi, one of Dryden's players: "When I started in the league, you fought to intimidate the other team. Now it's a natural reaction to certain situations, but I don't fight for self-satisfaction. I fight for my team . . . I'm respected enough that I don't have to drop the gloves all the time."

Ironically, in one of the most violent games of all, football, there aren't as many fights as there are in hockey—probably in part because players would injure their hands on another player's protective equipment. Equipment is not an issue in professional basketball, where players sometimes come to fisticuffs. A 1997 team brawl between the New York Knicks and the Miami Heat, in which players came to the aid of fallen teammates, probably cost the Knicks a shot at the NBA championship because they subsequently had several key players suspended. Even in a more cerebral game like major league baseball, bench-clearing brawls are common. A report on baseball violence indicated there were 41 such brawls in the American League in the 1993 season and 38 in the National League. Many players and managers say they are often ignited when it's believed a pitcher is throwing at a batter to keep him away from the plate.

It's believed such incidents have been on the rise in recent years, perhaps a sign that players don't have as much discipline, or respect, as they once did. In the 1940s, Hall of Fame pitcher Bob Feller hit 60 batters and not once did opponents charge his mound. And another former great player, Frank Robinson, was hit by pitches 198 times, but rather than fight, he'd dust himself off and make the pitcher pay for it with a base hit. Is it possible that many contemporary players have more respect for themselves than they do for the game?

War In Miniature

"The competitive orientation of athletics creates a dehumanized, stereotyped way of perceiving the opponent," wrote psychologists George Bach and Herb Goldberg in their book *Creative Aggression.* "We love our team and hate theirs. The game becomes a war in miniature."

If athletes can be an aggressive bunch, their coaches and managers can be as well. There have been many fights between players and their coaches over the years—in the NBA, Golden State Warriors guard Latrell Sprewell choked coach P. J. Carlesimo; in college basketball, Indiana coach Bob Knight appeared to kick one of his players (his son Patrick) on the bench; and in baseball, manager Dave Bristol of the San Francisco Giants gave his pitcher John Montefusco a black eye. "I did what I had to do," Bristol said. "I don't want anyone screaming at me, telling me this and that."

In the 1997 NHL playoffs, Colorado Avalanche coach Marc Crawford was fined $10,000 for losing his cool. Crawford's Avalanche were defending their Stanley Cup championship, but were on their way to falling back three games to one in the series with the Detroit Red Wings in a fight-filled game. Following one melee, Crawford and Detroit coach Scotty Bowman exchanged heated words across the partition separating the players' benches. "Obviously, emotions got out of whack," Crawford said later. "You say some stupid things, they say some stupid things. It happens. It happened to us earlier in the playoffs. Nobody's proud of it, but it's part of the game." Bowman said: "He was pretty emotional. I guess I've been that way before, too. But his eyes were coming out of his head. He was pretty excited."

Pittsburgh Steelers coach Bill Cowher admitted he considered tackling Jacksonville Jaguars Chris Hudson as he ran downfield to score on a game-ending blocked field goal in 1997. Cowher stepped briefly onto the field in an aggressive manner as Hudson passed by him. "I could have tackled him. It crossed my mind. But thank God I didn't," Cowher said.

Stress experts say that when athletes get angry, their testosterone and noradrenaline levels tend to rise and become hard to control. "Intense competition level produces an aggressive approach to the world," says Laura German, a lecturer with the Chico State University sociology department. "It's a compulsive nature you take with you off the field. Some studies are beginning to say that athletes may physiologically have higher levels of testosterone, a male hormone that has been linked to aggression," she said. Even fans can become violent. A study by Georgia State University scientists showed that watching a game can raise a fan's testosterone level, which might account for fans' rioting after games, the researchers said.

The problem for athletes may be perpetuated by steroid use, German added. "Steroid use increases your susceptibility to violence. The biggest problem with steroids and violence is that no long-term studies have been done."

Hideous things can occasionally happen in amateur sports, as well. In 1991 in East Saint Louis, Illinois, a baseball coach who shot at a teenage umpire for calling out a nine-year-old player on his team was sentenced to 12 years in prison for attempted murder. Just after another game in Illinois in 1990, a Little League coach and his father attacked the opposing coach, who had apparently usurped the authority of an umpire by calling plays at first base. The victim, who suffered broken bones, a lacerated kidney, and a scratched retina, was later awarded $758,000 in a civil court case. Larry Nicholson, a skinny and soft-spoken 17-year-old from Philadelphia, said he didn't know what made him throw a punch at a referee in a high school basketball game. Nicholson was carted away in handcuffs, jeopardizing his chance at a college scholarship. "I just lost control," he said. "All I can do now is grow, try to learn from it."

Sarah Morgan, a Mission League soccer player in Sherman Oaks, CA, said she becomes intense and even angry when she looks on their opponents as enemies. In 1995, she was suspended for allegedly kicking an opponent in the neck.

That Old Ego Again

It seems it's not uncommon for athletes to use primitive animal fighting tendencies to protect themselves, their image, or their careers, Redford Williams said. In 1996, Baltimore Orioles star second baseman Robbie Alomar got into a shouting match with umpire John Hirschbeck with both men allegedly hurling profane insults at one another after Alomar was called out on strikes. Alomar was ejected from the game, then flew out of the dugout to spit in the umpire's face, drawing a five-day suspension. Defense of ego is sometimes behind these incidents. When he was manager with the Cincinnati Reds, Lou Piniella and relief pitcher Rob Dibble had a showdown that left them swearing at one another, then wrestling on the clubhouse floor. "I sort of lose my cool," Piniella said. "It's just that simple. It happened. When my integrity gets questioned, it's not that easy of a situation to deal with."

In 1995, in front of a national television audience in South Africa, soccer player Ahmed Gora Ebrahim of the Rabali Blackpool team became angry because his manager, Walter Rautmann, took him out of the game after just 16 minutes for a substitute. The player kung-fu kicked Rautmann to the ground, damaging his kidney. Also that year in England, Manchester United soccer player Eric Cantona jumped into the stands to kick a spectator.

Self-Esteem Overdose

Many psychologists believe athletes with low self-esteem are susceptible to violence, but too much self-esteem can be a key factor in determining aggressive and violent behavior, according to three researchers who analyzed more than 150 studies in psychology and criminology. "You've got a lot of people running around with seriously inflated egos who come crashing down to earth all the time," said study co-author Joseph Boden, a post-doctoral research associate at the University of Virginia. When confronted with their weaknesses and failures, however, they lash out—typically at those who have challenged what the researchers call their "threatened egotism."

Being insulted by fans can send an athlete into a rage, like at an international cricket match in Toronto in 1997. A fan had been heckling Inziman Ul-Haq of the Pakistani team through a megaphone and calling him a "potato" when the cricketer suddenly leaped up into the stands and wielded a cricket bat during a wild melee. Police became involved and Ul-Haq was suspended.

Tyson, who sought psychiatric help to enable him to control his emotions, said he snapped and bit Evander Holyfield's ear in their 1997 match because he was mad at Holyfield for head-butting him and putting his career and family income in jeopardy. But Holyfield said it was all about controlling such animal instincts. "What happened opened people's eyes about how much pressure can happen when things are not going your way," Holyfield said. "Anytime you're accustomed to winning and it comes to a point where you meet your match, something like that can happen." When he was

Mike Tyson in 1997. Perhaps no boxer has had to overcome so much to gain first great success and then great notoriety in the ring.

bitten on the ear by Tyson, Holyfield first wanted to bite back. "That ran across my mind," he said. But Holyfield was in so much pain, jumping around the ring, that "it allowed me to think about how to get my composure."

And yet, even "composed" athletes may be susceptible. As an up-and-coming boxer in 1980, Holyfield bared his own teeth, according to his opponent Jakey Winters. It allegedly came during a Golden Gloves tournament in Atlanta and Holyfield later admitted he had bitten Winters. "I dropped him with a left hook to the body and doubled up to the head in the second round of a scheduled three rounder," Winters said. "At that point, he was hurt and angry." After Holyfield got up, composed himself and withstood another round of punches, he spit out his mouthpiece and bit Winters on the shoulder, breaking the skin and causing bleeding, Winters said. "It's hard to spit a mouthpiece out, but he was desperate . . . Evander is no angel. It can happen to anybody. A fighter is oblivious." Holyfield later admitted his mistake.

Defense of their livelihood can send an athlete into a rage. In 1997 near Pittsburgh, an amateur golfer trying to qualify for the Professional Golfers Association scored a very damaging quadruple bogey.

For a few moments, he wasn't a good person to be around, PGA official Thomas Beeler quickly found out when he warned the golfer about slow play. The golfer called the official names, then slugged him in the face. He was disqualified from the tournament and charged with assault. "I'm required to tell a player when they are moving slow, but I guess I shouldn't have done it after he shot nine on a par-five hole," Beeler said.

In 1996, competitive pressures described as "scorching" lay behind an attack on a hockey referee by members of the University of Moncton (New Brunswick) Blue Eagles following a controversial goal. Eight Moncton players swarmed the referee, backing him into a corner and taking turns throwing punches. The players issued an apology, saying they had lost control of their emotions. A study of the incident revealed that pressure was high for the Eagles to win, partly because of the competitive university recruiting system for hockey in Eastern Canada.

Fans may be getting tired of the antics of many athletes. In a 1997 *USA Weekend* poll, 86 percent of the 51,286 respondents said they believe misbehavior by players both on and off the field was the biggest problem facing sports. High-ticket prices (11 percent) were far behind, as was owners who move their teams (3 percent).

Maybe it's just an athlete's fierce desire to win which can obliterate his good sense when the pressure is on and the arousal hormones are pumping. Boxer Vinny Pazienza decked referee Tony Orlando during his 1996 bout with Dana Rosenblatt. "I wanted to knock everyone out," Pazienza said later. "Tony just got in the way."

Most incidents occur just after competition when noradrenaline levels are still high in an athlete's system, Williams said. More of these post-competition incidents are being reported these days because media are on the spot with their microphones and notepads. A special 150-meter race in 1997 between Olympic gold medallists Donovan Bailey and Michael Johnson was to decide who was "the world's fastest man." Johnson pulled up lame early in the race, which angered the winning Bailey. Seconds after he crossed the finish line, TV reporters interviewed Bailey, who sneered that Johnson was faking his injury because he knew he was going to lose anyway. Bailey said they should run the race over "so that I can kick his ass one more time." A day later, Bailey apologized for his remarks, but the damage was done and conservative Canadian fans were shocked.

The Amazing (-ly Explosive) Mets

Self-destructive behavior in New York Mets pitchers from 1992 to 1997:

- Jason Isringhausen punched a heavy-duty plastic trash can in the clubhouse after giving up two runs in the first inning of a minor league game, suffering a compression fracture of his wrist. "I was shocked at myself," he said.
- Dwight Gooden allowed three home runs on opening day of 1994 and kicked the dugout steps, breaking a toe.
- Left-handed John Franco punched the door to the sauna at the visiting clubhouse in Atlanta, cutting his right hand for seven stitches. But he retorted: "You can still get the anger out with the other hand."
- Anthony Young allowed a game-winning homer and injured his foot by kicking a water cooler.
- Bret Saberhagen was removed as starting pitcher in a game in Los Angeles for what was termed tendonitis in his finger, but it was learned later he had punched a wall or a locker in a fit of frustration.
- Pat Zachry broke a toe when he kicked the dugout after allowing a single by Pete Rose.

CHAPTER 16

Athlete Addictions

"I found out I wasn't perfect. I freaked out. I found an opposing player better at one of the things I set my sights on to be the best at."

Former NBA All-Star
John Lucas

Many athletes can become addicted to the arousal hormones that help make them so successful, said Archibald Hart, professor of psychology at Fuller Theological Seminary and the author of the book *The Hidden Link Between Adrenaline and Stress.* "There may be a psychological dependence or a physiological dependence to the chemistry involved," he said.

Is this "buzz" the reason many athletes continue to play long past their prime or with serious injuries—or get involved in other risk-taking ventures to try to replace the athletic high? Is this what attracts top athletes such as Michael Jordan, Pete Rose, and golfer Laura Davis to seek the highs of always winning or to other buzz-giving activities such as gambling, card-playing, and horse-racing? Is there also a connection to other "addictions" such as alcohol and drug abuse? Hart believes it's possible, although no research is available. "Many of us get hooked on some activity or interest, just as an alcoholic is addicted to alcohol and we depend on that activity for the kick it gives us," says Hart. "And this is very visible in athletics . . . whatever the underlying reason, the athletes don't feel normal unless they're doing their activity." For most people, their games and hobbies are harmless and provide an escape, he said, but they can be harmful if athletes rely on them too heavily. "Then, if you don't get your fix, you can suffer physical and / or emotional adrenaline withdrawal."

In some circles, a form of this is sometimes known as "addictive runner's syndrome," even though it may involve sports other than running. Hart said that in the arousal stage, it may be a psychological addiction to adrenaline or a chemical addiction to endorphin—or it may be addictive because of the power and control that athletes seek from it.

"There are a lot of adrenaline junkies," says Massad Ayoob, an expert in the mind-body's reaction to risk and stress. "We like feeling stronger and more aggressive than usual. After the rush, we feel relaxed and calm with euphoric aftermath."

Competitive sports breeds a kind of obsessiveness in elite and amateur athletes, psychologist say. J. Morrow, PhD, a professor in the psychology and physical education departments at John Jay College in Criminal Justice, City University of New York, said that the drive to exercise compulsively often masks deeper issues such as depression, a need for control, an unrealistic body image, or the inability to form relationships. "You don't need to be a sport psychologist to treat someone who's exercise-dependent," he said. "But you do need to be a good clinician and sensitive to the problem." (Morrow's treatment approach includes techniques from the cognitive behavioral school of psychology which involves repeating positive statements such as "I feel and look better when I don't overtrain" and "I can get pleasure out of a lot of things in life," and rewarding oneself for involvement in nonphysical activities). Later in this chapter, we'll discuss the related topic of elite athletes who overtrain.

Athletes involved in physical danger get a high that narcotics can't give them, said motorcycle racer and author George Jonas. "What motorcycle racers are looking for is 'that feeling,' a kind of addiction," he said. "It's a feeling that is only available in the shadow of mortal danger. You cannot get it from playing computer games. It is a flower that you want to pluck which grows on the edge of a cliff . . . I think it is probably a chemical addiction. In the shadow of death, your senses, like little neuro-transmitters, start firing like crazy. Adrenaline is pumping and it creates a high. You have to pass over that hump of being scared before you get that feeling. If you stayed scared, you couldn't get it, and you'd just white-knuckle it." Jonas said he'd smoked drugs—"but they don't come close to this feeling". Some mountain climbers may be adrenaline junkies, who keep challenging hazardous nature, according to Allan Derbyshire, who runs a mountain climbing school in the Canadian Rockies. "For them, it's the adventure, the danger, stepping off into the unknown. . .the risk of finding themselves in a situation that they're not totally in control of," he said. During a rescue, Derbyshire used an adrenaline rush as a life-saving tool to ski 14 kilometers "at what must have been record speed" to get help for a seriously injured man.

Some athletes are addicted to the hormonal high that comes with power and anger, said cardiologist Arnold Fox. "They feel strong, invincible, explosively powerful while riding the adrenaline wave."

Exercise Addiction

"Exercise can be a powerful medicine," says Robert Eliot, former director of the Institute of Stress Medicine International in Denver. "But too much can have bad effects. An athlete may have a superb cardiovascular system, but if he beat the daylights out of his feet and knees, he may get bone and joint disease." Yet endorphin and other natural painkillers can mask the pain of such injuries, he added. "When they're running or competing, they may feel no discomfort because the release of endorphin is like taking a fix of morphine. It masks ordinary messages and they run the risk of injury."

Athletes, like police officers, soldiers, type-A personalities, and workaholics may be more susceptible to disease and live shorter lives than other people, Massad Ayoob says. "Eventually, too much adrenaline stress is going to kill you," he said. "The cost of constant exposure to the body's fight-or-flight system is high. Your blood pressure is constantly quadrupling. There is hypertension and disease."

Hart said that constant stress can reduce the body's immune system, making it prone to sickness and heart disease. Excessive circulating adrenaline lies behind the risk factors that lead to heart disease, high blood pressure, high blood cholesterol level, and probably hardening of the arteries. On a minor level, it causes headaches, ulcers, digestive problems, and muscle spasms. Excessive exercise can lead to high blood pressure, too much cortisol release, and a decrease in eating habits, Eliot said.

"If athletes are exposed to adrenaline highs too much, they can get severe damage," said Mike Lashuk of the University of Calgary. To most amateur athletes and coaches, however, the effects are usually less severe, he said. "When their season is over, they suddenly come down with flu and other illnesses. Their system doesn't function normally without adrenaline."

Overtraining

Elite athletes expose themselves to intense arousal not only during competition, but in training as well, according to Jay T. Kearney, sport psychologist. And they don't have to get psyched up—arousal modes kick in as the body goes into intense exercise. Too much practice can send an athlete into a chronic syndrome called "overtraining," usually brought on when an athlete trains too much while he is "stale" and which can lead to high levels of stress, emotional instability, apathy, depression, and low self-esteem. Studies have shown that athletes can even go into the "fight or flight" mode during training.

World-class athletes must skirt a fine line between the intense training they need to keep up with the competition and the "overtraining" that can lead to their physical, mental, and emotional downfall, said Kearney, who helps athletes to try and reach their peak just before key competitions. "I'm convinced that to achieve at the highest level of world performance, you have to expose yourself to enormously high levels and volume of intensity," he said. "People can no longer perform at a world-class level without it. That's what separates the people who have identical genetic capability. The ones who fall behind are those who are unwilling to spend six to eight years at the Olympic level of training. If they come to work on the track and give 98.5 percent of their absolute best, people will say they had a great day, but they're going to lose to the guy who's giving 99 percent. And that's what's happening these days." Kearney believes that many elite athletes who put in these long hours of training are driven by internal issues. "A lot of them internalize their drives. They have strong drives, an emotional drive, a need for success," he said.

Other terms have been used to define excessive training techniques, such as "overload" training to condition athletes and to enhance their tolerance for stress. Such methods are the major reason—more than sports technology, coaching techniques, and nutritional strategies—why Olympic records have fallen one after another in recent times. Their burning drive often causes them to overtrain, Kearney said, resulting in physical and mental burnout. "Coaches of the best athletes have to be cautious of this." Even without the mental or emotional arousal, athletes go into physiological arousal during intense training, sometimes even the fight-or-flight mode in some cases, studies have shown.

Research has shown that at least 64 percent of female and 66 percent of male elite distance runners experienced some form of overtraining during their career. Alberto Salazar, winner of the Boston and New York marathons, stopped running at the peak of his career because of this syndrome. "Exercise is a stimulus that can have beneficial or deleterious psychological outcomes," says exercise physiologist Jack Raglin. "And the threshold that separates those two outcomes is poorly understood."

Salazar said his obsession with training resulted in mental and physical burnout in the 1980s. "I didn't know what to do with my life, but for much of the last 10 years, I hated running with a passion. I used to wish for a catastrophic injury in which I would lose one of my legs." But he was consumed with running well and other parts of his system broke down. "I was always sick and injured and I had three episodes of heatstroke. That, combined with all the years of hard training at such a high level without ever taking a break, damaged part of my brain. . . . My endocrine system was so screwed up that I had very low hormone levels." Salazar was able to make a comeback in the 1990s by taking the prescribed drug Prozac. "I took it to feel better, not to race better." Suddenly, he was able to handle the stress "that had overwhelmed me both physically and mentally."

Overtraining can lead to burnout, but so can an emotional drive that is too strong, psychologists say. Burnout has been called a state of emotional exhaustion that can result in depression and low self-esteem. Burnout is produced the moment that the costs of a sport outweigh its rewards if those costs are stress-induced, according to Daniel Gould, a professor of exercise and sport science at the University of North Carolina at Greensboro. His research revealed that many burned-out athletes were not able to cope with their own perfectionist personalities. The U.S. Tennis Association, which funded the study, is using its findings to help parents and coaches see the signs of burnout among young players.

"The competitive athletic setting can be a highly demanding one from both a physical and a psychological perspective, and one which is therefore capable of eliciting high levels of stress in participants," said Ronald E. Smith, a psychologist at the University of Washington in Seattle. "Elite athletes have dropped out of sports at the peak of their careers, maintaining they are burned out and that participation has become too aversive for them to continue. Concern about the large number of athletes who drop out of sports during the adolescent years has been fueled by speculation that years of inappropriately intense competitive pressures during childhood may cause some youngsters to burn out and abandon sport participation."

Stress is a symptom of burnout, not its cause, said sociologist Jay Coakley, PhD, a sociology professor at the University of Colorado at Colorado Springs. He studied competitive downhill skiers and tennis players who had burned out and found that their identity and self-esteem were wrapped up too much in their performance. He found that players in team sports were not as susceptible to burnout because "they would collectively get together to take more control of at least parts of their lives." Coakley believes that stress management could help such athletes to control burnout, at least in the short term.

Posttraumatic Stress Disorder

The aggressive, combat-style mentality of pro football can cause an emotional disorder among players similar to posttraumatic stress disorder that affects some war veterans, said psychiatrist Armanda M. Nicholi, Jr., who worked with the New England Patriots. They can develop anxiety from experiencing "a serious threat to their physical integrity . . . and seeing someone who is the victim of physical violence," he said. "The intense contact on the football field simulates hand-to-hand combat on the battlefield and meets the criteria of posttraumatic stress disorder," Nicholi wrote in the *The New England Journal of Medicine*. Nicholi treated some players who suffered from a sense of a shortened future, irritability, sudden outbursts of anger, and dreams of violence. "During my time with the Patriots, several players have consulted me to express alarm over dreams about death, plane crashes, and blood massacres," he said. "It's not as severe as when it occurs in the severe forms with [soldiers], but it nevertheless can lead to very similar symptoms." Nicholi was uncertain how widespread the problem is. "I think once something's identified like this, people may recognize it more—both the doctors and the players."

Boxer Gabriel Ruelas may have suffered a type of posttraumatic stress disorder in a 1996 bout. The year before, Ruelas had killed opponent Jimmy Garcia in the ring and subsequently he was haunted by the death. The next time Ruelas stepped into the ring, he was unable to perform. Although he later blamed it on the flu, he conceded that he thought he saw Garcia's face before him in the ring.

Ego Addiction

"I think that standing up there day in, day out and someone points at you saying, 'You are the world champion' and then you stand in the blocks and you realize that there are eight (opponents) every single time you step on the track that want to kick your butt. I've seen lots of people crack."

Olympic Sprint Champion Donovan Bailey

Ego defense is one of the strong motivators of elite athletes and a key in their athletic success, many experts say. But it can be off-putting, even dangerous. For one thing, if it turns to arrogance, it can lead to alienation of fans, foes, coaches, and teammates. And it can be harmful to the athletes themselves. As he stated earlier in this book, Toni Farrenkopf, PhD, a clinical and sport psychologist who works with athletes and coaches in Portland, Oregon, said that many super athletes are driven to great heights by issues of ego, but that can be hazardous. Often, he said, their emotional drive is fueled by an obsessive-compulsive disorder in which they over-compensate for their insecurities and emotional needs through incredible achievement. "They could be over-compensating because of neurosis, previous putdowns from others, poor self-esteem, or other psychological and emotional frailties," he said, adding that such mindsets can result in psychological and emotional problems, especially obsessive-compulsive disorder. "We're a pretty neurotic society. We're pushing people to the point of insecurity and anxiety and poor self-esteem." Even though they achieve greatness, many athletes suffer from depression, anxiety, and distress, he said.

Exercise physiologist Jack Raglin said that when they're not in the heat of competition, elite athletes tend to be in better mental health than the average person with generally lower levels of anger, depression and confusion—"but during competition, all bets are off. There's a remarkable shift. They turn their anger on and off, often by recalling events or situations which elicit strong emotions."

But even athletes who initially feel great about themselves and their careers can be getting set up for psychological pitfalls, says Dan Millman. "The undesirability of low self-concept may seem obvious, since it limits our achievement. Unrealistically high self-concept has its own unique problems," he says. "Young children who are constantly praised for everything and told they are 'the best' and 'great' get used to such praise, which represents the positive attention that all children crave. They will strive to maintain this praise as much as possible; maybe they'll even develop precocious abilities. The shadow side of this picture is that their sense of self-worth depends at first on the praise and later gets transferred to the achievement that earned the praise. They grow up to expect success and they project this expectation onto other people, that everyone in the world expects them to succeed. This expectation becomes a tremendous pressure not to let the world down. It can create brilliant students, star athletes . . . and suicides."

It is those who are most obsessed with winning who often achieve the world and yet they may suffer the most, according to John Douillard, who has advised tennis stars Martina Navratilova, Steffi Graf, and John McEnroe. The latter two do not enjoy the game unless they win a tournament, he added.

"Second place means nothing these days, especially with so much riding on a victory—trophies and earnings, corporate sponsors and self-esteem," Douillard said. "We've put so much pressure on winning, we've traded in the process of getting there, the enjoyment process of sports which many athletes these days never achieve. The fun has gone out of it. There may be some enjoyment in getting to the top, but no fun in trying to maintain it under those pressures."

Douillard said that in his prime, McEnroe often let anger work for him, especially to intimidate opponents, but that he could have been a better player for longer in his career if he had created an inner calm within himself. Other athletes risk mental and physical health, as well as their happiness all in the name of becoming the best in their fields, Douillard said. He recalled a Pan-American Games karate champion he once counseled:

> He was a very kind and soft-spoken man, but he said that one of his coaches in his youth had brainwashed him into thinking there was no such thing as defeat. He was not even allowed to think about it. But this became obsessive and before competitions, he would panic and hyperventilate. He couldn't sleep and suffered from anxiety and he couldn't even drive his car without his legs shaking, but he continued in karate because he had a gift and he couldn't let his coach down. At home, he was very aggressive with his family. He was burned out by the time he was in his mid-20s and had to take tranquilizers.

Not winning the big trophy leaves leftover feelings for many athletes, suggests psychologist Thomas Gilovich of Cornell University, who published a 1995 study in which he found that athletes apparently feel better about coming in third in a competition than second, because the pain of being so close to the top hurts so badly. Gilovich and his researchers studied winners and losers from the 1992 Olympic Games and found that athletes who won silver medals were much more unhappy than those who went home with bronze. Researchers were trained to numerically "rate" how athletes reacted when they finished their events, and when they accepted their prizes.

"The world seems obsessed with what's the best in an unhealthy way," he says. "For example, when you lose multiple times, you are written up as a loser, whereas people and teams that are worse don't even make it as a story." Self-esteem and winning are inextricably linked for athletes and fans, he adds.

Perfectionism

When winning becomes too important, when becoming and staying number one in sports becomes too important, it can lead to an athlete's downfall, says John Lucas, a former NBA all-star, coach, and general manager. He calls this a *disease of perfectionism* that afflicts the ego. And it nearly killed Lucas. The disease started in his college playing days and "led me on a collision course to kill myself with drugs (alcohol and cocaine)," he said.

"This disease that almost killed me was the disease that creates the drug and alcohol problem: I found out I wasn't perfect. I freaked out. I found an opposing player better at one of the things I set my sights on to be the best at. I always saw the negative in me instead of the positive. I could go 19 for 20 (shots) and be mad about the one I missed . . . it's a disease that strikes at the heart of the athlete. The Ego."

Sport psychologist Don Weiss said that the drive in some athletes is driven by a burning, uncompromising focus and it's impossible for them to see beyond that, he said. "They feel they must achieve because achieving defines who they are."

In 1987, talented 21-year-old runner Kathy Ormsby was the favorite to win a 10,000-meter race in North Carolina. When she fell behind, something snapped and the honors pre-med student ran off the course and jumped off a bridge. Both her legs were paralyzed and her promising athletic career was over.

"Some people are so obsessed with the idea of being the best that they are self-punitive," says psychologist Harvey Brooker of the Clarke Institute of Psychiatry in Toronto. "The danger with these people is that they may never be able to feel good about themselves." The more they strive, the more they succeed and that success comes at a great personal or physical cost. Heart disease, obsessive eating disorders, and the breaking apart of personal relationships can be the price of a narrowly defined success, Brooker adds. Such "overachievers" are often people who had trouble getting attention or affection as children, he said. The constant desire to achieve, to gain recognition, is a desperate attempt to fill that void and, for some, no matter how much attention the success generates, it's not enough, Brooker says.

Farrenkopf tells his clients to try to reduce the neurotic pressure in their lives and thus relieve their tension. "I tell them to play happy, play with a grin on their face." He believes it will not take the edge off their game.

> The so-called neurotic component in their lives may still be there subconsciously, and driving them, but when there is a conscious neurotic sense of achievement or failure, then the athlete does fail. I tell them to go out and enjoy themselves for the fun of it, then they don't worry so much about the scoreboard and being afraid of failure. . . . Research shows that when you're playing happy and in flow with the game, you perform better.

Eating Disorders

Perfectionism can lead to eating disorders, especially among female athletes who may fall victim to competitive pressures and risk contracting the disorders as they try to please fans, parents, coaches, or judges. A 1992 study by the American College of Sports Medicine showed that eating disorders affected 62 percent of females in sports such as figure skating and gymnastics. Another study found that 4.2 percent of female college athletes satisfied the criteria for anorexia nervosa and 39.2 percent for bulimia, compared to less than 1 percent and between 1 and 5 percent, respectively, of young women in general. American gymnast Cathy Rigby battled anorexia and bulimia for 12 years and suffered cardiac arrest twice. Christy Henrich, who missed making the U.S. Olympic gymnastic team by .0188 of a point, died in 1994 of multiple organ system failure related to eating disorders. She weighed 60 pounds. And Nadia Comaneci, the sweetheart of the 1976 Olympics with three gold medals and a perfect 10 score, suffered from bulimia and tried to commit suicide at age 15 by swallowing bleach. Her brother Adrian said his sister "must always be told that she is beautiful and good."

Too much attention on the results helps explain why young gymnasts fall prey to problems such as eating disorders and low self-esteem, said Joan Duda, a researcher at Purdue University who served as consultant to the USA Gymnastics Artistic National Team and Women's Program. "We want them to be able to handle the tough times so that they can rise above the performance slumps and, when injury occurs, they can sustain their involvement," she said.

These eating disorders have had devastating effects on the mental, emotional, and physical well-being of the athletes. It's estimated that 30 to 50 percent of bulimics abuse alcohol and drugs. A rarer fanaticism just being recognized by researchers is "exercise bulimia," in which excessive exercise becomes "payment in advance" for food bingeing or penance for foods already consumed. Another newly-discovered affliction is "muscle dysmorphia," in which bodybuilders are pathologically preoccupied with the appearance of their muscular bodies and yet falsely believe they are small and weak.

Denial

Many athletes deny injuries and even their creeping age in order to stroke their egos and need for attention and affection, Brooks Johnson said. In 1997, 69-year-old Gordie Howe played one shift with the Detroit Vipers of the International Hockey League, allowing him to have competed professionally in six decades. George Foreman and Sugar Ray Leonard competed for world boxing championships in their forties. Carl Lewis was in four Olympics. In 1992, 20 years after he won seven gold medals, 41-year-old swimmer Mark Spitz tried to make a comeback, but he failed to qualify for the Olympics.

Years of competitive drive can turn against an aging athlete if he feels the need to compete to compensate for other things that are lacking in his life, according to Brooks Johnson. "If athletics works for you, it should diminish the need for indiscriminate love, but if it heightens it, then it hasn't been successful . . . then you're never satisfied," he said. "Then you have no business going back into the game, then you have to get help. Many athletes get involved in alcohol and drug abuse and they can't function in society. Their psyches are stretched so tight, it can snap. One of the problems is we expected these elite athletes to be perfectly normal people with normal personas. But even a player like Wayne Gretzky is an abnormal personality. If he was to channel his aggression or psychology into nonproductive areas, we'd have him in jail.

Putting All Their Ego Into One Basket

The emotional drive to succeed at a sport can create a single-mindedness that can lead to lifestyle problems—in relationships, self-identity, and retirement. "It can be dangerous for athletes to put all their eggs in one basket," says sports researcher Dan Landers. "That can be dangerous off the field. You can lose focus about what life's about, so narrow in your thinking that your life is a failure if you don't win. Sometimes athletes need to take a break."

Former Olympic gold medallist Janet Evans admitted that late in her career she took defeats hard because her identity was wrapped up in her winning in the pool. "I was known as 'Janet, the Olympic Swimmer.' I lost my identity. Swimming became my identity. It was the way I was accepted. It became my entire life. And when I failed in the pool, I felt like a failure as a person. Swimming ate me up inside," she said. After winning in the Seoul Olympics, Evans didn't repeat at Barcelona, and she started to believe that people didn't like her as much. "I'd been trying to live up to my past and it was impossible," she said. "I was so into setting world records that I wasn't used to finishing second or third. I thought my life was going to be ruined."

Obsessive drive can cause problems in an athlete's family and social life, said 10-time Great Britain Grand Prix champion Stirling Moss. "The real competitor is not easy to live with when he is on his way up and when he is at the top because he is driven to compete with everyone," Moss said. "He wants to do everything better, he wants to dominate everyone around him — his friends, his associates, his employers, his wife. This is the deepest need in his nature and allowance must be made for it. It has made him what he is: without it, we would never have heard of him." Moss competed well enough in a 14-year career that he won 194 of the 466 races he entered. Looking back at his Hall of Fame basketball career, guard Bob Cousy said he regretted that he couldn't turn off his killer instinct off the court.

> The killer instinct brought me success as a player, but it also tempted me to run over people, to break the rules, and neglect my family to a point. I was on the edge of physical and emotional breakdown. . . .I'm no longer proud of killer instinct. It can kill the moral sense, happiness. It is not an instinct I can get rid of. It is something I must live with as best I can.

"When you're playing, you always have to be 'on,' whether it's practicing or playing games," says former NFL linebacker Marlin McKeever, divorced from his wife. "If you're not 'on' when there's a problem in the home, it tends to get magnified."

On the playing fields and in the arenas, elite athletes rise above others because they often become "monomaniacal" and make their profession their whole life, says clinical psychologist Selwyn Liderman. "They often times are mostly nonfunctional unless they are in complete control. If their boyfriend or wife or husband can accept that, it can work okay; otherwise, they are generally not good socially. They're only comfortable doing their own thing. They don't develop their full personal lives. There's more examples now of domestic violence and drug abuse among athletes and more verbal violence and so much sexual activity. When athletes are deified like they are today, it brings out grandiosity. When people are put into a special position, it's hard not to be seduced by people telling you how great you are. Some become greedy." When they get depressed, many athletes quickly get back into their sports routine "and that's their saving grace," Liderman says. "Michael Jordan has said that when he retires, he expects to sit back and become fat. My thought is unless he finds some other area that can be of strong interest to him, he is potentially setting himself up for trouble."

Ted Turner admits that his "unhealthy drive to achieve" carried him through the America's Cup yacht championship, then to founding CNN and the Goodwill Games and owning two professional sports teams. But he added that it ruined his relationships and personal life and, after seeing six psychotherapists, he's given up racing and forces himself to have noncompetitive hobbies like fishing. "I'm finally finding some peace," he said.

It's not easy for an elite athlete to turn off the competitive mode in other areas of life, says sociologist Monika Schloder. She found that she couldn't turn off her obsessive drive after her competing days were done. Schloder believes this "neurotically intense drive" can also cause physical problems. "I developed stress and then lymphatic cancer," she said. "Researchers need to address this problem among sports' high achievers." (Schloder eventually found help through psychotherapy).

Retirement

When they take that final break—retirement—obsessed athletes often have nothing else to fall back on. *Newsday* looked at life after football. Its survey responses from 1,425 former NFL players and interviews with more than 100 retirees, spouses, NFL executives, and psychologists found that almost one in five former players reported emotional problems, ranging from postcareer letdown to depression during their first year out of football. Only 16 percent of those who retired in the 1990s reported that they felt more successful after football.

"You go through a fog, an emotional depression," says former Redskins and Lions defensive tackle Eric Williams.

> It doesn't matter how many times you've been all-pro or all-world, the problems are the same. I think the whole thing stems from identity. All your life, you're known for what you do. Since the sixth grade, I was always known as Eric Williams the football player. The accolades, the ego strokes, are incredible when you're a football player. You don't pay for dinners. You go to a bar and they say "Drink

for free all night." You don't wait in lines. And that's just the tip of the iceberg.

From 1980 to 1997, seven former NFL players committed suicide. A common theme in almost every case was a difficult transition from life in the NFL. Five suicides were reported (combined) of retired players from pro basketball, baseball, and hockey.

From a family aspect, retirement is difficult because you have to have some place to focus that anger and energy and hostility," former NFL linebacker Brian Noble has said. "When that's gone, your time is spent with your family. Guess who's going to catch the brunt of a lot of that?"

Since his retirement in 1997, former undisputed heavyweight boxing champion Riddick Bowe has had numerous problems, including domestic disputes with his sister and his wife, a failed attempt to join the Marines, and separation from his wife and five children. At one point he was hospitalized for counseling and therapy for emotional stress.

Other Obsessions

Athletes' superior drive and obsessiveness to succeed can attach itself to other types of obsessions, said addiction expert Toni Farrenkopf. Those consumed with competing, especially with winning, are addicts, he said. Their "obsessive-compulsive behavior" can be seen as just another term for addictive, he said. "It's a type of emotional drive. Just as the drug addict is driven by pleasure and the sex addict is driven by lust, the elite athlete is driven by achievement and that could mean performance, excelling over competitors or boosting ego. . . . seeing one's name in print." This compulsion can spill over from an athlete's professional life to his hobbies and lifestyle, Farrenkopf said. "The achiever probably runs on that driven-ness all day long, no matter what he does, even cutting the lawn on weekends." This behavior can adapt to common addictions such as gambling and alcohol and drug abuse and even tobacco chewing, which was banned in minor professional baseball, he added.

Many athletes turn to gambling because it's competitive and risk-taking—just like their athletic lives, Farrenkopf said. "Someone could get addicted to gambling with a sense of wanting to win, but not in strictly a game of chance. It's a competitive kind of thing. They want to beat the numbers and the odds. Golfer Laura Davies, the world's top female golfer, admitted she lost $1 million gambling at casinos and race tracks, although she claimed it was a hobby, not an addiction. At home, she has a set up whereby she can watch up to 61 horse races on various TV screens. Baseball all-star Lenny Dykstra admitted he lost $78,000 playing poker. The same risk-taking attitude that made Pete Rose the winningest baseball player of all time and its career hits leader got him into trouble gambling, sport psychologist Tom Tutko said. Rose was indefinitely suspended for life for reportedly placing wagers on several major league baseball games, including some games he was involved in while acting as player/manager of the Cincinnati Reds.

Baseball should recognize that gambling is no different than other addictions that athletes fall prey to, says George Diaz, a writer for the *Orlando Sentinel*.

> Major league baseball treats its addicts, drunks, and cokeheads with compassion and understanding. It treats one of the greatest players in the history of the game as pond scum, casting its pretentious disapproval at the sins of man consumed by a different kind of addiction. In the eyes of baseball, it is a far lesser crime to sniff, snort, and shoot the substance of choice than it is to take the Atlanta Falcons plus 14 against the 49ers.

In England in the mid-1990s, soccer goalkeepers Bruce Grobbelaar and Hans Segers got mixed up with gamblers and were convicted of criminal match-fixing, although they later had the conviction overturned. They admitted they had been paid to forecast the results of games, a violation of Football Association rules. Michael Jordan admits he gets highs from competing in basketball, baseball, and golf. He has also admitted to being hooked on video games, especially those in his personal computer he carries around on airplanes between Bulls' games. Chicago Bulls fans may be inclined to agree. Some of them blamed Jordan's obsessiveness with golf for his unusual performance in a 1997 playoff loss to the Miami Heat. The day before the game, when many people stayed indoors to avoid the oppressive 95-degree heat and humidity, Jordan stayed on the golf course for 48 holes over 12 hours. His legs were spent the next day, and he missed most of his shots in the first half. In the second half, though, admittedly angered by his poor performance, he went wild and nearly brought the Bulls back to win. Psychologists might suggest that his adrenaline took over in the second half and gave him energy over the short term.

Many hockey players, including Wayne Gretzky, own racehorses. Former NHL goalie Gary "Suitcase" Smith claims that in the 1980s and 1990s he lost 130 straight photo finishes while betting horse races in Vancouver, British Columbia.

Alcohol and Drugs

The link to other forms of addiction are not as strong, but they can be there, Farrenkopf says. No studies have been done into drug and alcohol use among elite athletes. Many sport psychologists and coaches doubt there is heavy drug and alcohol use by professional athletes during their seasons because of the physical and mental toll it would take on their performance. However, in a 1997 article in the *New York Times*, which interviewed more than 25 former NBA players, agents, and basketball executives, many of them estimated that marijuana smoking and heavy drinking were rampant in the league, involving 60 to 70 percent of the players.

High expectations of talent and pressure of being a celebrity drive many athletes to drug and alcohol problems, said Steven Berglas, a clinical psychologist at Harvard Medical School. "Intense scrutiny keeps them in a chronically-stressed situation," he said. "Their success becomes not beneficial to their self-esteem." There's more pressure on athletes these days, he said—"To win, to fill the seats, to make the playoffs. Then they try too hard and get stress overload."

Several research articles have suggested an association exists between athletes' self-esteem and alcohol and drug use, contending that they use those substances to try and cope with threats to their self-esteem. At the high school level, a research team at Ball State University reported that 92 percent of the 337 male athletes at a large midwestern U.S. high school had used alcohol and 73 percent had been intoxicated. Both figures were markedly higher than those for the nonathlete male population. In college, a Michigan State study found that 88 percent of 2,048 athletes surveyed were drinkers. In professional sports, there have been many well-documented cases of heavy drinkers (Mickey Mantle, Darryl Strawberry, and Dennis Eckersley in baseball, Sugar Ray Leonard in boxing, and Chris Mullin in basketball) and cocaine users (Dwight Gooden and Steve

Howe in baseball, Grant Fuhr in hockey, Dexter Manley and Lawrence Taylor in football, and soccer's Maradona.) Green Bay Packers' quarterback Brett Favre became addicted to painkillers and spent 46 days at a drug rehabilitation clinic in 1996.

Golfer John Daly claims that golf has addictive qualities similar to those of heavy drinking. Daly has hit the highs and lows in his professional and personal life, winning the PGA and British Opens with his booming tee shots and falling into problems with drinking, chain-smoking, and domestic violence. "Golf and this disease (drinking) are pretty similar," he said. "Golf is an addiction. So is alcohol."

John Lucas said he was so addicted to winning, he transferred that attitude to taking drugs and would try to outdo fellow addicts. "It became a game of beating the game," he said. "People looked at me like I was nuts, but I wanted to be the best drug addict. If you had a little bit, I had to have more." Lucas, who is now off drugs but addicted to a diet soft drink, opened several drug and alcohol rehabilitation centers for professional athletes.

Of course, such obsessions and addictions can have a serious affect on an athlete's personal and social life. "The same obsessiveness in business is sometimes called workaholism," said John Douillard. "These [athletes] become completely dependent on constant activity and can run their health, marriages, and jobs into the ground. Their compulsive nature also makes them especially susceptible to over-training and, consequently, to injury." In Calgary, Alberta, a woman left her husband because he became obsessed with running every day, according to their physician, Bob Hatfield—"to the point he let his life and responsibilities fall apart. He was addicted to his running."

Addicted to Winning

When goalie Patrick Roy won hockey's Stanley Cup as a rookie with the Montreal Canadiens in 1986, he said it added to his hunger for winning. "There is no greater feeling than holding the Stanley Cup and knowing you have earned the right to hold it," he said. "You do that once, and you want to do it again and again." And he did, contributing heavily to another Montreal win in 1993 and a championship with the Colorado Avalanche in 1996.

According to Cal Botterill, a sport psychologist who worked with Canadian national teams, Canadian sprinter Ben Johnson was so addicted to winning that he cheated to stay on top. Off the track, Johnson was a shy and insecure stutterer, some say sheltered from reality by his family and coaches, another impoverished child who used his body to climb to the top of the sports world. On the track, he became superman in the 100 meters, the most explosive sprinter of all time. His duels with Carl Lewis in the 1980s were classic confrontations as well as bitter personality duels. In the 1988 Olympics, Johnson flew down the runway to a world record—but then it was revealed he had cheated by taking steroids, raising his testosterone levels to more than 10 times normal, and his gold medal was revoked. "More than anything, I think that success was addictive to him," Botterill said. "His whole life revolved around track and field and his whole identity is caught up in being a sports star."

Speaking of steroids, athletes who take large doses of steroids may risk addiction similar to narcotic abuse, doctors warned in a letter published in the *New England Journal of Medicine*. The letter told of a 23-year-old bodybuilder who could not stop taking anabolic steroids without experiencing withdrawal symptoms, depression, and disabling fatigue. The athlete said he sometimes felt uncontrollably violent, paranoid, and suicidal. After a week off steroids, he told doctors he couldn't bear his depression, fatigue, and drug craving and intended to resume taking drugs.

Many athletes carry other obsessions or addictions around with them. In soccer, former Brazilian greats Gerson and Socrates smoked two to three packages of cigarettes a day. Other "habits" are less severe—Pittsburgh Penguins hockey star Jaromir Jagr has been "addicted" to playing video games; former Olympic champion decathlete Daley Thompson was addicted to eating wine gums (candy); hockey great Wayne Gretzky was addicted to watching TV soap operas. And Sacramento Kings player Lionel Simmons missed two games from a sore wrist caused by too much Nintendo.

Not all "driven" athletes have problems in other areas of life, said clinical psychologist Ron Thompson, of Bloomington, Indiana. "There's a difference between being obsessive and being focused," he said. "There's a perfectionism that's part of being an elite athlete. Some have the ability to channel their obsessiveness. It's an adaptive type of obsessive-compulsiveness. They can adapt their obsessiveness in ways that are helpful to them and they can control it." Thompson believes that perfectionism is more related to low self-esteem rather than any other quality.

"The strive for perfection can be a defensive reaction, an over-compensation for low self-esteem."

Clinical psychologist Robert Grant agrees that some athletes can limit their "dysfunctional thinking" to parts of a match. "They may have enough personal stability to have their egos wounded or tarnished only during their performances—and they may even make that work for them," Grant said. But for many athletes, Grant added, weak links in their identity often show up away from the playing fields in the form of addictions or domestic violence. Yet elite athletes can attain good mental health and still be productive professionally by seeking therapy, he said. "They need somebody to help them sort out the wounds and emotional injuries they've suffered. If they did, they'd be a lot more balanced and stable and could achieve higher performance longer in their careers."

Some athletes seem to thrive professionally with their insecurities and unresolved issues and their coaches often keep them in this "on the edge" state because they believe it's good for business, Grant said. If anything, the athlete may get help from a sport psychologist for performance only while their deeper mental and emotional disorders are left untreated.

Grant said that a good comparison for his argument is the careers of Mark McGwire and Jose Canseco, known as "the Bash Brothers" when they were swatting home runs for the Oakland A's. Both had problems off the field, especially Canseco, who had numerous domestic disputes and arrests. "Canseco was a better player early in their careers, but he never got [clinical] help and he dropped from superstar status, but McGwire did, and look at his career now," Grant said.

For years McGwire kept his feelings and his problems bottled up; his self-doubt, fluctuating self-esteem, his claustrophobia, his hitting slumps, and relationship difficulties. "I was all closed in," McGwire recalled. "I didn't like myself. I wasn't a very secure person. I could never face the truth. I always ran away from it. It's like sometimes I look back at myself in those days and think, 'Who the f—' was I?'" Following the 1991 season, in which he hit a pitiful .201 for the Oakland A's, McGwire drove from Oakland to his home in Los Angeles. "I was at a crossroads in my life. I remember driving home. I knew I had five hours by myself to think. I didn't turn the radio on." When he got to his house, McGwire called the A's employee assistance program and they set him up with a psychotherapist. The next season, his home run total jumped from 22 to 42, and he continued to flourish while seeing the therapist over the next four years. "It took failure for me to understand myself," he said. "I'm not afraid to talk about therapy. [Other players] tell me they'll never go to therapy. That's bull. Hey, everybody needs therapy. It brought so many things to my life. I can face the music now. I can face the truth." (Those quotes came prior to the 1998 season, when everything came together for McGwire—his confidence and his willingness to face the truth, the pressure and the failure—and he smashed a record-setting 70 homers.

Emotions Off the Field

Just as problems of violence and overarousal have been well documented on the playing fields and in the arenas, so too have the many problems away from sports. Some of these problems seem to be sociological, but others may involve athletes' inability to control their arousal as well as attitudes of superiority and dominance in everyday life.

Some examples:

• Former middleweight boxing champion Sugar Ray Leonard admitted in 1991 he had abused his first wife and threatened to burn her house down.

• Florida Panthers goaltender Mark Fitzpatrick was charged with aggravated domestic battery in 1994 after his wife, eight months pregnant, told police he pushed her head back and kicked her in the back. He agreed to counseling.

• John Daly, champion of the PGA and British Opens, was charged with assaulting his wife and trashing their home in a drunken stupor. He pleaded guilty to harassment.

• In 1994, figure skater Tonya Harding was sentenced to commnity service for her role in the clubbing of rival Nancy Kerrigan.

Some researchers and sociologists are cautious, stressing that there is still not enough firm evidence to prove that athletes are higher crime risks, but Todd Crosset, assistant professor of sport management at the University of Massachusetts, who helped author the study at Northeastern and the University of Massachusetts, said that there is solid evidence of a problem in sport. "What this study does is show that we have a problem," he said. "It demonstrates the need to address that problem and to study it further."

Sociologists believe many athletes may be susceptible to violence for several reasons, some of them perhaps intertwined:

1. An inability to control aggressive urges, especially during domestic situations

2. A high level of testosterone and sometimes steroids

3. Attitudes of superiority and dominance over others, particularly women

4. A society and a sports system that treats the athletes as special with less accountability than nonathletes

5. A dysfunctional upbringing

Richard Rodriguez, a former amateur wrestler and author of the book *Days of Obligation,* believes there is increasingly more violence on and off the playing fields because it is a reflection of society. "The athlete—the ideal about which the ancients sang—is becoming rarer in our society. Our real world is slipping into the playing field," he says.

And yet athletes teach society how to take control of animal instincts, sometimes brutal instincts, Rodriguez says. "The athlete literally minds his muscles, governs fury, manages exhaustion, channels rage. The athlete turns contest into an exercise of the mind and will," he says. Even in boxing, the most savage sport, athletes can learn to hold back their animal killer instinct, he says. "Here is a sport of naked and brutal intent. But for all its muscularity, boxing demands intelligence, restraint, and self-control. Is there anything more extraordinary than a boxer's ability to stop, midswing, at the sound of a bell?"

In a world like the competitive sports world, where aggression and arousal are often keys to victory, where an athlete's "contradictory" mindsets of insecurity and superiority loom large, it may remain a tightrope act between miracle and mayhem for many athletes. "The athlete," Richard Rodriguez says, "straddles some line between the realm of the animal and the realm of the angel."

Bibliography

Books

Cohn, Patrick J. 1994. *The Mental Game of Golf*. South Bend, IN: Diamond Communications, Inc.

Csikszentmihalyi, Mihaly. 1990. *Flow: The Psychology of Optimal Experience*. New York: Harper and Row.

Douillard, John. 1994. *Body, Mind and Sport*. New York: Harmony Books.

Ferguson, Howard E. 1990. *The Edge*. Cleveland, OH: Getting the Edge, Company.

Goldberg, Alan S. 1998. *Sports Slump Busting*. Champaign, IL: Human Kinetics.

Goleman, Daniel. 1995. *Emotional Intelligence*. New York: Bantam.

Grant, Robert W. 1988. *The Psychology of Sport: Facing One's True Opponent*. Jefferson, NC: McFarland and Company.

Gretzky, Wayne. 1990. *Gretzky: An Autobiography*. New York: HarperCollins.

Gross, Richard. 1992. *Psychology: The Science of Mind and Behaviour*. London: Hodder and Stoughton.

Hackfort, Dieter and Spielberger, Charles D. *Anxiety in Sports*.1989. New York: Hemisphere.

Johnson, Brooks. 1985. *The Winning Edge*. New York: Atheneum.

Kohn, Alfie. 1986, 1992. *No Contest: The Case Against Competition*. Boston: Houghton Mifflin.

Loehr, James E. 1994. *The New Toughness Training for Sports*. New York: Dutton.

Mackenzie, Marlin M. 1993. *Skiing: The Mind Game*. New York: Dell.

Millman, Dan. 1994. *The Inner Athlete*. Walpole, NH: Stillpoint.

Murphy, Shane. 1996. *The Achievement Zone. An 8-Step Guide to Peak Performance in All Arenas of Life*. New York: Berkley Books.

Tutko, Thomas, and Tosi, Umberto. 1976. *Sports Psyching*. New York: Tarcher/Putnam.

Ungerleider, Steven. 1996. *Mental Training for Peak Performance*. Emmaus, PA: Rodale Press.

Index